W9-DEV-896

TRAVELERS' TALES GUIDES

FAMILY TRAVEL

✿

The Farther You Go,
the Closer You Get

"This captivating treasure chest of dazzling, first-person essays will touch your heart, soothe your soul, and stir you to travel the world with those you love. This is family travel at its finest."
—Judsen Culbreth, editor-in-chief, *Working Mother*

"In Laura Manske's beautiful collection, familial ties examined in unfamiliar contexts prove to be just what travel writer Bob Sipchen says they are: All we've got in this difficult, fabulous life."
—Jessica Maxwell, author, *Femme d'Adventure: Travel Tales from Inner Montana to Outer Mongolia*

"Laura Manske's appreciation of the discovery, adventure, and sheer delight of travel is abundantly clear in the essays she has selected here. A wonderful read for passionate voyagers."
—Cathy Cavender, executive editor, *McCall's*

"A treasure of sincerely told remembrances. They illuminate how travel enhances us as individuals and lead to a perhaps unexpected insight: Best friends can be found within families."
—Martin Hollander, travel columnist, *Newsday*

"All parents will relate to these remarkable stories. They say home is where the heart is, but this moving tribute to family travel proves that some of our fondest memories and strongest bonds are created on the road."
—Sally Lee, editor-in-chief, *Parents*

"The next best thing to a great family vacation is cuddling up with this collection of stellar essays. Inspiring, heartwarming, entertaining, and finally useful, this is a book for any parent who travels—or wants to dream about it."
—Pam Abrams, editor-in-chief, *Child*

"A wonderful collection of family stories! It made me wish we'd traveled ore—and to more exotic destinations—when my children were young."
—Nancy Clark, deputy editor, *Family Circle*

TRAVELERS' TALES GUIDES

FAMILY TRAVEL

The Farther You Go, the Closer You Get

Collected and Edited by
LAURA MANSKE

Series Editors
JAMES O'REILLY AND LARRY HABEGGER

TRAVELERS' TALES
SAN FRANCISCO

Nothing can match the treasure
of common memories...

—ANTOINE DE SAINT-EXUPERY,
Wind, Sand, and Stars

To Chet,
Max and Natasha,
my magnificent traveling team,
without whom this book would never have taken flight.
Thank you so much for the journey.

Table of Contents

Part Two
SOME THINGS TO DO

Part Three
GOING YOUR OWN WAY

Part Four
IN THE SHADOWS

Part Five
THE LAST WORD

Family Travel: An Introduction

On the road, across the sea, in the air, my family has found count-less moments of the purest joy. We have sailed near pale blue, calving Alaskan glaciers and trekked through steamy Costa Rican rainforests verdant with exotic flora and fauna. Aboard an ocean liner plowing the choppy Atlantic, we witnessed majestic hump-back whales and, finally, spied the castle-crowned coast of England. Off a catamaran in the Pacific, we splashed with playful dolphins and dodged stingrays. These memories fuse and define our family. And along the way, we've met countless other clans who feel the same need to be together en route.

At times it baffles me how travel *en famille* today is viewed by some people as a nuisance. And then I remind myself that those who avoid such adventures perhaps aren't passionate enough about both seeing the world and holding their loved ones near to commit to the experience, and to make it a positive one.

Because you've picked up this book, you either understand that unique family travel thrill or want to learn how to create it.

These heartfelt, personal stories tell tales of devotion and affec-tion, fervor and yearning, laughter and surprise—about embrac-ing family history, about better understanding the immediate family, about becoming a new family. Read on and you'll be transported, transformed. Discover that even when expeditions don't go as planned, something poignant can be born, a turning point realized, a funny twist of fate revealed. All worth the price of admission, whether it's a journey abroad long saved for, or a spontaneous weekend outing to the mountains.

Certainly, the travel gestalt is changed when a child, an aging parent, or a sibling tags along. Eyes and hearts venture down unfamiliar avenues, emotions intensify. Exploring with family in tow may be more time-consuming, but it is also time-enhancing. Traveling together as my family does is about connecting on different age levels with people, with ideas, with landscapes. For me, as a mother, it's about giving my children a sense of why governments, cultures, religions, foods, and architecture are diverse. (And why that diversity is good.) My eleven-year-old son, Max, and my seven-year-old daughter, Natasha, ask why when I would have otherwise moved on. I would have missed so much if I hadn't had these little magnifying-glass people with me. They give me balance. They give me roots. They give me stronger wings. They encourage me to look under the leaves in the proverbial forest. So I explain and explain again, and consider my children's innocent and often insightful queries as precious gifts that open doors.

My children will not remember everything about these adventures. Nor, at their still-tender ages, will they even recall taking some of them. But that's looking at travel—and the family travel experience—in the Small Picture. The Big Picture is that travel has contributed to who Max and Natasha are. For instance, Natasha has developed compassion for less-fortunate children—she's seen their Third World lives firsthand. When Max studies history from schoolbooks, he also has tangible connections with the past from which to draw: the barracks he touched in Valley Forge, Pennsylvania; the Colosseum he explored in Rome, Italy; the stone starting line he bolted from in Olympia, Greece; Lenin's desk at the former Bolshevik headquarters he gazed upon in awe in St. Petersburg, Russia. There have been new cuisines to try, new languages to speak, new sunsets to replicate with a box of Crayolas. And traveling with those I love has been a priceless education for me as well. By stretching their horizons, they've stretched mine farther than I ever thought possible. It was family that made the difference.

The equation for fruitful family travel is really quite simple: the desire to be together plus a desire to see the world. Money helps smooth the way, of course. Behold my friend Michael, who, along with his wife and two daughters, travels with his brother and sister and their families every summer to some far-flung locale—a roaring white-water jungle river, a lush French countryside, a Galapagoan islet blanketed with wildlife. But deep pockets don't guarantee that kin will get along. He talks of the bond that travel inspires in his family. "Everyone's lives are so busy today," says Michael. "Travel gives us a shared opportunity to pause the stopwatch. To touch base again. Perhaps our best family memories have been forged on trips—so we do whatever is necessary to make them work. We each adjust our needs for the collective good."

My friend Anne, whose purse strings are far tighter, makes travel a priority as well for her husband and four children. They don't own Nintendos, see first-run movies, buy the latest fashions ,or eat regularly in restaurants. Instead, money is saved for getaways. So they rent videos, play board games, shop yard sales, buy cereal in bulk, and fix their small home's clanging pipes and leaky roof themselves. And then Anne's troupe climbs into their nine-year-old van nearly every month for long weekend wanderings, and plan a major North American drive—replete with secondhand camping gear—every August. In the last five summers, they've explored Nova Scotia, British Columbia, the Southwest, the Yucatán, and the Mid-Atlantic States, each trip costing less than what many Americans spend on an entertainment system. Ask the kids to name some of their favorite things in life, and they enthusiastically chime in: maps, small-town diners, and quirky museums.

The Big Picture. In this book, Kate Divine McAnaney's "My Child, Our Vacation" illustrates how a mother's love transcends even the most formidable travel obstacles. In the lovely "The Certificate of Virginity," Tim Parks describes the life of children in Italy—and explains why he desires his own children to grow up there. Jane Myers, in "Past Imperfect, Future Not So Tense," agrees to go on a Mediterranean family sojourn with a long-ago-divorced husband to please her grown children—and is serenely surprised. In "Pieve San Giacomo," Jason Wilson, an exchange student in Italy, puts the wishes of his host family above his own—and is repaid. Andre Aciman's vivid "Alexandria's Ghosts" tries to make sense of his family's past. And thoughtful Chelsea Cain, in "A Room in Oaxaca," gives her dying, Mexico-loving mother the freedom she needs at the end of her life.

In these and other stories, I hope you'll find the inspiration to hold hands with those you cherish as you explore the world. Think about the shape you want your family map to take.

I wish you much joy on journeys ahead.

—LAURA MANSKE

PART ONE

ESSENCE
OF FAMILY TRAVEL

MARY MORRIS

Blessed

*An itinerant traveler plants
the seed for her child.*

I DREAMED MY DAUGHTER BEFORE I HAD HER. I DREAMED her on a Yangtze River cruise where the dead bodies of pigs and cattle and humans floated by. I dreamed her in a sweltering heat where the stench of urine rose into our cabin from deck class below. On the river that the Chinese say is the river of life and of death, I imagined my daughter, and there I conceived her.

On that journey through China with my companion, I met a young girl with copper-colored hair who liked to paint with watercolors to pass the time. The girl, Axelle, was eleven years old, and her family, which lived in Fiji, traveled all over the world. I admired this family of intrepid travelers—each child with a pack of his or her own things—and I knew I wanted to have a child to journey with, to see the world. In the afternoons, as our boat sailed down the Yangtze, Axelle came to my room, and we sat on the floor and painted. We painted river gorges and the farms that lined the river banks. We painted the sailboats and the sunsets we saw. We exchanged paintings and promised to write.

I wrote in my journal: "May 23. Arrived Wuhan 6 p.m. Spent day painting and reading with Axelle. I long for a little girl—I have a deep desire for a child, boy or girl, but a girl would be best." In Shanghai, I left my companion and traveled on by rail, from Beijing to Berlin via Mongolia, feeling sick and tired the whole way.

Nine months later to the day of my journal entry, my daughter, Kate, was born. She had already been around the world. During my pregnancy, I imagined other journeys I would take with her. The plains of Africa, the highlands of Nepal, the islands of the Galapagos. "Your traveling days are over," some friends said. But one wise woman who had raised many children told me: "Start her early. Make her sleep in different places. She'll go anywhere you go." Since her birth, she has been to restaurants and parties, board meetings and museums. She has taken trains and buses, subways and cars and several airplane rides.

Six weeks after her birth, we went to Florida. I had gotten an aisle seat far back in the plane. A man in a business suit was assigned the seat next to me. At first he did not see the child strapped to my chest. But when he did, he was chagrined. "Oh," he said, "You should sit in the front of the plane." I thought he was being kind, but then I realized he was annoyed.

"What if she wakes up," he said. "What if she misbehaves."

She can't misbehave worse than you, I wanted to say. But I held back. "She'll sleep the whole way," I promised, and she did.

When you travel with a child, help comes in ways you never imagined. The disgruntled man changed his seat, and a young woman sat beside me. She turned out to be a flight attendant on vacation and taught me how to buckle my seat belt with a baby. She told me to put a bottle in Kate's mouth during takeoff and landing to protect her ears. She took my carry-on luggage off the plane, gave it to my father, and disappeared into the crowd.

Kate was born in the dead of winter and had lived cooped up in a New York apartment. When we left the terminal, Kate breathed fresh air and saw the full light of day for the first time. I held her up, high into the air. "That is a tree," I said. "This is the sky. Here is the world."

When I was a child, our parents took my brother and me to Idaho from the Midwest by rail. The train had a dome car, and I sat there for hours looking up and watching the sky go by. I remember my first mountain. It seemed to come out of nowhere at all, and my mother said to me: "That is a mountain. We are coming to the Rocky Mountains." I always remembered that mountain.

I remember everything about that trip—the mountains, the horses, the duck pond my brother fell into, a cowboy named Ray, the endless Western sky.

For a child, the world is a foreign country where everything is new. But to travel with a child can be an ordeal. You need more patience and paraphernalia than you've ever needed before. There are bottles where my books used to be. There is all the furniture—the stroller, the backpack, the Kanga-Rocka-Roo. The car seat, the Port-a-crib. What you can't rent, you carry. You need four hands and a very strong back. Once in an airport, while checking my luggage, I saw a man with a toddler clutching one hand, a newborn with his other arm, and a pacifier in his own mouth. I thought he was an idiot, but I understand that man only too well now. What you get is this: you get to see a child's eyes the first time she sees an ocean or an elephant, smells a pine forest or gazes at the ongoing narrative told from the window of a train. You experience the world as the child experiences it, for the first time, all over again.

In Florida, we walked the beach, and I told Kate tales of pirates. We searched for bits of gold, broken glass, relics of shipwrecks.

Going home in a packed airplane, Kate woke up. She didn't cry as I removed her from the Snugli, and the man beside me—a nice man who said his name was Leonard and told me "it only gets better"—got up so I could change her. I changed her, and she never cried. Instead, she looked at everything. At the call buttons, at the seat belts, at the other passengers, at the windows. "This is an airplane," I told her. "Get used to it."

As we were leaving the plane, a woman came up to me. "Your daughter is a traveler," she said. "You are blessed." My daughter is a traveler. She already loves her wanderings through the world. It's true; life is a journey. I see it in my daughter's eyes.

Mary Morris is the author of four novels, two collections of short stories, and two travel memoirs, Wall to Wall: From Beijing to Berlin by Rail *and* Nothing to Declare: Memoirs of a Woman Traveling Alone. *She has also co-edited* Maiden Voyages, *an anthology of the travel writings by women. She lives with her husband, Larry O'Connor, and daughter, Kate, in Brooklyn, New York.*

✳

One of my most deeply imprinted memories of childhood is being taken up in a small plane by my father; tightly buckled in the front seat of a two-seater Piper Cub as my father in the cockpit behind me taxis us along the bumpy runway of a small country airport outside Lockport...and suddenly the rattling plane leaves the ground, lifts above a line of trees at the end of the runway...climbing, banking, miraculously riding the air currents...until the roaring noise of the engine seems to subside, and we're airborne, and below is a familiar landscape made increasingly exotic as we climb. Transit Road and its traffic...farmland, wooded land, hedgerows...houses, barns, pastureland, intersecting roads...creeks and streams...and the sky opening above us oceanic, unfathomable.

—Joyce Carol Oates, *Fathers*

JAMES O'REILLY

* * *

Road Scholars

Eight thousand miles in France with three kids, a van, and no hotel reservations.

OUR PLAN WAS TO SHIP OUR VW VAN—STUFFED AS THOUGH it were an indecently large suitcase—to France, drive around for six weeks, find a town to our liking, and settle down for two years so our three girls, aged three, five, and seven, could learn French while I finished a book. Not exactly *A Year in Provence*, but maybe a year or two in Montpellier, Pont-Aven, or Grenoble. Of course, it didn't work out quite like that. Well, to be honest, it didn't work out like that at all.

To begin with, there was the obligatory French dock strike. Our van would be two weeks late, we were told, and it wasn't going to arrive in France after all. Maybe Belgium, perhaps the Netherlands. *Normalement* the boat would head for Antwerp after bypassing Le Havre (where it was supposed to go), but for obscure reasons it might have to unload in Rotterdam. So, sitting on lumpy mattresses in an atmospheric but squalid Left Bank hotel, my wife Wenda and I took a deep breath and decided to enjoy our fate while matters maritime sorted themselves out.

We explored Paris, bitterly cold in early January but devoid
of tourists. There were no lines anywhere. The Eiffel Tower in
a rainstorm was ours. So too the Musée d'Orsay, the Louvre,
and Notre-Dame. There was nobody waiting for ice cream
cones outside Berthillon on L'Isle St-Louis. We were cheated
by cab drivers and snubbed by waiters. We rode boats on the
Seine, wandered the streets, visited Jacques Cousteau's Parc
Océanique under Les
Halles, spent exorbitant
sums on mediocre snacks,
and in general had a won-
derful time. We decided
Paris was indeed extraordinary, oozing history and
beauty like no other place,
but that Parisians who deal
with tourists bear a distinct

> *Traveling in the
> company of those
> we love is home in motion.*
>
> ◆
>
> —Leigh Hunt,
> *The Indicator* (1821)

behavioral resemblance to New Yorkers, Paris not being France
the same way New York is not America. Or is it? The question
had too many layers to sort out when a three year old wants
to be carried through all six million miles of the Louvre.

We rented a little red Peugeot, stuffed dolls, bears, and children into it and set off to find the real France, where we would
set up shop. No sooner had we left Paris than one of the girls
threw up all over the back seat. We pulled off the road next to
a nice-looking *auberge* by the Seine and cleaned the car. By
then everyone was hungry and cold, so we trotted past ducks
and up stone steps and inquired if the establishment was open.
It was, *bien sûr*. We were warmly welcomed, served great food
at a reasonable price, and left feeling that perhaps we had not
made a mistake after all, that in fact Parisians were only as
good ambassadors as New Yorkers.

We headed for Normandy, where we stayed with friends in

a farmhouse near Caen. We visited the Peace Museum, walked Sword Beach, and told the girls about World War II and the approaching fleet had this been D-Day so many years ago. One evening I achieved *satori*, or, as Spalding Gray might have it, a perfect moment, sharing wine and camembert with our friends. I am by no means a food-oriented person, but the French—if I may generalize—do indeed have a remarkable and communicable way with food. The next evening, however, I made the mistake of expressing too much enthusiasm for *tripe à la mode de Caen* and needed to eat a lot to convince our hosts. In the morning, as I groaned, my daughters entertained me with a dance they called "Let's Do the Cow Stomach."

In Villedieu-les-Poêles we visited a foundry where the church bells of France and other countries are made. We explored an empty, windswept Mont St-Michel and listened to organ practice in a chapel. One of the girls fell down a flight of stairs. A Mirage fighter roared overhead. The bay was magnificent, the solitude extraordinary.

We drove to Blois, on the Loire River, arriving late in the evening. By now the children had become night owls, but if we didn't feed them by eight, rebellion was at hand. We staggered into a full and too-expensive restaurant and asked if the chef could produce something for the children. He presented exquisite little steaks at a fraction of the cost of a Paris snack. Wenda and I ruefully settled for shallow bowls of seafood soup, but after one mouthful it was apparent this was no ordinary soup. (In fact, many months later, on the Alaska Railroad, I struck up a conversation with one of the dining car waiters— he was French, from Blois—where he said there was a restaurant with this soup…. How could soup be that good? I still wonder. But somehow it was.)

We stayed in a hotel next to Château de Chambord, where we were fawned over by a staff who acted as though they hadn't had guests in years. In fact, we were the only guests. It had become clear to us that one of the merits of traveling in winter with children was that hotel and restaurant staffs were more indulgent—and forgiving—than they might have been at peak season. But apart from the pros and cons of winter travel, we found people all over France to be warm and caring, especially toward children. Wherever we went, people seemed to look out for our daughters. It felt safe to let them out of our sight in a way that it doesn't in America.

In the morning, we explored the Château and its extraordinary ramparts and double-helix staircase. Huge fires blazed in the fireplaces, but couldn't chase the chill. I scattered a friend's ashes on the frozen Cosson River nearby; when spring came, he'd be carried into the Loire.

That night we walked the perimeter of Chambord, vast, dark, mysterious, Orion bright and hard in the January sky. We heard the laughter of the Château's guardians floating from their living quarters, mocking the excesses of the dead. It occurred to me like a bell struck in the night that the only legacy worth having is one of kindness.

We headed south, past the sprawl of Lyon, to a walled farmhouse high over vineyards near Orange in northern Provence. The mistral howled all night but we slept well, aided by our hosts' own wine.

By now we had seen dozens of towns and were adept at squeezing the car late at night down alleys meant for people and horses, in search of shelter. But a disturbing theme began to appear—we liked many places, but we couldn't see ourselves living in them. "Let's check out the next town," became our mantra. The girls protested, but by now they were beginning to qualify as Road Warriors, if not Road Scholars quite yet. When they tired of history lessons, we reminded them they could be at school back in the States instead of eating chocolate for lunch and driving around France. Life could be worse. We told ourselves the same thing, but the fact is, we were getting worried. Little did we know we would be doing the same thing four months and thousands of miles later.

We thought we'd like Aix-en-Provence, but there were an alarming number of tollbooths straddling the *autoroute* outside of town warning of the hordes to come once the weather turned warm. We drove around for an hour before finding a parking spot and then stepped out into a pile of dog *merde*, and were immediately panhandled. These incidents, we decided, did not constitute good omens, and after looking around the admittedly lovely city, we decided it would be a great place to live in as a student, but that it was too crowded for us. So it was back to the road.

Near Bordeaux, we stayed on a farm where the girls saw hours-old baby goats and drank fresh warm goat's milk. Later, on another farm, they made butter with the farmer's wife and mother and saw a calf still steaming from birth. These farm experiences came to be an important part of the Road Scholar Curriculum, along with almost daily tutoring from Wenda.

We hastened on, for it was time to pick up our van, which we had been told was in Belgium. We dropped by our friends' Normandy home to recuperate, and then headed back to Paris. We stayed in a miserable establishment, more flophouse than hotel, and took the train to Antwerp the following misty grey morning.

On the way to the shipping office, we had a cab driver who spoke French, Dutch, Flemish, German, and English. By now I think the utility of knowing another language was beginning to sink into the girls' minds and their games had a mixture of French and pretend French. They could see how ineffective I was with only minimal French, but how well their mother—

fluent in French and Italian—could communicate. To be monolingual is to be socially hobbled, no matter how much of the world speaks English. The next morning, Wenda asked them if they wanted to wash their hair, and the three responses were, *"Oui, bien sûr," "Weird, bien sûr,"* and *"Oui, bien sure."* Clearly progress was being made towards the parental Holy Grail of bilingualism.

We drove through stack after towering stack of sea-freight containers until we arrived at one which mercifully contained our van and manifold contents. The children were delighted to renew acquaintance with toys and clothes; we were astounded at the quantity of stuff we'd thrown at the last minute into our capacious van, so full that if we parked on an incline and opened the door, goods to stock a Wal-Mart tumbled out.

We sallied forth again, crossing Belgium and Luxembourg to the Alps and Chamonix, where we were to meet friends for a week of skiing near Mt. Blanc. Our often-prescient oldest daughter suggested that this was the town we should live in. The people were friendly, it was the right size, and even though there were tourists, the outlying villages were appealing. But adults are a thick-headed lot, and we said no, there were other places more appropriate (sniff) than a ski town. We crossed the Massif Central, visited Lourdes in its exquisite Pyrenean setting, congratulating ourselves that we didn't buy even one ashtray of the Virgin, saw vineyards covered in snow, drove through innumerable hamlets that charmed but didn't hold us.

The fact is, we were on a driving jag. The *autoroutes* were empty, the hotels still empty, the prices off-season low, and the children were seeing more of France than many French do in a lifetime. We completed our second circuit of the country and drove into Switzerland. In Geneva, the girls watched a friend work the floor of the U.N., lobbying for a human rights resolution on behalf of Tibet. We drove to Lausanne with its Transport Museum, Vevey and its Alimentarium, Interlaken, Zurich, and into Austria. But as much as we enjoyed everything, we were happy to leave highway *ausfahrts* behind and return to French *sorties*. At least we were in the right country, learning about France and the French if not much French itself.

By now we had hit upon our best tactic for ensuring the girls' cooperation in exploring historic and religious sites—we bought postcards before entering and had the kids look for what was on the cards. It was also becoming clear to us, the more we roamed, that parents too routinely surrender the job of teaching to schools. There is great joy in seeing how your children learn, in a way you can't when you just help with homework at night. We also gained renewed respect for the work teachers do.

Heading south again, we committed cultural heresy by visiting EuroDisney

*Y*ou have to accustom yourself to sightseeing at a child's pace, to pointing out every camel or elephant or horse or donkey or cow along the way, and also searching out animals in sculptures, temple carvings, and cave paintings. And if you find yourself settling down in a little niche on the outside of the Taj Mahal to read aloud *Madeline*, well, probably you will always remember the beauty of the pietra dura stone inlay work that you stared at as you intoned: "In an old house in Paris that was covered with vines, lived twelve little girls in two straight lines."

♦

—Perri Klass, "Asia on Ten Diapers a Day," *The New York Times*

(now Disneyland Paris), feeling it was small payback for months of good behavior in the back of the van. Nonetheless, to make up for our sins we hastened to Versailles. In the vast cobbled courtyard, my oldest daughter took me aback by pointing at the palace and asking "Daddy, can we buy one of those?" Their favored mode of viewing the Sun King's treasures was to lie on the floor and study the splendid, intricate ceilings.

On our third Tour de France now, we thought seriously about settling in Pont-Aven, the lovely town in Brittany where Paul Gauguin once lived, but a bizarre April Fool's day encounter with a potential and emotionally disturbed landlord, replete with symbolism that would have us laughing later—a huge spider in a closet, mold, a rainy funeral, a dead horse, *deviation* road signs, and the fact that I was reading Stephen King's *Dead Zone*—sent us back to the *autoroute* with a sigh of relief.

But by now we had been driving for more than four months with only a week's letup here and there in a *gîte* (a country place for rent), and everyone's nerves were fraying. One night our three-year-old shouted in a restaurant at the top of her lungs, "I hate menus! Just bring me food!" We, slow-to-learn grownups, began to wonder—perhaps we were overdoing this.

We went back to Normandy and left our van in a barn surrounded by chickens and bales of hay, and took the train to Paris. We rented an apartment for a week, an expensive proposition at first blush, but cost-effective for a family when you consider meals not eaten in restaurants. Our place was directly across the Seine from Notre-Dame Cathedral, which filled our living room windows.

One night, *Vertigo*, Hitchcock's evocative San Francisco masterpiece, was on TV, and I discovered I could watch it in the dining room mirror with Notre-Dame also reflected there. A heady combination of wonders sent my head spinning, places and names scrolling before my eyes: Pont Neuf, North

Beach, Pont-Aven, Mission San Juan Bautista, Pont d'Avignon, and Jimmy Stewart and Kim Novak struggling under the Golden Gate Bridge....

It was time to go.

Although we never did find a home on that first trip, we've since returned to France many times. And of course, my daughter was right. We returned to a village in the Haute Savoie a few kilometers from Chamonix, where she and her sisters attended a public school. PE included instruction in downhill and cross-country skiing and they are now correcting their mother's pronunciation. Mine, they just laugh at.

James O'Reilly is co-editor of the Travelers' Tales series. He is also co-author of "World Travel Watch," a syndicated newspaper column.

✦

It's just before midnight on a clear cold Christmas Eve, and the bells of Les Baux-de-Provence—an eerily lovely, half-ruined medieval town perched on the peak of a mountain—toll solemnly over the valleys. Inside the centuries-old church of St. Vincent, a cluster of little girls in white robes, angel wings, and halos huddle in the Nativity crèche near the altar. In their high heartbreaking voices they sing ancient Provençal carols, accompanied by the music of a flute and a drum. The teenage boy and girl chosen to play Mary and Joseph in this midnight Mass are themselves not much older than children. Joseph's voice is changing, and when it breaks and he falters halfway through an extended solo, the village priest appears at his side and patiently guides him through it.

I have come with my husband, our two sons, and my mother to Les Baux, in the Alpilles range, nine miles from Arles. We're spending Christmas in the south of France partly as a vacation, partly as an escape. We chose Provence after French friends told us that the holidays are celebrated here with particularly rich traditions, so unlike the ritual of the evening news at home: the interviews with shoppers and merchants at the suburban mall, the worried reports on holiday spending as an index of national fiscal health. Our hope, too, is to spare our sons, ages eleven and fifteen, the Christmas Day phone calls from friends wanting to compare notes on the number, variety, and magnificence of their presents.

Indeed, all that seems very far away from the church at Les Baux where the dim interior suddenly darkens even more. A hush falls over the congregation during the slow grave lighting of candles which signals the beginning of the ceremony of the pastrage. In this procession, reenacting the bringing of gifts to the manger at Bethlehem, men in shepherds' robes and women in folk costumes approach the altar to kiss the doll that represents the Christ child. The most precious of their offerings is the lamb that the worshipers lead through the church in a wooden cart decorated with green boughs and surrounded by burning candles.

By now the crowded chapel has fallen silent; the only sounds are the quiet bleating of the lamb and the slightly melancholy ringing of the bell around its neck. I turn and look at my sons—and I see that their eyes are shining.

—Francine Prose, "Christmas in Provence,"
Travel & Leisure

⭑ ⭑ ⭑

For the Birds

In Tanzania, the author's
feathers get ruffled.

MY FATHER STANDS BEAMING ON THE TARMAC. "WELCOME,"
he says, "to Tanzania."

I have just deplaned at the Kilimanjaro airport. Curiously,
so has he. In fact, neither of us has ever set foot in Tanzania
before. But if he sounds proprietary, the expansiveness is
characteristic.

Inside the terminal we join a line behind a young Dutch
woman. "End of a *long journey*," he says to her, grinning
broadly. She smiles and looks around, as if to gauge the airport's security presence. Not to worry. His attention has already
shifted: something large is batting at a ceiling light. He leans
over toward me. "First moth," he confides.

And I think, *Only sixteen days to go.*

Don't misunderstand. My dad and I are close. But we're
about to become dangerously close. If travel has a way of reducing personalities to their essence, then a certain kind of
travel—say, two weeks in the same tent on a safari—does the
job that much faster.

17

Even more worrisome: in many ways, we're opposites. Charming, gregarious, and tenaciously cheerful, he takes a welcome-humankind-my-name-is-Mike-and-I'll-be-your-host-this-evening approach to life; I might as well walk around dangling a sign that says, "Fine, but don't crowd me." Clearly we are going to have to tap deep resources of humor and goodwill just to keep from bopping each other over the head with flashlights. Will it be a happy trip, an echo of childhood experiences—my dad, after all, is the one who long ago first got me interested in both travel and wildlife—or more like *The Two Stooges Go to Africa?*

The issues were piling on the table well before we landed in Kilimanjaro. It's a long-running gag in my family that Dad is a desultory reader, reliably whipping through several books per decade. For this trip, he'd packed *Portrait of the Artist as a Young Man,* which was taking him longer to read than it took Joyce to write. Available evidence suggests that he first cracked the paperback sometime in 1994 and by late '95 had gotten midway through. Half a novel, even a slim one, would normally hold him for a couple of weeks—a couple of years, conceivably—but at Kennedy Airport he panics. "I think I'll go find a book stand," he says abruptly, after watching me read for a while. He returns ten minutes later carrying a brown paper bag. I don't even hazard a guess. His bookcase at home is divided between psychiatry and birding—vocation and avocation—subjects assigned precious little rack space at JFK's boarding-gate stalls. How would Dad manage book shopping alone, under pressure, and without a net? He plops down next to me.

"Dante's *Inferno* and *Beowulf,*" he says. For a moment I think he's kidding.

During most of the journey over, he confines his reading to crossword puzzle clues and the mileage updates on the cabin

screens ("Two hundred miles to go…five letters, beginning
with E…a hundred and fifty miles to go"). I know this because much of it is read aloud. Somewhere over the Sudan
he completes the puzzle and fishes the *Inferno* from his knapsack. The knapsack, at least, makes sense; the rest of his luggage, packed with the aid of my mother, does not. By the time
our small group, Treks Ltd., led by the naturalist Jim Brett,
assembles for breakfast the first morning in Arusha ("The adventure begins," declares my father, who happens to be looking at his eggs), it's clear that Dad's is the only blue vinyl suitcase in East Africa. It juts up stiffly from an acre of duffel bags,
like a prezoning high-rise in a neighborhood of brownstones.

The owners of all this luggage have more or less been hand-
picked by Brett, who was for 25 years the director of the Hawk
Mountain Sanctuary in Pennsylvania. Brett is a legend, probably the only hell-raiser-turned-birder-turned-wildlife advo-
cate who nevertheless soothes himself in stressful moments
with daydreams of climbing onto a Lawn Chief and mowing
the Serengeti ("I'd go right up to Lake Victoria and come
back"). It's a great group, though Pennsylvania-heavy, which
leads to more conversations about the restaurants of greater
Reading than would seem humanly possible in two weeks.

We ride in three Land Rovers provided by our local connection, Bjorn Figenschou, and his company, Tanzania Guides.
Of the drivers, Lawrence Mbay has drawn the short straw.
Lawrence has the bad luck to be an excellent birder, and so has
been assigned the group's two obsessives, my father and an affable chamber of commerce director named Tony Grimm.
Both compile life lists of species and, I'm sure, would gladly
sign up to have binoculars surgically attached to their eye
sockets, if only that wouldn't make their turn at the telescope
problematic. I'm just a casual birder, but I'm allowed in the
vehicle anyway, and Lawrence suffers us all with remarkable

grace and patience. Our jeep is soon dubbed the Bird Cage by the dilettantes in the less specialized "mammal cars."

"They driving you crazy yet?" Jim Brett asks me, as we all stretch our legs at the entrance to Tarangire National Park, our first stop. Well, no, although two days later, while my father leads a protracted discussion about wheatears, I nearly eat my sunglasses. For anyone not sitting in it, the Bird Cage would be indistinguishable from the other two Land Rovers but for the fact that it advances in increments of ten or twenty yards, Lawrence being under strict orders to brake at the slightest rustle of tiny feathers in distant baobab trees. Cheetahs, elephants, and prides of lions sweep past, earning our grudging glances if they're lucky; the chirp of a putative terrestrial bulbul, on the other hand, stops us dead, and then we tend to settle in for lengthy symposia on eye rings and median primary coverts.

In fact, the Tanzanian birdlife is incredible, and Dad and Tony nail 100 species by the third day. But soon there's a group revolt, precipitated by one endless, caravan-halting debate. With the thermometer and the tsetse population inside the Cage both hovering around three digits, the experts page laboriously through the half-dozen field guides scattered on the front seat until my father is finally heard to utter what, under the circumstances, are the three most terrifying words in the English language: "But *which* lark?" It's the proverbial last straw, and the Bird Cage self-imposes a three-minute rule: name the bird in that time, or drive on.

My father is actually showing great tolerance for the shortcomings of the nonbirding population, and doesn't take offense when I continue to refer to something called a pratincole as "that profiterole." He even remains good-natured in the aftermath of the Lake Manyara Hippo Pond Incident, which marks him for permanent group ridicule. Briefly, he's so distracted by some shorebirds that he fails to notice 30 or

40 hippos lolling and yawning among the plovers and avocets. "Hey, there's a hippo!" he cries out, after the rest of us have been quietly watching the enormous mammals in awe for several minutes. It takes a tough man to live that down. And he does.

For my part, I'm getting better at tuning out his ongoing exterior-interior monologue ("Binoculars at the ready" "Should I have the lamb or the beef?" "We're kicking up a lot of dust, but I think I'll leave the lens cap on" "The dawn breaketh" "Good-bye to the Tarangire plains") while paying enough attention to pick up useful fatherly advice (he converts me to an excellent new razor) and wisdom: "When dung is plentiful," he says one day, gazing pensively at the horizon from under his Tilley safari hat, "elephants cannot be far away." Words to live by. And I'm no longer disconcerted to notice, for instance, that he and I often find ourselves sitting with arms and legs folded and arranged identically. It seems the apple doesn't fall far from the tree, after all (although it can roll quite some distance). Standing up in the open hatch of the Land Rover as we speed toward our campsite at dusk, I feel like an ecstatic kid. What I want badly, I realize, is to spot a leopard and impress my dad.

I quickly learned that no matter how old a child is, no matter how successful he or she has been in professional life, around your family it takes approximately twenty-four hours to regress into the behaviors of a fourteen-year-old.

◆

—Laura Muha, "Picture Perfect," *Newsday*

We visit Olduvai Gorge, where the Leakeys did their digging and made all that trouble for future creationists, and our group hikes down to the site, happy for the chance to get a little exercise without becoming part of the region's glorious food chain. I fall naturally in line behind my father, carrying the bird book—essentially replaying a family scene you could carbon-date to maybe 1965, only transposed from the Botanical Gardens in the Bronx. When *Australopithecus* went out to look for birds early on Sunday morning 1.7 million years ago—in the Bronx or elsewhere—did *Australopithecus Jr.* trail behind him, kicking at pebbles and clutching a prehistoric Peterson's?

Back in our tent one day, after a huge lunch, my father produces a chocolate bar the size of a two-by-four, which my mother had packed. I'm amazed—sated, we'd pushed back our dessert dishes literally seconds earlier—but, of course, I take a piece. We munch without speaking, sitting on our beds. My father, who remains in constant touch with his outer child, suggests devouring another hunk; I refuse. "That's why you and I stay trim," he says, without a trace of irony. "We know when to stop." With a proud flourish, he bends the foil around the rest of the bar, places it in the suitcase, and returns to the *Inferno*. Judging from the bookmark, I'd say he's just about reached Canto VI, Circle 3 ("The Gluttons").

A week or so into the safari, we have a travel day and spend a single night at a lodge. That's where Dad discovers that he can't locate his return airplane ticket ("The hell. Where did I put that?"). Together we check off the likeliest spots to search, and then he glumly begins to reorganize his packing in the desperate hope that a boarding pass can accidentally get balled, undetected, into a pair of socks. I watch from across the room. Atop one pile of his clothes is a shirt reading I'M FOR THE BIRDS; draped over a chair is a green t-shirt spattered white with representations of bird droppings, which are identified by species. I start to wonder what kind of father I've raised.

There are moments during our trip when the parent-child

relationship does appear to have reversed itself—notably when I remind him not to switch horses in mid-cocktail hour—but even then, the essential nature of the discourse remains fixed, as if we're just reading each other's lines. Because for all the familiar and affectionate head-pat/knee-slap/neck-clap combinations he bestows upon me, as if I were a particularly delightful eight-year-old, our relationship is more traveler-to-traveler than son-to-father. The pleasures and demands of a trip take precedence—always.

My parents have always fancied themselves smooth travel professionals. But over nearly half a century together, they've divided their responsibilities so completely that neither can function dependably without the other. My father's explanation, when he finally reports the loss of the ticket to our group, is, "My wife usually takes care of that stuff"—the same as it is a week later when it's learned that he hasn't bothered to sign his traveler's checks. At this point—for deep down he is a sensible man—he wordlessly hands me his passport for safe-keeping. It's a symbolic moment, but a confusing one. Am I turning into my father? Into my father's father? Or am I really turning into my mother?

"The mood must be upon us," Dad says that evening, "because I woke up from my nap and I'd dreamed of my father—that he was still alive and that they'd been keeping it from me." The mood must indeed be upon us: even as he was dreaming of his father, gone twenty years now, I was in fact busy writing a postcard to my son.

Halfway through the trip, during a day spent kopje-hopping out on the Serengeti, the Bird Cage ticks its two hundredth bird. In unrelated developments, Dad reports that he is (a) plowing through the *Inferno* with real pleasure and (b) suffering from scores of chiggerlike bites. Eventually most of the group will succumb—to the chiggers, or whatever, not to the

Dante—but for a couple of days my dad feels singled out, joking that they must have been planted on him. Nonsense. But I confess: had I had a chigger in my possession when we first looked out from the lush rim of the Ngorongoro Crater and my father said, "There it is, George, the Serengeti. From the book...to your real experience," I believe I would have used it.

By the time we leave Ngorongoro behind (Dad: "A crater to remember"), the Cage has shifted to "hard birding" mode, and the remaining days are spent scrambling pell-mell toward 300 species. We feel like hunters. "Now I want a bittern," my father says, staring at some weeds. "Or a rail." The tally finally stops at 299, when a barnyard rooster glimpsed from the highway as we speed to the airport is disallowed. Another goal left not quite attained, I suspect, is the *Inferno*, though I'm too polite to ask.

In the end, my father had a blast. He always does—but so did I, with him. He's a piece of work. Maybe travel, in the way it trashes patterns and routine, can also coax surprises from people you thought you understood all too well. Wildebeests never even know their fathers. How, then, could I not appreciate knowing mine as I watched him glance almost nightly at the sky and never fail to find, and point out, the Belt of Orion? So what if he had a harder time locating the belt of Mike, even in a smallish tent with the aid of two candle lanterns, a powerful kerosene lamp, and a pair of flashlights? ("The hell. Where did I put that?") Because there's something to appreciate about that, too.

Returning to our campsite at the base of Mount Meru on our final evening in Tanzania, we're both up in the hatch, the wind in our faces, the acacias whipping past. Giraffes strike dramatic poses against pink clouds, and nightjars slice the air. For once, and for a little while, even Dad doesn't feel the need to comment. Finally he does speak:

"I'm starting to get the bug for Antarctica. Arusha National Park, Momella Gate."

I lose him after Antarctica, and it takes me a few seconds to realize what has happened: we've just gone through a checkpoint and he's obligingly read the signs out loud. Still, I'm going to think seriously about Antarctica, if he can stand to have me along. Among other things, I want to see how it goes with *Beowulf*.

George Kalogerakis has worked as an editor and writer at New York, Vogue, Vanity Fair, *and* Spy. *He lives in New York City.*

✳

Before we left South Africa for Rhodesia [now Zimbabwe], our girls wanted us to buy them South African safari suits. The outfits looked so smart and were cool and tough. Most men and all small boys wore them—steel gray, khaki, or blue safari jackets with matching shorts and cuffed knee socks. But the department store clerk was scandalized that the girls would even consider them. She was emphatic: only boys wore safari suits. She flatly refused to sell them to us.

Thinking quickly, I said, "Oh well, the girls have cousins 'upcountry,' so they can try them on for size. I didn't know only boys wore safari suits. The girls will get something else."

Alzada and Kymry eagerly set about deciding what "John" and "Peter" would like. There was not much of a choice, with only three colors available. Each selected a steel gray set and a blue set. Once out of the store, they wore nothing else for the rest of the trip. The safari suits were washed in buckets and dried on bushes, and they always looked great. I was tempted to get some myself. The girls always had trouble keeping their knee socks up until we learned that South African schoolchildren glued their knee socks to their legs with a glue stick. No droopy socks here!

At dinner that night, Kymry refused to swallow her vile-tasting malaria pill and spat it into her soup, making the soup virtually inedible. Her father looked at her steadily and said, "Kymry, we know the pills are awful, but we all must take them. You have three options.

You may finish every drop of your soup. You may take another pill and have the rest of your dinner. Or you may go upstairs and take your pill before breakfast." Dave had spoken; this was the last time Kymry would revolt over her malaria medicine. Oddly enough, she chose to finish the soup.

—Alzada Carlisle Kistner, *An Affair with Africa: Expeditions and Adventures Across a Continent*

JASON WILSON

* * *

Pieve San Giacomo

*Embraced by an Italian family and a terry cloth
bathrobe, an American student experiences
a different kind of family travel.*

ON MORNINGS LIKE THIS, WHEN YOU WEAR MY MUSTY OLD
bathrobe, I can feel the terry cloth weight of responsibility. I
can smell obligation in those damp sleeves. I can see simple
truths revealed in the way it hangs slightly opened, untied, as
you blow-dry your golden hair.

Make no mistake, the robe is ugly. Heavy and not quite soft,
it's cut too big, the unnatural material too unabsorbent for
drying completely after a shower. The pocket sits too high for
any hand to rest comfortably inside. A mixed floral pattern,
muted goldenrod and dirty white, extends from the collar to
the knees. From a distance the color is reminiscent of used
manila envelopes. Yet you continue to grab for the robe behind the bathroom door as you shiver on cold days and it often
appears burdensome as it drapes over your smooth skin.

But there is another thing. These mornings, when I see you
in that robe, I also am reminded how lucky I am to have not
one, but several families—including one in a dusty little village in Italy's Po Valley. There, on a hot July day, I lounged in

my pretend aunt's whitewashed courtyard with my pretend mother while the sun reflected off tins of biscotti and bottles of sparkling water. The two women watched, giggling in Cremonese dialect, as I ate meats and breads and pastries they'd carefully prepared and drank the Coca-Cola bought special for me in the city.

And on these mornings, when you smile at me in the mirror as you brush your teeth, I'm once again nineteen years old, studying abroad for the first time. Once again I am sitting in that Italian courtyard, not quite mature enough to grasp the complex familial duties I'm expected to carry out. Once again, for just a moment, I live in Pieve San Giacomo.

"The Bernabé family specifically asked for the boy," Professor Causa said with a wink when she greeted me at the elaborate arched doorway of the Circolo Fodri, our school in the small city of Cremona. Inside, a dozen men and women attired in designer suits and silk dresses smoked and drank coffee and nibbled treats. They filled the hot, muggy air with Italian language in a way I'd never heard before—certainly not the laborious *"amo, ami, ama"* I was accustomed to hearing in the black headphones of the college language lab back at the University of Vermont. I was lost as I shook hands and uttered a meek *piacere* when presented to a man wearing Gucci sunglasses standing next to his bleached blonde wife.

I heard my professor repeat to Sara and Jen, two of my fellow students, that "the Bernabé family specifically asked for the boy." I scanned the room and realized I was the only male out of seven students. And since I was also the youngest—just a sophomore—I assumed that also made me the only boy. All around the room, fellow students were paired up with the well-dressed couples smoking cigarettes.

Then, as if they simply materialized from the swirl of language and heat and smoke and silk and laughter, the Bernabé family was thrust before me. A round, red-faced bald man with a giant mole on his thick neck waddled over, dressed in neatly pressed polyester pants and a short-sleeved dress shirt. The man reached for his gray-haired wife's arm, tugging instead at her stiff blue housedress. The two of them beamed as they approached while behind them trailed one of the stylishly dressed young women with long brown hair. Professor Causa introduced the family: Paolo, Anna, and their 27-year-old daughter, Daniela. Paolo slapped my shoulder and put his arm around me. Anna kissed my cheeks. Daniela took my hand.

From then, I can only remember the stern warning from my professor: "Daniela works in the local tourist office," she said. "She speaks perfect English, but I've explicitly told her that she's not to help you at all unless there's a real emergency. You are to have total immersion."

I was whisked away in a dark blue Fiat and we rode through the busy streets of

*A*s all classical music lovers know, Cremona is world famous for its exquisite violins. Antonio Stradivari is the most renowned of Cremona's violin makers. His secret formula for violin varnish allegedly gives the Stradivarius its distinct sound.

◆

—LM

Cremona into the countryside. I sat in the back with Daniela, and Paolo kept looking at me in the rear view mirror with a big grin on his face. Anna asked me dozens of questions, little of which I truly understood. When I turned to Daniela for help in translation, she smirked and shrugged her shoulders.

At great speeds, we passed yellow and green fields, patches of blood red flowers, and farmhouses with terra cotta roofs.

Fifteen minutes outside of Cremona, I began to worry about where the Bernabé family was taking me: all of the other students were staying with families only a few blocks from the Circolo Fodri. Anna started speaking louder and slower, as if I was retarded or deaf. I was dripping with sweat, but I couldn't think of how to ask Paolo to roll down the windows.

Soon, I saw a little blue sign for Pieve San Giacomo and Anna turned, tapped my hand, and shouted, "We are here!" The Fiat pulled into the gates of a dusty yard, past farm equipment. We parked beside a lush vegetable garden, more red flowers, and a patio with a fountain. Puppies and kittens roamed freely.

Paolo grabbed my bags, escorting me through the red drape hanging over the door and onto the cool stone floor of the house. Anna led me into my room, showing me my towels, my drawers in an ancient oak wardrobe, my orderly bed. Outside my window, chickens strutted in the yard next to a doghouse.

That night, at dinner, Paolo passed around a plate of prosciutto he'd cut on the meat slicer in the kitchen. He uncorked an unmarked bottle of red wine. The television news on RAI UNO droned as white noise in the background. Anna disappeared and reappeared from the kitchen with plates of melon, spinach, pasta, *fagiuolo*, veal, bowls of the sharp Grana Padano cheese of the region. By my third glass of wine, I was beginning to understand more and more of what everyone was saying. Every time a dish was served, Paolo slowly explained where it came from. "All of this meat, it comes from my cows. The vegetables, from my garden. The grain, from my field. And the wine, it comes from my grapes." In fact, the only thing in the kitchen that looked store-bought was the Coca-Cola Anna had offered me when we walked in the door.

Between the pasta and the main course, I carried my dish

into the kitchen. Anna quickly shooed me away saying, "No, no, no, no," and dragged me by my arm back to the table, laughing.

Later, as we drank coffee and Paolo poured Cognac onto the fresh kiwi gelato, Anna turned to Daniela and asked, "Americans eat breakfast, right?"

My ears perked up. It was the first phrase—spoken at normal speed—which I completely understood. I was elated.

"Sì!" I said, nearly jumping across the table. "We eat breakfast every morning at home." *Colazione. Colazione.* Breakfast. Oddly enough, it is still perhaps the most beautiful Italian word I know.

Anna smiled. Her wide blue eyes flashed at Daniela with a look of pride. She spread her arms. "Big?"

"Sì," I replied.

"Tell me," she said. "What do you eat for breakfast?"

That's when I was stuck. Visions of pancakes, waffles, muffins, Pop Tarts, and Cap'n Crunch floated through my head. But I had no dictionary nearby and I didn't know any of those words. Everyone at the table watched patiently as I stammered. Then suddenly, I remembered a vocabulary list from the previous semester. *"Uova!"* I shouted.

"Uova?" Anna said. "Very good. There will be eggs tomorrow morning at seven o'clock." Things had been settled. After coffee, we all went to bed.

The next morning, the following headline appeared in a local newspaper: "Vermont college students are Cremona's guests."

During our first days at Circolo Fodri, I asked Professor Causa, "Why do they say things like *Cuma veet* instead of *Come vai?*"

She chuckled. We were on our morning coffee break and English was allowed. "I assumed that might happen," she replied. "Signor and Signora Bernabé speak in dialect. It's probably been a long time since they studied the Italian you're learning. In many ways they are meeting you in the middle when it comes to language."

"It's difficult to follow."

"Maybe they will teach you their dialect, as well." Professor Causa finished her cappuccino. "Back to class," she said. *"Allora, parliamo italiano."*

That first week, we reviewed nouns and present tense verbs. We wrote out dictation quizzes. I tried to do my homework the best I could after drinking many glasses of wine at dinner each night and then grappa in my coffee.

The reading from the first chapter of our textbook, *Vivere all'italiana: A Cultural Reader,* was due on Friday and I translated it at lunchtime on a park bench near Cremona's cathedral while Sara and Jen and Lisa drank aperitifs at the cafe near school. The translated essay was entitled *"La Famiglia Italiana"*:

> *Italy, therefore, presents the character of a society in transition, divided between the old and the new, between tradition and modernity. The family reflects this contradiction and strains to compromise. Many parents today are more open to dialogue with their children and inclined toward self-criticism.... The majority of young people maintain affectionate relations with their parents, and in general the profound sense of devotion and responsibility between them remains unchanged.*

"Su! Su! Jason!" shouted Anna at 7:12 a.m. *"Tardi! Tardi!"* The light switch for my room was situated in the hall. Anna flicked the light on and off to wake me even though I'd only overslept a few minutes.

When I sat at the table, two fried eggs were waiting for me—just as they were each day for twelve weeks. Paolo returned from the morning inspection of his fields and read the newspaper, RAI UNO still droning on the television. Paolo poured a shot of grappa into his coffee cup. Meanwhile, Anna raced back and forth, urging me to eat faster or I'd miss my train.

This was the routine, established from day one when I inadvertently left myself an extra 45 minutes to catch the thirteen-minute train from Pieve San Giacomo to Cremona. After that, no matter how late I stayed up the night before, my bedroom light flicked on and off some time around seven o'clock. Every day, I arrived in the city much too early for class.

On that first day of school, Anna gave me a green child's book bag—complete with a colorful tag on the flap for my name and address. Daniela left for work in Milan later than usual so she could escort me into Cremona. I tailed along like a little brother, book bag on shoulder, as Daniela showed me how to purchase tickets. Then she showed me to a compartment where she introduced her friends, Mariangela and Christina, both stunning with long, curly black hair, dressed in chic Milan outfits, and wearing sunglasses.

When we arrived in Cremona, the four of us walked to Daniela's favorite coffee bar and ate brioches with other fashionable people, me in shorts, sandals, and a FREE SOUTH AFRICA t-shirt. The women introduced me to the *barista* as "Jason, our American friend" and everybody laughed when he yelled, "Ah, Friday the 13th!" and ducked behind the bar. After coffee, Daniela slipped me a few lire to make sure I had enough money for lunch and instructed me on which afternoon train to ride.

Each morning after that, in Daniela's absence, Mariangela and Christina doted on me as they went to work at the hair salon and the shoe store. The two of them didn't speak English, but wanted me to tell them all about New York and its nightclubs and they laughed and flirted and invited me out to discos at night, even though they knew Paolo and Anna would never have allowed it.

I usually returned home to Pieve San Giacomo alone on the train. Paolo was often in the garden, with tall rubber boots glistening in the bright sun, picking asparagus or spinach for dinner. Inside, a Coke was poured and waiting. Anna ironed in the living room or worked on the sewing machine or stood in the kitchen shaping tortellini with her finger. My laundry sat neatly folded on the bed. Once, I had located the washer, but was chased away by Anna, who squealed and said, "Men don't know how to use this."

On those hot afternoons, young men, Bernabé cousins, stopped over on motor bikes and scooters to discuss Rambo and Schwarzenegger and auto racing. Shy little neighborhood girls came to the patio so they could play with the puppies. They blushed and giggled when I poked my head outside. The television was tuned every afternoon to World Cup games, which Italy hosted that summer, or to an Italian version of "The Price Is Right" called "OK!"

One day, I met Daniela after school and she took me to meet her boyfriend, Massimo, who lived in Cremona near a violin-making school which Stradivari had attended. Massimo was a painter who shared a studio with several other artists and Daniela was obviously smitten with him.

We hung around all afternoon, as Massimo, in paint-splattered clothes, wild hair, and a goatee, sketched and paid little attention to me. Meanwhile another young artist painted a watercolor of me on brown paper.

When we arrived home after dusk, dinner was ready. Bowls of minestrone were served and I mentioned to Anna that I'd met Massimo. She smirked and glanced at Paolo. "Do you like him?" she asked. "His long hair?"

"Sure," I said.

"He's an artist, you know." Her smile grew and she raised her hand to shoulder level. "With long hair."

Anna poked me in the side and chuckled while Daniela blushed and tried to sink into her chair. I smiled, now reveling in the role of annoying little brother. Daniela was thoroughly mortified.

"Oh, Massimo is nice enough," Anna said.

Paolo grunted. "He's crazy," he said with a wave of his arm. "Just crazy."

At that, Daniela sat straight up and loudly began defending her Massimo. Paolo winked at me and shook his head. "Crazy!"

Late that night, Daniela brewed coffee and the two of us stayed up and, for the first time, really discussed anything in English. "You seem tired," Daniela said.

We talked about Jack Kerouac, whom she had just read. Then we joked about the DE LA SOUL t-shirt she wore and how she hadn't realized the phrase was the name of an American rap group.

When my train stopped in Pieve San Giacomo each afternoon, the remaining mile home I often traveled alone. Sometimes, I heard the children who rode their bikes nearby tell each other in loud whispers, "That's the American," and I waved. But most often, the walk was a chance to clear my head from a full day of lecturing and to prepare for a full night of conversation.

My classmates could stay at the cafes in Cremona until late, drinking and complaining about what a task master our professor had become. Afternoon after class, we sat and watched German tourists come in and out of the cathedral and spoke English in purposeful slang so no one could understand us. I generally was compelled to leave after only one or two bottles of Danish beer.

And so I would return to my family. In the fiery sunlight of the late afternoon, I followed the road home between fields and grain towers. Golden brown dust levitated in the hot air. On some particularly tough days at class, I would walk the road cursing my situation, angry that the Bernabés frowned upon me staying in town to hang out with my friends. Instead, I had to phone my friends and plan to be dropped off and picked up or arrange a sleepover as though I were thirteen. If I took a different afternoon train home, even if it was six minutes later, I made sure to call.

The road to Bernabés' eventually brought me past a white iron gate and the home of Daniela's aunt. Once she'd learned my daily schedule, Aunt Gina would be waiting for me in the yard. "Jason! Jason! Come here! It's your *zia*," she said, her jet black hair pulled straight back, her eyebrows meticulously plucked, and her make-up unmarred by the heat. She gripped at the white bars of the gate and asked me if I liked the flowers in her yard. Every day, Auntie begged me to come in for a snack and I always evaded her by politely declining, saying Paolo and Anna were awaiting me at home.

But soon, Aunt Gina appeared at the gate with treats. A bottled water or a Coke in the afternoon. Then, she began waiting in the mornings, as well. She dangled bags of cookies through the gate. "Share them at school," she said.

And, always, she implored: "Please, some day, come by. I'll make you lunch or dinner or just a snack."

After about a week of this, I asked Paolo and Anna about Aunt Gina. They smiled sadly and shook their head. *"Che peccato,"* Anna said. Paolo told me she'd lost her husband the year before.

One morning, when I stepped outside on my way to school, Paolo was sitting on the patio smoking a cigarette. He stood and waved for me to follow him. We walked along the edge of the farmyard and then toward a shed. "In here," he said, motioning at the door. I walked through the shed door and immediately faced a slaughtered cow carcass hanging on the wall, blood dripping on the floor. A half-dozen women from the village, including Anna, sat at a long table slicing slimy pieces of red meat and dividing the good stuff amongst themselves. My stomach wretched in the stale air.

Paolo said something in dialect while all the women looked at me and giggled. He then put his arm around my shoulder and explained that this was one of his cows. I was too shaken to really listen to his explanation, but it was obvious Paolo was proud that one cow could provide food for so many families.

When we returned outside, Paolo lit another cigarette and returned to the patio, quite pleased with himself for giving me such a shock so early in the morning. "The men, we only slaughter the cow," he chuckled. "It's the women who have to do the rest."

This was not the first time the men of Pieve San Giacomo tested me.

Earlier in the week, two of the Bernabé cousins—young Paolo and Mirco—stopped by on their motor bikes and asked me to play soccer. Since I'd already bragged about playing the sport since age five, and since no one believed me, I was forced to prove myself. We rode through tiny streets to the dried-out fields where a dozen teenage boys kicked a ball around. Mirco introduced me as an exchange student and one of the older boys asked, "What is he, German?"

"No," Mirco replied. "American."

"American? What does he know about *calcio*?"

We played six a side and, right from the first touch, everyone on my team passed the ball to me. Meanwhile, everyone on the opposing team rushed to defend me. It must have been

*M*y mother was brought to live in Italy by my father, but she was raised and bred in Oregon. She grew up on abundant corn-on-the-cob and strict Lutheran morals. One time, after a decade of doing without, her craving for corn got the best of her. We were driving past a luscious cornfield in July. Mom abruptly pulled over and said, "I've just got to get some. You stay in the car." Astonished, I watched her run to the edge of the cornfield and begin stripping away ears of corn. Unfortunately, the farmer seated in his high tractor saw her. A chase ensued. My mother leapt into the car, throwing corn ears hither and thither, and drove off at high speed. I watched the gesticulating farmer grow smaller and smaller. That evening, she boiled the corn for 15, 20, 30 minutes but the kernels remained hard. It turns out she had stolen hog corn, unfit for human consumption. "God got me yet," Mom mused. She hasn't been seen stealing corn since.

◆

—Anne Calcagno,
Travelers' Tales Italy

because I was at least three years older than the other kids, but I easily dribbled through the defenders. I drew the goalie out of the net and rocketed a shot past him that hit the upper corner of the net.

"Are you sure he is not German?" asked the older boy.

I scored several more times that afternoon and the boys invited me to play in their big weekend match. I returned home for dinner with dirty knees and grass stains on my shorts.

Paolo returned from the local cafe not long after I did. He entered the dining room and said, "The word in town is that the American is very skilled, a great player." He smiled. "You could play in the first division." This was exaggerating quite a bit. But still, the words he used— *un bravo giocatore*—filled me with the kind of pride only a father can bestow on a son.

*

It is six years later and my family—my real American family—is seated in a restaurant. I have just finished translating the words "rabbit" and "apple" from the Italian menu and now my real mother understands what's in the risotto special.

"It's a shame you don't practice your Italian more often," she says. My real father and real brother rip off hunks of bread and dip them in oil.

"When is the last time you contacted Paolo and Anna?" my mother asks.

"Two years ago," I reply. "During the World Cup when Italy was in the finals."

"That's a shame," she says. "They were both so good to you."

An uncomfortable silence hangs over the white tablecloth. My mother smiles and pretends as if this is just small talk. Just normal dinner chit-chat.

My father tries to fill the silence. "Didn't you tell me Paolo had his leg amputated a while ago?" he says.

"Yeah," I mumble with a mouth full of bread.

"Well, I hope you go back there some day soon," my mother says with a sigh. "You'll regret it if something happens to one of them."

I chew my food knowing that I've had opportunities to return to Pieve San Giocomo but have chosen to travel elsewhere for many reasons. My family has moved on to another conversation but I am far away, wallowing in regret.

I am reminded of the night I decided to stay in Cremona and drink in bars with my friends. I believed I'd clearly explained my intentions that afternoon over the phone to Anna. That I'd miss dinner, but not to worry, I'd eat a pizza in town. Sara, an Italian friend Pietro, and I drank bottle after bottle of wine beginning directly after school. When I finally decided to go home, dusk had been hours ago. Daniela and Paolo were waiting for me at the train station, headlights on in the pitch black. Both frowned. "Did you have a nice adventure?" snapped Paolo.

"I'm sorry," I said. Daniela remained silent.

At home, Anna was standing in the doorway, her face flushed with fear. Inside, dinner was sitting on the table, cold. I sat down to eat it. I tried to say that I'd explained myself over the phone, that we'd had a communication breakdown. But my Italian failed me. All I could do was repeat, "I'm sorry, I'm sorry," over and over. I went to bed. The next day, two eggs sat on the table, Anna flashed her smiling eyes, and Paolo returned from the bakery with a brioche. And nothing more was ever mentioned of the incident.

Salad is served in the restaurant and I've yet to say a word since we ordered. My mother tries to bring my head back to the table. "Don't worry," she says. "They know you'll come back to visit."

But what about the robe? you ask. What does the robe have to do with all this?

Everything, I tell you.

On a hot Saturday in her courtyard, I was finally ensnared by Aunt Gina. On that day, Anna and I rode bicycles—Paolo was off in the fields and Daniela working in Milan—and arrived at Aunt Gina's house to find a great feast prepared. Aunt Gina pulled me into the yard by my arm and I wasn't allowed to leave my seat until I had gorged myself on every dish set in front of me. Sweat trickled from my every pore while the women carried trays back and forth.

Then, when I could eat no more, Aunt Gina insisted I tour her house. The three of us entered the cool, dark living room, lighted solely by strips of sunlight through nearly-drawn drapes. Aunt Gina fingered a yellowed photograph of a young man in a soldier's uniform, and told me it was her husband. There were no other photographs of sons or daughters, only Jesus Christ hanging over the sofa.

Aunt Gina motioned for me to stay where I was and shuffled down a long hallway. *"Che peccato,"* Anna whispered and crossed herself. We waited for what seemed like twenty minutes and could hear her rummaging through the bedroom, calling, *"Un momento, un momento!"* Finally, she emerged from the hallway—gently carrying the robe.

She thrust it into my hands and urged me to slide it on over my clothes. I complied, wrapping it around my GRATEFUL DEAD t-shirt and tying the sash tight around my waist. Silence enveloped the dark room. I stood with my arms wide, modeling the same robe her dead husband had worn each morning while he sipped his coffee and read *La Gazzetta dello Sport.*

"Che bello!" she exclaimed. Then she burst into tears and hugged Anna, whose eyes also welled up.

"You'll promise to wear this?" she asked.

I stood dumbfounded, staring at the sleeves of the huge, ugly robe, not believing this whole presentation could be for me. Me. The one with the already stuffed backpack. The one preparing to shove off in two days for the rest of Europe. I knew I had no choice but to make room. To smash down what clothes I could and inevitably leave some of my other things behind. I had no choice but to carry the heavy robe.

And I have. I've carried it through more than ten moves— from dorms to apartments to houses. I've carried it in trunks, in trash bags, in a box shipped by my real American mother, a woman who has always understood the value of things like robes and small feasts in widows' courtyards.

Now, years after the semester abroad, Aunt Gina is dead. Paolo walks with a prosthetic leg and doesn't leave the house much. Daniela still lives at home, and she and Massimo are still only friends. I hear from Anna infrequently, but from what I can read, she still makes sure the Bernabé house runs smoothly. The few letters I send are written in English for Daniela to translate; any Italian proficiency I once possessed is certainly long gone.

Yet each morning, at our home so far away from Pieve San Giacomo, you reach for that robe behind our bathroom door. I chuckle to think this is what you wear before dressing in your fashionable skirts and pants. At times, the robe makes me hungry for fried eggs—a food we never eat because, of course, eggs are much too high in cholesterol and because we have promised each other to try to stay healthy.

Other times, I can't help but ask if there is something else you'd rather wrap around your body. "I don't want a new robe," you say, so simply and beautifully. You giggle, amused to watch me fumble while learning my new role as husband. Right then, I know I am hopelessly entangled by my families—all of them—including the one the two of us are just beginning.

Jason Wilson teaches writing and is a contributing editor for the New Jersey Reporter.

★

My husband and I took our boys, Ryan and Matthew, to Ireland. My parents were born there, and I have more aunts, uncles, and cousins living there than in the States. When we announced our plans, my father was delighted and said to four-year-old Matthew, "Isn't it grand. Now you're going to see the 'Old Country.'"

Later on, Matthew asked me, "How old is Ireland going to be?"

We explored caves and the Cliffs of Moher. We stayed at a castle in the room where two of the Beatles had slept. But the memories that my children still talk most about revolve around working the cash register in my Aunt Susan and Uncle Dan's shop, meeting Uncle John

Joe's cows, looking up at the bird that sat on his head, and spending a night at a pub with cousins galore.

This is the life lesson that my children know best: it's the people you're with and the folks you meet that make travel wonderful; scenery is just background.

—Susan Ungaro, editor-in-chief, *Family Circle*

KATHRYN MAKRIS

* * *

Breakfast in a Vineyard

A granddaughter returns to the island
of her Greek ancestors.

It was the sort of thing my grandmother had warned me against—sitting alone on the very spot where her father had died, in the ruins of the vineyard cottage from which a band of mountain brigands had once threatened to kidnap her and hold her for ransom.

She had left Greece for the United States in 1916 during a time of political turmoil. In the 1990s, as I prepared for a trip back to her home island, she was full of trepidation for me.

Yet on my last morning on the island of Cephalonia, there was no place I could be but exactly there, serenaded by nearby church bells, amid what had long ago been a green sea of grapevines. I ate an orange, watching steam rise from the old stone well, with the spirit of Mihalakis, my grandmother's father, to keep me company.

A month earlier, when I'd first found Mihalakis' vibrant presence in the vineyard waiting for me, I didn't believe in ghosts. Now I had no choice but to believe in the uncanny and powerful sense of well-being that just being in his vineyard gave me.

Of course I had to explain to Mihalakis why I hadn't come sooner, why my Greek was that of an *Amerikanaki*, and why, at age 35, I still didn't quite know my purpose on the planet. In return he waved away my grandmother's warnings and gave me all he possessed, embodied in the form of his favorite piece of land among his many holdings on the island—his beloved Lakomatia.

At the turn of the century the hillside property had produced some of the finest *robolla* wine in Greece. Now it sprouted thorny, tumbleweed-like bushes, stunted little trees and controversy over its ownership. The eight decades since my grandmother's emigration had meant eight decades of neglect, and now anyone might attempt a claim to the estate if my family didn't.

To me, Lakomatia was the landscape of forgotten love, its sunburned, stony soil as fertile ground for my imagination as Provence for Cezanne or baby lettuce for Alice Waters. It was the territory of my heart.

A bowl of acreage sloping up from both sides of the road, Lakomatia nestled inside a larger bowl of gray mountain foothills. In the bottom of both bowls, in the roofless ruins of the cottage by the road, I was sheltered from even the sun at that early hour, and from the view of the occasional car puttering down toward the monastery. The mist of the cool October morning provided a heavier veil. It condensed in a silky sheen on my hair and skin, blending me in with the land, so that I could, if I wanted, pretend to be a tree or a part of the crumbling rock wall I sat on.

The only intrusion from the world beyond was the insistent summons of the bells at the Monastery of Agios Gerasimos a mile away, and also the knowledge that in a few hours I would have to leave Lakomatia, leave Mihalakis, and leave the island.

For the moment, I closed my eyes and filled my lungs with the air that had nourished my grandmother's childhood summers, when dense heat in the port town sent her family in retreat to the vineyard. A small breeze brought me the tang of wild thyme and rosemary, the salty whip of the sea beyond the hills and fresh evergreen down from the mountain. From somewhere, I was sure, I caught a whiff of wine.

Ghosts populated the land: Mihalakis beside me, the shouts of his workers in the fields, their slapping feet in the wine press cottage near the house and the quiet laughter of his only child, my grandmother, playing with a puppy, forever safe under his burly, bearded visage from the villainous mountain men.

The bells began their litany again, calling to me from the church at the monastery that is five centuries old, the church where my grandmother met my grandfather the year after Mihalakis's death. There they decided to marry; there they decided to leave the island of Cephalonia, cross the Ionian Sea and the Mediterranean and sail the Atlantic for America.

Now it was time for me to leave, too. From my backpack I pulled the wedge of *galatoboureko* I had brought for breakfast— a honeyed concoction of cream of wheat and phyllo pastry, fragrant with cinnamon. I left it on a fallen slab of the old house. In exchange, I took into my palm a wind-pocked, dew-drenched shard of roof tile, bony on my skin, a talisman from our vineyard, from Mihalakis, from our family of ghosts.

Nowhere on earth could I be safer than in that place. My grandmother would have to understand. Time had trans-formed her danger into my solace.

Remember, my great-grandfather said, *this is the land of your dreams.* His voice rolled through me, as resonant, as true, and as fortifying as the steady, singing clang of the monastery's bronze bells.

Kathryn Makris is the author of seventeen novels for young readers
and a CBS-TV Schoolbreak Special adapted from her Children's
Choice Award winner Crosstown. Currently she is at work on a
book and a screenplay set in Greece's Ionian Islands.

*

I see everywhere in the world the inevitable expression of the concept
of infinity…. The idea of God is nothing more than one form of the
idea of infinity. So long as the mystery of the infinite weighs on the
human mind, so long will temples be raised to the cult of the infinite,
whether it be called Brahmah, Allah, Jehovah, or Jesus…. The Greeks
understood the mysterious power of the hidden side of things. They
bequeathed to us one of the most beautiful words in our language—
the word "enthusiasm"—*en theos*—a god within. The grandeur of
human actions is measured by the inspiration from which they spring.
Happy is he who bears a god within, and who obeys it. The ideals of
art, or science, are lighted by reflection from the infinite.

—Louis Pasteur

* * *

Wee Airborne Advice

*At 35,000 feet, a new father
discovers a simple truth.*

WHEN WE GOT ON THE PLANE, I FINALLY UNDERSTOOD WHY
they let people with small children get on board first. It's not
because you need more time to put things away; it's because
they want to spare you all those dirty looks. When we stepped
onto the plane, my wife holding our son, me lugging three
bags, a collapsible stroller, a car seat, a video camera, and a
panda bear the size of Buddy Hackett, every person on the
plane looked up with an expression that said, "Please, whatever
you do, don't sit near us."

There's a palpable discrimination you face when you travel
with an infant. Like hotels that happily took our reservations
until we mentioned we needed a crib.

"A crib? Why did you say 'crib'?"

"Because we're circus people and we're traveling with a seal.
Whadaya think—we have a baby."

"Oh, I'm sorry, we don't accept babies."

"What do you mean you don't 'accept' babies? There's
nothing to accept. This is not some crazy kid running around

vandalizing your ice machine. This is an infant. And not just any infant—this is our infant. Perhaps the sweetest boy working the country today. What kind of sick people are you?"

Never mind the fact that less than a year ago, I myself would call up hotel managers and ask them to relocate the people with the screaming kids to another side of town because my wife and I—"regular people"—were trying to get some rest.

Settling into her seat, my wife began to breastfeed our son to relieve his ear pressure during takeoff (which, I understand, hands-down beats the hell out of chewing gum).

"Honey," she said, "could you get his jacket? I think it's in the canvas bag"—which I had just finished cramming into the overhead compartment, behind the...stroller, two puffy down jackets, and our four-hundred-pound diaper bag.

I hoisted myself up, gathering a lap full of stuffed animals and assorted containers of half-chewed oranges, gummed bananas, and sampled-but-rejected soggy crackers, and dumped them on my seat. Yanking open the compartment, I was hit in the eye with a rubber duck. As I swatted him away, I noticed—directly across the aisle—a young couple who'd been watching the whole show.

"How are ya?" I mumbled politely, knowing full well what they were thinking.

"Our lives are sooo wonderful and simple and carefree, and we're so much happier than you poor slobs with your baby." That's what they were thinking—I just knew it. But I was on to them.

"Have you any kids yourself?" I asked, like I didn't already know.

"No," the guy said, "but we're thinking about it."

A short while later, somewhere over the Great Lakes, I imagine, I had my son in my lap and was reading him one of his favorite books. When you're very young, by the way, your favorite book isn't necessarily the one with the best story or even the prettiest pictures. It's the one whose pages taste best. The book that goes easy on your gums is a good read.

"I enjoy Faulkner's storytelling, but his novellas tend to cut me in the roof of the mouth. Dickens, on the other hand, is soft and nice."

As I read my boy his book, and he chewed on the chewiest chapters, I noticed the couple looking at me, but now a little less condescendingly.

"He's a beautiful boy," the guy said.

"Oh, thanks," I acknowledged politely.

"Is this your first child?"

"Yup…first one…"

My son, who must have sensed that he was not only the object of discussion but also the floor model for this couple on the brink of their big decision, took the book out of his mouth and offered it to them, while smiling one of his hard-to-argue-with killer smiles.

They both melted. The woman reached over to caress my son's cheek.

"I could eat you up with a big spoon," she cooed.

"What's it like?" the guy asked.

"What's what like?" I said, making him work for it a little.

"Kids. Having kids. Is it good? I mean, we want to have kids, but everybody says it changes your whole life and everything. So, I was just wondering if it's really true. If, y'know… is it good?"

Having been there myself, I knew how vulnerable they were. I could make 'em or break 'em. I turned to my wife.

"What do you think, honey?"

"About what?"

"These nice people are thinking about having a baby."

"Oh," she said. "Good for you guys."

Then turning back to me, she said, "Well, that's a darn good question. What do you think we should tell them?"

We looked at each other and smiled. What should we tell them? Should we tell them it's the hardest and scariest thing any sane people could ever do? Do we let them know that having a child drains you, depletes you, exhausts you, and frustrates you until you end up hiding in your car whimpering like a puppy?

How can you explain that having a child drives you as far apart as you've ever been, yet draws you together more deeply and magically than ever before—all at the same time?

That after you've both spent an aggravating, mind-numbing hour-and-a-half rocking, walking, patting, begging your child to sleep, there's nothing you'd rather do than spend the next hour and a half together, watching this angel sleep.

How can you explain that in the midst of a cranky discussion over who's not "being supportive" of whom, you notice how adorably and hilariously your child is eating a bowl of spaghetti, and suddenly all the things you fret about just don't matter.

You can't.

I turned to the couple and said, "Yeah, it's good. You'll see."

They nodded and drifted into their own conversation.

I held my boy's face in my hands and planted a juicy kiss on his cheek. I leaned over and kissed my wife, too.

"What did we do before we had this boy?" I asked.

"That…," she said, smiling at the other couple.

I couldn't believe how a handful of months could obliterate everything that had come before.

"But now we're this," she said.

Our son sat in his mother's lap, one hand wrapped around her fingers, one hand on my nose.

"You know what?" I said. "I like this better."

Paul Reiser is the star, co-creater, and executive producer of the NBC-TV series Mad About You. *He's also the author of* Couplehood *and* Babyhood.

★

Two weeks before her first birthday, we took Ella to Istanbul, Turkey. This was during Ella's Cheerios period, and her father and I boarded the flight with cereal-filled plastic bags stuffed throughout our carry-on luggage. Each tiny circle provided not only nourishment but also a moment's entertainment as we parceled them out one by one, often with comic fanfare. By the return flight, our Cheerios supply was exhausted. During the layover in Germany, my husband struck upon one equally small food. He plied her with raisins. An hour into the flight, we were suddenly reminded of the laxative power of dried fruit. Halfway to New York, Ella had spent her entire diaper supply and had gone through all three changes of clothes allotted for the flight. When we finally landed at Kennedy Airport, she was wearing a t-shirt and two airline blankets.

—Sue Warner, "Fear of Crying," *Los Angeles Times*

TIM PARKS

* * *

The Certificate
of Virginity

*A lapsed Anglo-Saxon takes his
children to the Italian seashore.*

I PLUNGE INTO THE WATER, FOLLOWED BY THE CHILDREN. IT'S
around nine o'clock. The sea is shallow, tepid, motionless. Yet
most bathers turn back, or just walk the shallows parallel
with the shore: grandmothers with straw hats and sunglasses,
fat men deep in conversation. In the first stretch of water, the
older boys play games of volleyball or *tamburello*. Almost
nobody ventures out of their depth.

I encourage my own children to swim. I have mock fights
with them. I persuade them to paddle out to the rocky break-
water and even to dive on the other side, in the open sea,
where nobody goes. In doing so I am constantly aware of
obeying a different cultural programming, of not being relaxed
enough. Other parents just like to stand in the warm shallows,
admiring their own brown skins glistening with sun and
water, ignoring their children, enjoying the mill of people near
the shore.

And if someone does swim seriously, it is a boy. None of
the girls seem to swim. The girls stand at wading depth and

make a gesture I don't remember seeing in England. In up to their thighs, they lift handfuls of water and let it dribble down over their bodies. They repeat the gesture perhaps three or four times. You imagine they're getting acclimatized, ready for the plunge, but just when you think they're going to plunge, they turn round and wade out again. Watching them, realizing the motions are habitual, I'm reminded of something I once translated, about a mythical girl called Iphimedeia. She had fallen in love with Poseidon and would often walk along the beach, go down into the sea, rise the water from the waves, and let it flow down over her body. It was a gesture of love, of seduction. And it worked. Finally, Poseidon emerged from the water, wrapped himself round her, and promptly generated two children. After which Iphimedeia no doubt became just another of the young mothers on the beach. "Do you want a banana, Benedetta? Come on, you need some fruit after your *pizzetta*. Don't throw sand. Don't bother your little sister. No, you can't go in the water till ten o'clock. You haven't digested yet. And you need some cream on your tummy, you're burning, can't you feel you're burning?"

Iphemedeia, the Medusa, the eternal return, the sharpness of figures against the light, like stark silhouettes on Greek vases, it seems one always has half a sense of myth by the Mediterranean, the land's edge is also the edge of a timeless world of Latin archetypes.

Though I'm always lapsing back into my practical workaday Anglo-Saxon mentality. Having crawled exhausted out of the sea, I'm now toiling over a huge round sandcastle in several tiers with moat and perimeter wall and secret tunnels and dungeons. It's a very English-looking thing. The kids join in. They love it, as I loved to do this with my own father and mother. So do other people's kids. A tiny Patrizia helps Stefi find shells for the battlements. Somebody's little Marcello is running back and forth with a bucket for water for the moat. Eventually, to my surprise a small crowd forms by the water's edge to admire the flying buttresses, the crenelated walls. We've got it up to about three feet now. It's a pretty big castle. People break off their strolls to stand and stare. Endeavor of this magnitude has considerable curiosity value here.

Later, back at the sunshade, we find Aunt Paola. Since we're not in Pescara for long this year, she is letting us share her sunshade, a gesture almost as generous as letting somebody share your bathroom. And given that my father- and mother-in-law are away for a few days, she is eager to help me and, like all the Baldassarre family, to offer advice. After all, it's a generally acknowledged truth in Italy that a man can't be expected to look after children on his own for more than a couple of hours.

Zia Paola is old, white-haired, slightly hunched, discreet, gracious. Her voice is pleasantly low and gravelly. And the first thing she says is not to buy mozzarella on a Monday. It would be a mistake to buy mozzarella on a Monday because they might well have been keeping it in the shop over the weekend, and in this heat…

Also, I should be very careful about salad. She can tell me a place where I can get good fresh tomatoes and lettuces at a cheap price.

She speaks for some time and in great detail about shopping and menus. Rather than myself, it is

*I*talians treasure children. Sophisticated career women kiss and coddle little ones on the street, crusty old farmers gush as school kids stroll past; even teenage boys pause to admire a sleeping baby. Again and again, families are greeted with the proverbial blessing *auguri*, wishing them well.

◆

—Valerie Wolf Deutsch and Laura Sutherland, *Innocents Abroad: Traveling with Kids in Europe* the children who join in, already better at discussing food than I am: they explain how Mamma dresses the salad, which pasta they like best. Stefi is particularly eager. She always drinks some of Daddy's wine, she says.

Paola promises she will bring me some local wine a friend makes. Then she warns me that I mustn't use the towel after laying it in the sand. One can catch skin irritations in this way. God only knows what funguses there are in the sand. I shall have to wash it now and leave it to dry in direct sunlight. And on second thought perhaps it would be better not to give the children mozzarella at all in this weather, not even if I buy it fresh on Tuesdays or Wednesdays, since in this kind of heat those things tend to ferment in the stomach.

Paola has been so kind I feel I must return the favor some-how, and seeing that she talks so constantly about food, I invite her to a restaurant. Perhaps tomorrow. With her daughter. But she declines the offer. She is too *fastidiosa*, she says. There are too many things she doesn't like or can't eat. Stefi says she feels exactly the same way. The little girl nods very sagely, damp hair falling over her eyes. For example, she doesn't like runner beans, and Michele doesn't like peas... "You never know," Paola is saying, "in a restaurant, how long the food has been in the freezer, whether they've washed their hands or not, what they've put in it to make it look nice. Eating out is so unhealthy." I decide I'd better not tell her that I am about to take the kids up to the terrace bar for their much-loved antipasto of *pizzetta* and Coca-Cola.

For this is what the routine now demands: shower, *aperitivo*, antipasto, computer games, home.

I can't recall the presence of showers on English beaches, but in today's anal post-peasant Italy it is unthinkable that one should be in contact with something organic like seawater without then taking a thorough shower to clean off. More practically, there is the problem that salt on the skin can be very unpleasant when the temperature is up in the high thirties.

Here, then, is the only part of my children's beach experience that involves something approaching heroism. As I said, the Medusa's showers are cold, and what's more, powerful. Either they're off or they're full on, drenching you with a pounding delivery of freezing water. Yet everybody seems to love it. People queue up by the four showers between terrace and bathing huts. They stand under the cold water and shriek. The children dance and scream. Then after only a minute, perhaps even less, of intense cold on burning skin, they're out already, laughing and shivering their way into bathrobes. It's as if all that excitement of contact with the elements, that thrill of endurance, hardship, all those qualities our English parents hoped we would thrive on as children, were condensed here into a few shockingly icy seconds, the better to enjoy the sensual pressure of the sun afterwards, the splendid sense of well-being brought on by bright light and color and abundant food.

"*Una pizzetta rossa,*" Stefi says, "*e quattro gettoni.*" Four tokens.

We're standing at the bar. I order a *bicicletta*, a bicycle, which actually is nothing more than a mixture of a pink *gingerino*, some kind of bittersweet soda, and a very large glass of white wine, the kind of drink that would look out of place on a Saturday night

---

*A*fter we had been in Italy for a couple of weeks, and had learned the *gelati* ordering ritual, eight-year-old Spencer, ever the independent child, marched into a *gelateria* in Siena and ordered, in a perfect accent: "*Due mille lire gelati citrone, per favore. Grazie signor, ciao.*"

◆

—Judith Schultze,
"Family Vacations: Europe,"
Los Angeles Times

in the Queen's Head or the Pig and Donkey in Clapham or
Stoke Newington, but that winks very colorfully here in the
dazzling sun.

The fat boy serving has a t-shirt on that says, I'M A LATIN
LOVER. I wish him well. His mother remembers to ask where
my wife is and, on hearing the news that she's expecting,
expresses amazement at our *coraggio*. Secretly, I know she is
imagining that this third child, six years after the second, is
a mistake. Every Italian adult I have spoken to is convinced of
that and will be all the more so if I bother to deny it.

"It's another girl," I tell her, since we know from the scan.

"Oh well," she smiles, "you already have your *maschietto*."

It's so reassuring to know beforehand what people are going
to say.

And the children's boyish and girlish personalities are so
evident now! Michele has grabbed his tokens to go and play
his computer game at the far end of the terrace. He's anxious
to get in there before the crowd arrives. Stefi waits behind at
the bar to pick up his pizza and Coca-Cola for him. Then she
will go and stand by the machine, and she will feed him and
water him as he plays. It's touching and somewhat frightening
this sweet femininity she has. Obviously, she's terribly impressed by the way he attacks the machine's buttons and tog-
gles, generating improbable martial arts in a figure called
"The Vigilante," who strides up and down New York subway
cars battering well-equipped crooks. Then the other children
who huddle round are impressed because Michele can read the
instructions and comments in English. Especially the bit when
the Vigilante finally hits the deck and a doctor appears with
caricature rimless glasses on his forehead and starts pressing
fiercely on his barrel chest, while red letters flash: "If you want
your hero to revive, you have thirty seconds to insert another
token." Michele reads the message to the other boys. He has a

way I have never managed to cure him of slightly over accenting the ends of the words. "Iff you wanta yourr hero to revive...," so that for a moment it seems the action really is happening in the Bronx. "You have thirty...." Stefi gets in the second token just in time, then claps when a particularly ugly thug goes down under a hail of spanner blows. Her admiration, her quiet supporting presence, holding her brother's pizza and Coke, isn't so far away from that of the *bagnino's* [lifeguard's] girlfriend.

All I have to do now, while the children get their daily dose of electronics, is sit and eat my *pizzetta* and drink my *bicicletta* and wonder what I'm going to make for lunch. I sit. A large crowd of fifteen-year-olds are hanging around the jukebox, putting on favorite songs. By the end of the week, I'll know which girls are going to put on which songs. For it's always the girls who put on the songs, though sometimes they may beg the money off a boy. One girl, still a child but with a woman's body and elegance, is dancing, in a bikini that says MORE ENERGY round the waistband and again on a sort of tight sash affair beneath her breasts. She is beautiful. But the boys are perfectly relaxed about it. Like the *bagnino* and his girl perhaps, it's not so much that they're unimpressed as that they haven't really noticed yet. They're eating *pizzetta* and discussing the exams they just finished. Then I realize that more interesting to them than the women are all the fashion accessories they have about them: the silvered sunglasses hung over top pockets, the gold chains round neck and wrist, the Swatches and fluorescent headbands and pinhead earrings and purple money pouches and leather key rings.

All of a sudden the whole group decides to move over to the other side of the terrace and the phone, where everybody crowds round the dancing girl with her MORE ENERGY costume. She is about to make an important call. She lifts the receiver and dials. As she speaks, the others mouth encouragement or pull faces. Is she phoning a boyfriend? Is she trying to get her parents to let her stay out? She's struggling not to laugh. The others are clowning wildly. And I think, one of the reasons I've stayed in Italy is that I believe, perhaps erroneously, perhaps sentimentally, perhaps merely in reaction to my own childhood of church halls and rainy weekends—I do believe that kids have a better time here, that adolescence is more fun here. Certainly, I never saw a group of people so confident and at ease with themselves and their youth. I wish it for my children.

Then you pick up the paper someone has left and read a story that knocks you out, that prompts revisions. Still licking the pizza grease off my fingertips and sucking the iceblock from the *bicicletta*, I've got half an eye on the kids, half on two men complaining about refereeing standards, one with *"Amo Lucia"* tattooed on his shoulder—I love Lucia—when my attention is caught by the fact that this is the very same name as the one in the big headline on the page I've turned. "LUCIA IMMACOLATA?" it asks.

Lucia.... *Corriere della Sera* describes her with endearing enthusiasm as a splendid Calabrian blonde, eighteen years old, the most sought after of her neighborhood.... The story goes like this. For reasons unspecified, Mother sent Lucia away to her aunt in Naples for a while at the beginning of summer. Result: everybody in her apartment block and street assumed that she was being quietly removed from the scene to have an abortion, or even to give birth. There's a nice expression in Italian here, *"malelingue"*—evil tongues, gossips—and what these evil tongues were saying was that Lucia was a slut. This distressed the mother, who was afraid that if everybody believed this slander, the girl wouldn't easily be able to get married. She thus went to a gynecologist at the main hospital in

Reggio Calabria to have him examine the girl and give her an official, yes, official, *"Certificato di Verginità."* With this in her hand she then went round to knock on all the doors in the housing project and show it to people. Her daughter was a virgin, she said. She had the proof. The rumors must stop. But this was a mistake. Not only were the *malelingue* not impressed by this, but they immediately began to put it about that the mother must have paid the gynecologist to produce the document, and given that she was a poor woman and widowed, the only way she could possibly have paid a professional man like that was in kind…her daughter's, of course. Lucia went to bed with the gynecologist to get her certificate of virginity! Understandably, this spicy paradox was all too much for the mother, who was now demonstrating that she did indeed have some savings by taking out legal action against the *malelingue*.

Reading this story under the shade of a tamarisk tree, sprawled in this lounge of light and shade, of dazzling color and domesticated outsideness, I start to think about the whole question of virginity and what it might mean: is it different in different countries? I think of the age people lose it, the age my children will lose it…. Do I want to know when they do? No. No, I most certainly don't. And this seems to me the point of the story. That surely we should not know whether Lucia is a virgin or not. It is none of our business. And we most certainly shouldn't ask. A facade of innocence must be maintained while Lucia is allowed to do as she wishes, if she wishes, hopefully with good sense and within limits. Really, *il certificato di verginità*, like so many documents in Italian life (the one indicating the price of my house, for example), is only a rather crude means of shoring up that facade, reestablishing a generous official version that it would be folly to question. There may be elements of hypocrisy, but it does seem to me that this is the most civilized approach, and the most exciting. Lucia is a game lass and a virgin....

The girls and boys are still round the phone. Another young maiden is calling now. She has a butterfly tattooed just above her breast. Did Iphimedeia have a tattoo? One of the boys is trying to tickle the inside of her legs with a seagull feather. MORE ENERGY meanwhile has bought an ice lolly, which has made her lips swell to bright strawberry. Then the *bagnino's* girlfriend, amazingly without *bagnino*, comes up to her and links arms. Ah, so they're friends! And there is such a complicity and craft in their smiles, such female guile, can you really believe that they...

But then you see that expression in ten year olds sometimes, in six year olds even. As now when my little daughter comes up to me, consciously flouncing her pleated blue dress, and she says, "Papà, o Papà-a, wake up, Papà." She pops the sweetest kiss right on my lips, and immediately I know that she too wants an ice lolly. And that Michele has finished his game. Another morning at the beach is over. Now I must get back and make them lunch. Except that I'm overtaken by an extraordinary languor. Has the Medusa turned me to stone? It takes a heroic effort to recover such concepts as responsibility, to deny the children their lollies, to insist on salad and mozzarella back home.

"And it won't ferment in your stomach," I manage to say, when Stefi objects. "That's just Zia Paola fussing too much." I love mozzarella. And it's easy. As we walk past three rocking horses, past the bubble gum machine, past MORE ENERGY examining some unimaginable blemish on the *bagnino's* girl's shoulder, Michele describes with the most innocent enthusiasm how he just beat more than twenty crooks to death with a crowbar.

Tim Parks has won international acclaim for his work. He is the author of Shear, Italian Neighbors *or* A Lapsed Anglo-Saxon in Verona, Goodness, Juggling the Stars, *and* An Italian Education: The Further Adventures of an Expatriate in Verona, *from which this story was excerpted.*

✳

It is tempting to say that one visits the islands of Italy simply because they are beautiful and because they are there, which would of course be reason enough—except that no act has a single motive.

I went because of my love of water, which is mingled with and almost indistinguishable from a fear of water (I can float in a vertical position—I enter a fugue state—but I cannot bear to bury my face in water).

I went as a kind of memorial gift to my father, who, though he lived ten miles from the sea in Calabria, never saw the sea until he crossed it to come to America....

I went, as a supplicant, to search once again for my mother and ask forgiveness of her spirit...which is to say, to try once again to comprehend the mystery of her life....

I went for my Grandma DiNardo, fat and rosy and jolly in her long black wool bathing suit with remarkable décolletage, who played Ring Around the Rosie with me—just with me—at Coney Island, the froth of waves licking at our ankles. I cherish this image of play, and my gratitude to her was a driving force, too.

—Barbara Grizzuti Harrison, *Desiring Italy*

JANE MYERS

✦ ✦ ✦

Past Imperfect, Future Not So Tense

Years after a divorce, a family comes together
in the Mediterranean to explore what
once was and what could now be.

I LOOK AT THE PHOTOS AGAIN AND AGAIN, SEEKING ANSWERS. Here we are, four people seated under an umbrella at an outdoor cafe, the golden afternoon sunlight casting a soft glow on our faces as we look at the camera. We are all smiling. I see two younger adults who are tall and tan and look quite alike, and an older man and woman whom they resemble in some ways.

It looks like a family. But is it?

I am the older woman in the picture, the mother, and even I don't know. Once, we were a family. But are these photos, taken last summer, images of a family? I do not live with the man in the picture, the father of the children. I am happily married to someone else and have been for nearly a decade. The children's father and I are bound now only by the slender historical thread of shared parenthood. Our marriage ended more than fifteen years ago. When we agreed, separately, to our children's request to spend a vacation together on the Mediterranean, we had not seen each other for three years—

and then only briefly, on the occasion of our son's graduation from college.

We four shared no illusions about being the family we once were. We explored no feelings: in our days together we skated safely above the dark waters of the past as if gliding over well-frozen ice. If we had fallen below the surface we would have risked losing the family we all seemed in unspoken concert to have: the family the children wanted for one brief moment in time, a happy family without any of the pain, the anguish, the chaos that had led to its sundering years before.

It felt unreal only because we were all on our best behavior nearly always. Even in the most harmonious of families, vacations often bring moments of high tension and fatigue. But for most of the trip we could have been a Disneyland model of family perfection. It was clear we had all made individual pacts with ourselves to be happy. We willed it so.

Most of my friends couldn't imagine such a trip, happy or not. "How did you do it?" they asked. "And why?" "What was it like?" "Did you find yourself attracted to the children's father again?" "What did your husband think of all this?"

Their questions were not the questions I asked myself when I returned home. Theirs were the easier questions, with the easier answers. I knew why I had gone: because the children, especially my son, wanted us to be together, wanted it with a depth of desire that made the effort worth the risk. We didn't exactly plan it: perhaps we wouldn't have had the courage to try it if we had. My son, who had worked in Europe for three years, wanted us to visit him before his return to the United States for graduate school. The trip evolved through various permutations, via transatlantic calls and faxes over several months.

How was such a gathering possible? Certainly the passage of time was important. The children's father and I had had many years in which to build separate lives. In the process, we had developed a shared forgiveness, a mutual letting go that allowed us to seal off the past, as though all the ego-battering despair we had known had been put into a chest and sunk to the bottom of the sea that glistened before us each day. Why this was possible is, like love, a mystery. We knew ourselves better, certainly, and accepted on some level that our relationship could never have survived.

No, I didn't find myself attracted anew to the man I once loved. Forgiveness can create compassion, but it doesn't erase the memory of the pain. And my present husband? He is a wise man, a compassionate man, a man with whom I share a profound mutual respect. He didn't question the children's deep longing or my desire—out of love, perhaps out of guilt—to honor their request. He did not want to be there himself.

My own questions were more difficult, the answers less clear. Why was this coming together of their family so important to my children, and what did it mean?

As we traveled from one lovely little resort town to another, I tried to make sense of it. But the terrain was so unfamiliar. I didn't know of other families that had done this, put the pieces back together for a few brief moments for the sheer pleasure of it, compelled not by the social dictates of a wedding or a funeral but only by the desire to be together. Eventually, as I struggled for comprehension, I came up with a word that seemed to be the right one: "re-creation."

With our unspoken contract to ignore the emotional freight we all carried from the past, we were re-creating an earlier time of comfort and joy, of safety and refuge, of everything good that families mean to the children who are part of them. Or was it only a miracle, a fantasy, a sad pretending? I forced myself to ask those questions, to ask, too, if perhaps the children had some hidden agenda I had chosen to overlook.

Yes, like so many children of their generation, they will

always wish their family had not come apart. Yes, like so many children of their generation, they have not rushed to create families the way their twenty-something parents did. But they seem to have few illusions. They have worked hard to become far more self-aware than either I or their father was at their age.

Even the trip's single incident of high tension—a father-daughter interchange on the last day—brought satisfaction for my son. Like many revealing events in a family's life, the trigger seemed innocuous but signified much more. This time, with all of us present, my son confronted his father with honesty and feeling. And what he and his sister got back from their father was honest and full of feeling.

But the power imbalance was gone. And the children and the parents were all different people, people who had been lucky enough and brave enough to have grown each in his own way. What my son achieved in that moment was what to him would have been a perfect family: not one of constant harmony (children are realists after all), but a family in which all the members knew themselves truly and knew their feelings truly and could speak those truths.

When I think back on the trip, studying the photographs, I finally come to an answer, one that an archaeologist might understand best. It has to do with the joy of discovery that archaeologists experience when they uncover a pot shard or the suggestion of meaningful pattern in the dust. From such seemingly spare details, but knowing much more, they are able to reconstruct the past.

If, as the writer Pat Conroy observed when his own marriage fell apart, "Each divorce is the death of a small civilization," then perhaps our days together can best be understood as the reconstruction, if only momentarily, of a small civilization, a civilization more filled with splendor, more intriguing to the children who were part of it than Pompeii or Troy or King Tut's tomb could ever be. I now have a fuller appreciation of what the psychologist Judith Wallerstein meant when she wrote in *Second Chances*, her study of divorced families, that "children are the self-appointed guardians of family history."

Children do not forget. They do not want to forget. And what they most desperately want to remember, for all of their lives, are their family's happy times. In some small but important way, our trip was for my children and for me and for their father, an affirmation that once, yes once, long ago, we were a small and happy civilization.

Jane Myers is a writer who lives in Ann Arbor, Michigan.

★

It had rained hard all night at Denali's Savage River campground, and in the morning, when the downpour turned to drizzle, my daughter Ashley and I decided to bicycle the twelve miles out of the park. Buried in rain gear, we took off pedaling across a bleak, gray landscape. But as soon as we were alone, the sky opened like parting curtains as if to show us—look quickly, please—that the jagged brown mountains had been powdered with the season's first low-elevation snow.

When those holes filled, other clouds lifted and sunbeams spotlighted the tundra—an incredibly rich red, orange, yellow, and green autumnal mosaic. The hills were so bright that, at first, we had to stop and squint through billows of steamy breath to distinguish background from the thick rainbow fragments arching over the canyons. Then the whole scene vanished again into cold and fog.

Metaphors are tricky, but to me that's a good one.

The world is unruly, dazzling, dangerous, lovely, unpleasant, and perfect.

Families are also perfect, because strange as they can be, always changing, they're all we've got to negotiate this difficult, fabulous life.

—Bob Sipchen, "On the Road with the Sipchens,"
Los Angeles Times

* * *

Travels with Mom

When this mother and daughter
travel together, they leave their
baggage at home.

I ALWAYS THOUGHT THAT IF I EVER FOUND MYSELF AT THE RITZ in some foreign city ordering room-service raspberries from a phone in the marble bath, it would be with someone I love.

And that's exactly how it happened, except that someone special turned out to be my mother.

Our trip to Madrid was the start of a recurring role for me: my mother's traveling companion. Over the years, we've traveled as a team at least a half-dozen times.

I always figured other people thought it was weird that I went on trips with my mother. When we spent a week together at a Club Med, I was twenty and, believe you me, absolutely the only young adult accompanied by her parent. The resort's swinging-single scene was hardly a PG affair, "affair" being the operative word there.

But that's all changed. Those wild and crazy beachcombers at Club Med are, ugh, grownups now who aren't embarrassed anymore to be seen stepping out with their parents. More and more aging boomers like me are discovering that traveling with a retired or flexible mom—or dad—is a neat solution to the problem of finding a travel mate who can conform to your limited vacation schedule. One friend convinced her mother to explore the South with her and leave dad behind (he doesn't like to travel).

But for me, going away with my mother has turned out to be more than a matter of convenience.

On our last outing, a long weekend in historic Charlottesville, Virginia, I was an overwhelmed new mom on maternity leave. I welcomed the chance to escape the house with a built-in babysitter. For her part, my mother was planning a trip to visit an old friend on a fellowship at the University of Virginia, only three hours from my home. Mom was ecstatic when I suggested I come along with Anna, her new granddaughter.

As it happened, it was Mother's Day weekend. We thought we were the ultimate three-generation threesome at dinner—Anna asleep in her little carrier, Mom and I eating tournedos by candlelight. Everyone commented. We both gushed like Niagara Falls with our newly discovered pride.

We've found that something almost magical happens when we travel together. We don't fight. Instead of adversaries, we become adventurers, conquering new lands together.

It comes down to this: my mother and I have your standard amount of parent-child baggage, but when we travel, we don't take it. (Of course, that could be because my mother always overpacks to begin with and doesn't have room for any extras.)

The neutral territory of foreign soil somehow gives our relationship a clean slate. It gives us a chance to rediscover our common likes, and to revel without guilt in the high adventure of it all: shopping, eating, napping, room service! Indiana Jones should have such thrills.

We also get a kick out of little neuroses we share: we both

always want dessert, no matter how many courses precede. We both always want to change hotel rooms for reasons we consider utterly reasonable. We both always hit the museum gift shop before the museum. At home, we simply don't get a chance to focus on all the fun trivia of our relationship.

While on the road, we also put refreshing new twists on our old mother-daughter roles. I'm generally boss on our outings—I honcho the trips. My mother picks up the tab. It's a good deal, all the way around.

Our trips may not have unearthed any apocalyptic revelations about the true nature of our relationship or helped us discover any profound new things about each other. They've just given us a chance to have a little fun together, and maybe that's most important of all.

Carol Clurman is associate editor of USA Weekend *magazine. She swears that someday soon she will: 1) take a bike ride through the Loire Valley with her husband and two children, and 2) rent fabulous villas for a month every summer in beautiful foreign countries.*

*

It was my mother who made a traveler out of me, not so much because of the places where she went as because of her yearning to go. She used to buy globes and maps and plan dream journeys she'd never take while her "real life" was ensconced in the PTA, the Girl Scouts, suburban lawn parties, and barbecues. She had many reasons—and sometimes, I think, excuses—for not going anywhere, but her main reason was that my father would not go.

Once, when I was a child, my parents were invited to a Suppressed Desire Ball. You were to come in a costume that depicted your secret wish, your heart's desire, that which you'd always yearned to do or be. My mother went into a kind of trance, then came home one day with blue taffeta, white fishnet gauze, travel posters, and brochures, and began to construct the most remarkable costume I've ever seen.

She spent weeks on it. I would go down to the workroom, where she sewed, and she'd say to me, "Where should I put the Taj Mahal? Where should the pyramids go?" On and on into the night, she pasted and sewed and cursed my father, who it seemed would have no costume at all (though in the end my bald father would win first prize with a toupee his barber lent him).

But it is my mother I remember. The night of the ball, she descended the stairs. On her head sat a tiny, silver rotating globe. Her skirts were the oceans, her body the land, and interlaced between all the layers of taffeta and fishnet were Paris, Tokyo, Istanbul, Tashkent. Instead of seeing the world, my mother became it.

—Mary Morris, *Nothing to Declare: Memoirs of a Woman Traveling Alone*

✦ ✦ ✦

Bambina, Bambina!

When in Rome, a child is a bonus.

THE FRUIT VENDOR AT THE OUTDOOR MARKET IN THE HEART of Rome stared at me as I picked up one of his little baskets of strawberries.

"Those for her?" he asked gruffly, pointing to my six-year-old daughter, who was smiling up at him. Yes, I nodded.

"Don't buy them. They taste bad," he barked, waving us away from his fruit and vegetable stall.

Dumbfounded, I put down the strawberries and stammered my thanks. *"Ciao, Ciao,"* chanted my daughter, waving good-bye and practicing one of her few newly learned words of Italian as we headed down the narrow, cobbled street. The grizzled fruit-seller grinned.

During the eight years I lived in Rome, and in frequent return visits, I had never met a vendor who told me not to buy his produce. Quite the opposite; unless you're a regular customer, many vendors will slip in some crummy produce or overcharge.

But on a recent visit to Rome with my daughter, Stephanie, we encountered kindness at every turn.

In the little food stores where we shopped for our picnic lunches, the grocers frequently slipped her a free chunk of Parmesan cheese. At the ice cream shop where we often stopped, her serving grew more massive each time, great spoonfuls of homemade strawberry, lemon, and chocolate draping the cone.

At the restaurant where we became evening regulars, the waiters took her into the kitchen to watch the chefs cooking pasta. On our last night each waiter gave her a little gift—a necklace, a pen holder—and hugs and the biggest plate of seafood I have even seen served in a Roman restaurant.

In Rome, the importance of eating is matched, barely, by the importance of religion. And again, traveling with a child opened doors. Just down the block from where we stayed was a convent. Each morning, a nun, in her long gray and white habit, swept the outdoor steps and sidewalk.

"*Ciao,*" chirped my daughter cheerfully as we walked past. A conversation began, and soon we were invited through the tall wood door that seals off the convent from the world.

One thing led to another. We were asked to stay for lunch, then two smiling young nuns whisked Stephanie through marble corridors to introduce her to other nuns.

Traveling with a child also got me the closest I've ever been to the Pope.

We'd gone to St. Peter's to see the church and the Pope, who was scheduled to hold an audience that day outdoors in the basilica's vast square.

He sat under a burgundy canopy on the steps of the church; the square teemed with thousands of people cheering as he addressed them in a dozen different languages.

We wormed our way forward to a barricade where police checked credentials, admitting only dignitaries and parish groups who had prearranged their seating in rows of folding chairs near the Pope.

I asked a stern-faced policeman if we could go through, just for a moment. He impatiently shook his head no, then saw my daughter looking beseechingly up at him. He took her hand, ushered her through the crowd, and pointed us to seats a dozen rows from the Pope.

Our days weren't always so sweet. There were times when my daughter was overwhelmed by the urban bustle of Rome, when the manic traffic and jammed buses were frightening, when she longed for some green space to play in this park-poor city.

Not understanding me when I spoke Italian confused her; not being able to speak with children she met frustrated her. But she soon found she could play without words.

At one of central Rome's few playgrounds, she shrieked and climbed and played tag for hours with three Roman children. And at almost every piazza we found a soccer game she could join.

One day, after watching shyly from the sidelines, she was invited into a soccer game in Piazza Navona. Soon she was part of the pack, chasing the ball around a centuries-old foundation in the majestic square.

The tough Roman boys, fierce and devoted players twice her age and size, slowed the game to her pace. And I sat on the steps of a church and watched, marveling how a child brings out kindnesses that drown the differences of culture and language.

Kristin Jackson is a travel writer and editor for the Seattle Times. *She has lived and traveled extensively overseas, with and without her daughter.*

*

My husband, Rob, always loved skiing, but I didn't ski, so after we married he gave up the sport. When our son, Jed, was in grade school, he was invited with an aunt on a ski vacation, and quickly became an excellent skier. This brought Rob back to the sport and my two guys bonded on the slopes. Then we had another son, Rory, who soon learned to ski as well. Suddenly, it wasn't so much fun being the mom left at home. Despite my fears—those slopes are high and cold—I learned to ski.

The first time all of us were together on a quad chairlift, Rob told me that it was the happiest moment he could remember in our family's life.

Since then, we've taken many ski vacations around the world, even though I'm always terrified the first day out on the slopes. But I treasure those times when we've whooshed together in beautiful, serene mountains. I swell with pride at how handsome and graceful my husband and sons look as they ski. And most of all, I cherish the cozy feeling we get after the day is done, when we loosen up our boots and sip cocoa in front of a roaring fire.

—Sally Koslow, editor-in-chief, *McCall's*

NICHOLAS D. KRISTOF

✦ ✦ ✦

The Girl in the Photo

*On a visit to the Philippines, a foster father
embraces his sponsored daughter.*

FOR FOUR YEARS I HAD BEEN WRITING TO THE BONGBONGA
family, who live in the middle of the jungle on an island in the
Philippines. It was somewhat eerie to walk down a narrow dirt
path and finally arrive at their thatch-roofed bungalow beside
a banana tree. "Joy," my escort called out. "Joy Bongbonga!
Your foster father is here!"

The door opened, and Joy appeared: an eleven-year-old girl
with thick black hair, light brown skin, and bright black eyes.
She looked just as she did in the pictures that I had received
periodically from Childreach, through which I sponsored her
as a "foster parent"—except, of course, in real life, scampering
around barefoot, she was cuter.

Like more than 1.1 million other Americans, I had sponsored a needy child abroad through contributions to a relief
agency; in my case this involved sending $22 a month and
exchanging letters with the family. When my work took me
to the Philippines, I decided to make a side trip to visit.

A dozen years before in the Sudan, I had visited another

foster child, Aziza Ali, sponsored by my parents. At the time I was studying Arabic in Egypt, and made a ten-day trip to the Blue Nile Valley where Aziza lived. I was so impressed with the foster parent program and the way it was improving the villagers' health and economic opportunities, that when I got a job and became solvent I sponsored a child in Haiti.

I was never able to visit that boy, Yves Jean-Baptiste; letters describing life in his remote village and pictures showing him as a frail teenager in neatly pressed clothes had to suffice. After he reached eighteen and graduated from the program, I sponsored George Bongbonga, Joy's elder brother, and when George left home to go to a city school, I was assigned to Joy.

We exchanged letters several times a year in English about our lives and families, her schoolwork and my job, and the customs in our countries for Christmas or Valentine's Day.

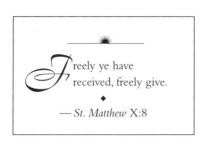

Childreach encourages sponsors to make these visits, and about 200 or 300 do so each year. The woman who answered the organization's phone in Warwick, Rhode Island, was most accommodating when I explained what I wanted to do. She sent me information about visiting a sponsored child and gave me the phone number of a Philippine branch office of Plan International, the organization of which Childreach is the American member.

reely ye have received, freely give.

♦

— *St. Matthew* X:8

I called the local Plan office, in the Philippine city of Calapan, and set a date to visit. The Calapan office gets only three or four visits a year from foster parents, and the staff seemed delighted that I wanted to see the child I sponsored.

So one day at the end of March I set off from Manila at

4:30 a.m. in a car that I had rented with a driver to take me three hours south to the city of Batangas. There I took a hydrofoil for an hour to the island of Mindoro, and when I walked down the gangplank I saw a couple of men holding a sign with my name. It always surprises me when things work out as planned in the Third World, but the whole day went like clockwork.

My escorts, Restie Consigo and Rene Pineda, both Plan employees on Mindoro, loaded me into the cab of a pickup truck, and we began bouncing our way to the Bongbongas' village. It was a three-hour drive on terrible roads, consisting of potholes interspersed with pavement at first, then disintegrating into dirt; where one bridge had washed out we had to drive through a wide creek with rushing water about a foot deep.

Mindoro is a beautiful tropical island of rice paddies and jungle, its verdant greens interspersed with the brown trunks of palm trees, the deep blue of a vast lake, the dark gray of a few somber water buffalo. We occasionally passed other vehicles, mostly private minibuses decorated with chrome and uplifting words—Peace be with You—as they roared down the roads with less inspiring manners. Restie and Rene kept the pickup's cassette player filled with Philippine love songs and Julio Iglesias, because Iglesias is also a foster parent of a child on Mindoro. He sends letters regularly, Rene said, as well as gifts of his music, but has not visited yet.

We stopped the pickup at a small Plan outpost near Joy's village, and about fifteen local volunteers were there to welcome me. The volunteers are central to the programs, doing much of the work at the local level: interviewing sponsored families; taking photographs; writing progress reports to foster parents; distributing letters and money; and planning community projects.

The volunteers all piled in the back of the pickup, and we bounced on up the road to Joy's village. Finally we parked the truck by the side of the road and trudged down a dirt path for a third of a mile to reach the Bongbongas' house.

Teresita Bongbonga, Joy's mother, opened the door, beaming, and a moment later Joy and two younger children appeared. None of us really knew how to behave. They had the idea that Americans are terribly demonstrative, so they seemed ready to plaster me with hugs and kisses, while I had the notion that Filipinos are a bit restrained, so I was ready to shake hands. But the volunteers began laughing and telling Joy to "give a kiss to your second father," and she gave me a peck on the cheek. I thought that Mrs. Bongbonga—her husband, Danilo, was away, working near Manila as a security guard and sending money home—would be offended by the references to me as a foster parent and second father, but she welcomed me in.

I sat down, and Joy sat down next to me, while Restie interpreted. Actually, Joy understood most of my questions—she's a top student in the local elementary school—but she said I was the first foreigner she had ever met, and she was nervous. She said that her favorite subject at school was English and that she wanted to be a teacher. She also showed me around the house, which, it turned out, I had helped to build.

Although sponsors send monthly checks, Plan International does not relay this money directly to the families. Instead, the sponsors' money is used in various projects. The Bongbongas' house, for example, was built three years ago when Plan offered materials valued at $400 if the family would put in labor and supplies worth $160. Made of concrete blocks with a roof partly tin and partly thatch, the house has four tiny rooms with doors and linoleum floors. Although it does not have electricity or glass windows, it is a huge improvement over the family's previous hut.

Plan also provided a water pump, on the condition that the family provide the labor to install it, so that now the Bongbongas have a 40-foot well and a reliable source of potable water. The organization provided a toilet that would prevent contamination of ground water; the Bongbongas built the outhouse around it. Likewise, Plan provides immunizations for Joy's younger brother and sister, Kris and Nikki, as well as family planning counseling to the parents and money to help Joy buy school clothes and scholarships to keep her siblings in school as long as possible.

This day, though, I felt that it was the Bongbongas who were sponsoring me. They treated me to a feast that Joy had helped prepare: bananas from their tree, coconut salad from their coconut palm, fish from a nearby river, rice, and a delicious fruit called star apple. The food was wonderful, although I did pause to collect myself when I took a bite of the fruit salad and found half a worm wriggling in protest.

Afterward, Joy showed me around the village, taking particular pride in displaying the family's pig. She pointed out the radishes, tomatoes, and various vegetables in the family's garden, and she tolerated my insistence at taking photos from every angle.

Finally, after two and a half hours, it was time to go. I first distributed presents: two blouses, a hair clasp, and stamp picture book for Joy; a toy truck apiece for Kris and Nikki; a dress for Mrs. Bongbonga; and a shirt for her husband. Plan had recommended not giving expensive gifts, and everybody seemed delighted—and immediately changed clothes.

Joy and her mother walked me back down the path to the pickup, and we said our goodbyes. The volunteers egged Joy on and she gave me another farewell peck and an embarrassed hug.

Now, when I get letters from Joy, she is not just a face in a photograph, but a vivid, smiling child showing off her pump and outhouse and pig. She is my window into a different world; when I write to her, I can conjure that bungalow beside a banana tree, and I now know I helped build it.

Nicholas D. Kristof is the Tokyo bureau chief of The New York Times.

★

There can be hope only for a society which acts as one big family, and not as many separate ones.

—Anwar al-Sadat

* * *

Harvest Out of Africa

*Across oceans and cultures, family
is the universal bond.*

THERE IS A PLACE IN THE HEART OF AFRICA'S GREAT RIFT
Valley where wine grapes grow. The Masai named this place
E-Nai-Posha, "that which is heaving, that which flows to and
fro." Perhaps it is the ancestral way of describing Lake
Naivasha, a remarkably beautiful place and the home of Elli,
my sister-in-law, and her husband, John. In 1982 they started
Kenya's first commercial winery with vines from some of
California's most prestigious wineries, purchased or generously
donated by friends in the winemaking trade.

Many might think it foolhardy to start a winery 50 miles
south of the equator; and yet, it is easy to explain why a vineyard can thrive there. With the exception of two rainy seasons,
most of the days in the valley are hot and dry. The evenings
are cool because of the high altitude and moist breezes off
Lake Naivasha, whose waters are used to irrigate the vines.

Elli is from Los Angeles. She met John, a third-generation
Kenyan farmer of Irish-English descent, on a blind date while
visiting Kenya. Elli's letters were full of stories about her life

and the progress and perils of the young vineyard. She wrote about the giraffe that wandered through the grapevines, dining on the tops of thorn trees, and the hippopotamus that chased her from the lake to the steps of her verandah. Her letters contained as much real-life drama as any that Karen Blixen sent out of Africa.

Her letters and love of family, wine, and travel made a visit inevitable.

As we approached Lake Naivasha Vineyards, riding over the crest of the escarpment, we had a breathtaking view of the Great Rift Valley and Mt. Longonot rising 9,000 feet above sea level amid the vast, endless plains. This enormous seismic fault in the earth's crust, we learned, provided the sandy volcanic soil that nurtures the vines.

The harvest was well underway when my husband and I arrived. The crop of sauvignon blanc grapes had already been harvested and was fermenting in thousand-gallon fiberglass vats inside the winery. But there were rows and rows of vines—thirteen acres in all—burdened with clusters of green-gold colombard grapes waiting to be picked. We had come to Kenya to go on safari, but for a few weeks we would harvest wine grapes with Elli and John and the crew.

"*Habarai asubuhi.*" The melodious Swahili greeting rang out from the workers gathered outside the winery ready to begin the day's tasks.

"*Jambo sana,*" I answered, enjoying the opportunity to use the Swahili I was learning.

"*Kazi mengi,*" the workers said, and I knew that had to mean "lots of work."

We picked the grapes in the cool morning hours between six and ten when they are freshest. As the sun rose over the vineyard, there was singing and laughter. The men sang com-ical songs about women and love, often raising their voices in falsetto to mimic the women they were singing about.

I looked forward to my mornings with the harvest because it was a chance for me to become acquainted with people who live and work in the surrounding villages. (These were mostly men, the majority of whom were from the Luo, Kikuyu, and Kamba tribes. Few women participated.) They were curious about the cost of things in the United States, everything from t-shirts and blue jeans to a plane ticket to Kenya. I told them the *kikapus* (colorfully woven straw bags) we were filling with grapes sold for as much as $25 in many stores. For these men who earn a few dollars a month as grape pickers and farm laborers, America seemed like a place where only millionaires could live. But they didn't believe anyone with so much money could be happy.

I was also curious about them. "What is the cost of a child's education?" I asked a man whose child was attending the village school. "A bag of flour," he told me. "Women walk with children and firewood strapped on their backs," I said. "It is such a heavy load. How far do you walk in a day?" The answer came with arms and palms opened wide.

One of the chores around the homestead was to collect firewood and straight branches that could be used to stake the vines. One day I accompanied a couple of men, riding in a trailer hitched to a tractor to Kedong Ranch, a communal Masai farm that spreads for many miles below the slopes of Mt. Longonot. Hudson, a Kamba, was our driver and unofficial guide.

Over the tractor's loud engine, Hudson would shout, *"Twiga!"* and point to a giraffe. He would frequently stop so that I could take pictures of zebra herds galloping across the brown, grassy plains or catch a glimpse of a gazelle darting into the bush. When we stopped for the men to clear away the bush, Hudson warned I should look out for *simba mkubwa*, a big lion. But his smile told me he was only teasing. The ride on the tractor pulling a trailer full of wood was slow and rough across the unpaved trails. At the end of the day, every muscle ached.

I had taken along a small photo album filled with pictures of my family and friends, my home, even my cat. These were a comfort to me but they were also invaluable in my efforts to talk with people. Whenever the lack of a common language rose as a barrier, I'd pull out my book and share the pictures of my parents and grandparents on their farm in North Carolina. In a place where wealth is measured in children, land, and live-stock, I had found a common bond. One by one the curious would gather around to look at the pictures, some even to touch, as if tracing the faces within the photographs might bring them to life.

There was one picture that everyone from women in the marketplaces to Masai warriors, to workers in the vineyards held up in surprise. It was a photograph of my grandfather standing in the yard in front of his home dressed in the dark khaki pants and shirt he wore to work in the fields. "He is Kikuyu!" they'd exclaim over and over again. It was spoken definitely and with pride.

Barbara Ellis-Van de Water, currently a public affairs officer for the Federal Emergency Management Agency, has worked as a writer, pro-ducer, and editor of television and film. This story was excerpted from Go Girl! The Black Woman's Book of Travel and Adventure, *edited by Elaine Lee. Barbara lives in St. John, U.S. Virgin Islands.*

✳

The girls kept watch while Dave dug because a lion moves through the tawny grass like a whisper, a shadow, a disconcerting thought. On the Edenesque plains dappled with grazing impalas, barely a stem moves as the stalking beast approaches. At night, my mind was flooded with disastrous scenarios. During the day, our carefree family clustered around termite mounds, while our guard sat under a tree, picking stickers out of his socks. We rarely mentioned the danger; there was no reason to call attention to the obvious. If we laughed and joked, the kids felt more secure and less threatened. But it was always there, that whisper in the grass.

—Alzada Carlisle Kistner, *An Affair with Africa: Expeditions and Adventures Across a Continent*

* ✶ *

The Road to Balbriggan

Tracing roots leads to an unexpected conclusion.

BALBRIGGAN IS NOT A TOURIST DESTINATION. FORTY-FIVE minutes from Dublin, it is possibly the only town in Ireland that does not have a quaint pub or a house with a thatched roof.

Instead of Aran sweaters and keychains made of old Guinness advertisements, its shops sell pork chops and discontinued shoe styles. It has a beach, but the only thing that appears to go near it is the train up from Dublin. We were the only people to get off that train at Balbriggan station. My father and his second wife, Ellie. My husband, Ken, and our two-year-old son, Alex. Me. American tourists with new sneakers and money belts that made our sweaters bulge out in odd places. We had come to Balbriggan in search of family.

At least those of us with Irish blood had. Ellie was German by way of Kentucky, Ken was a Jew whose ancestors had come from a small town near the Polish border, and Alex was a little Russian boy who'd spent the first fifteen months of his life in a Moscow orphanage.

My father looked over the concrete wall of the train station and took a deep breath of Balbriggan's foggy air, as if it might awaken some forgotten genetic memory. His mostly black hair was squashed down into the shape of the Irish tweed cap he'd bought almost as soon as he'd gotten off the plane. The same cap that was now on Alex's blond head, floating around his ears. Ellie was singing to Alex, a country-and-western song about a lonesome train, while Ken tried to open the stroller without damaging the print, slide, and video cameras he had slung around his neck like the bandoliers of a Mexican bandit. I, too, tried to wake a sleeping genetic memory with a deep breath of Balbriggan's damp air. It smelled mostly of car exhaust.

My father spoke to the stationmaster. "We're from the United States," he said, as if he thought the man might find the news surprising.

"Tony McCormick," the stationmaster said, reaching up to shake my father's hand. He was a small man with white hair and a blue uniform.

"My family came from this town," my father said, "name of Harford."

"And would you be knowing old Freddy Harford then?" stationmaster McCormick asked. "He'd be living just up the road next to the hairdresser's."

"Freddy, huh?" my father said. "We should invite him to the pub."

"You'll not be wanting to do that," the stationmaster told him. "Freddy's a pioneer."

"A pioneer?" my father asked.

"Have you not heard of the pioneers? They never take a drink."

"Freddy doesn't drink?" My father sounded as if the stationmaster had just told him that our new-found relation had been born with three legs. "Are you sure he's a Harford?"

"Oh, is it Harford you're saying? I thought it was Harper.

Old Freddy Harper's the one lives next to the hairdresser's. I guess he wouldn't be a relation of yours then, would he?"

We decided to ask stationmaster McCormick for directions out to the old cemetery, where we'd been told we would find a family grave, and leave it at that. Like all Irish directions, they were as dense, as beautiful, as baffling as a page of *Ulysses*.

"What you'll be wanting is the road that bends and leads off the main road, past the video store where the wall is painted a yellow-gold like sun shining and sends you down past the old factory where there's been no work for a good long time now, to the butcher shop on the corner where the Benson and Hedges advert's been painted over the old kiln bricks," he told us. We set off walking, Ken pushing the videocamera in the stroller, Ellie looking in the windows of Balbriggan's stationery shops and newstands for an Irish sweater.

Up ahead, my father had taken Alex's hand, and it made me think of the things we'd done together when I was a child. How he would lie in my bed at night and tell me stories until he fell asleep, how he'd put on his plaid bathing trunks and join me in the bathtub, how one time we'd stayed up all night filming pictures of World War I battlefields with an eight millimeter camera for my history project.

The old cemetery was perched on a green hill off the main road to Dublin. An ancient church stood at the top, and the white headstones of

> *E*ver since I was a child at my mother's knee, I heard her speak of the beauty of open fields and woods and the wise and endless sea. Truly a dreamer and seer she was, for then she had only known the sea from pictures. And so I am just walking her way.
>
> ◆
>
> —William Willis, from *Travel That Can Change Your Life* edited by Jeffrey A. Kottler

the graves marched up in neat rows like a small army. My father and I walked through wet grass looking for a headstone with an inscription that matched the one his mother had recited from memory before she'd died. It was her grandparent's grave.

My father found it almost immediately.

It was a rectangular stone with a large Celtic cross on top, and the family history carved into it. Listed among those who had died in America, was Marianne, my father's grandmother.

My father ran his fingers over the carved letters on the headstone. "In a few more years," he said, "you won't be able to read it at all."

I found drawing paper and a green crayon in Alex's diaperbag. I put the paper over the rough stone and rubbed with the crayon. The words *Erected in loving memory* appeared.

As I rubbed, the words came letter by letter, the way they do on a Ouija board. I felt as if I were receiving a message from the grave.

When I reached the last line, it started to rain, and I gave the crayoned rubbing to my father, who rolled it up and tucked it under his jacket as if it were a rare and valuable parchment. Then we crossed the road to a modern pub that had a sign advertising conference rooms.

The pub was paneled and carpeted and had two color televisions tuned to the same soccer match. We sat in a corner booth and ate oxtail soup, while Alex walked behind us and made animal sounds into the backs of our necks.

"If it's living relations you're looking for," the bartender, a tall man with red hair and a pink face said, "you should be talking to Sean McNally the Undertaker. He knows everybody."

We took a taxi to McNally's Drapery Shop, an old-fashioned clothing store, with racks of men's sports coats with plastic covers over the shoulders.

"You'll be finding Sean at home," the man behind the counter told us. "Just go back up the road away from Dublin, past the Church of our Savior, and look for the tallest of three tall houses all in a row." His shirt still had creases where it had been folded in its package.

My father and I wanted to go off in search of the undertaker, but the last train back to Dublin was leaving in fifteen minutes, so we headed back to the station.

"Did you have any luck?" stationmaster McCormick asked when we returned.

"Not really," my father told him.

"This might be of some help to you then." He was holding a small white piece of paper. "It's the phone number of Monica Harford. She reckons her husband Patrick might be a relation."

Two days later, the five of us returned to Balbriggan in a rented car to have lunch with Monica Harford at the Mile Stone pub.

The Mile Stone smelled like old cigarette smoke and gravy. There were dead flies caught between the screen and the window behind our table, and a small color television set tuned to the sheep dog trials above the bar.

Monica arrived in a flurry of face powder and conversation. "I'm expecting a fax from the Fingal Heritage Group," she said. "I've a friend over there looking up Harfords in their database. They'll send it round about three-thirty." She pronounced it *tree-turty*.

"Would you like a drink, Monica?" my father asked.

"Vodka and white lemonade," she said.

"Just white lemonade?" my father repeated, not having heard the rest.

"Now what good would that do me?" Monica told him.

Her hair was standing straight up on one side of her head, as if that was the side she slept on.

Between bites of the turkey and ham special, Monica told us about the Harfords who were still in Balbriggan.

"Of course, there's my Patrick, and Patrick's three brothers," she said. "And Christy Harford, the bomb maker, sure and he's dead now."

"The bomb maker?" my father said.

"Have you not heard of Christy Harford?" she asked. "Made up bombs for the IRA, he did. Made them right in his basement." A large drop of brown gravy fell onto the front of Monica's pink blouse. "The Gardai arrested him ten years ago. A pub owner in town paid his bail, and sure and if Christy didn't disappear right after."

"How did he die?" my father asked.

"One night, about five years after, men in *balaclavas* brought his body back to his house. He'd died of natural causes," she said. "Sure and there's still bombs today they call a Harford, after Christy."

The fax from the heritage society arrived, a document that traced the Harfords back to my great-great-grandmother's baptism in 1847. My father poured over it.

"It's grand what you Americans do," Monica said. "Tracing your ancestry. It's important to know who you belong to." She smoothed the curled pages of the fax flat on the table. "Not like some. A school teacher and his wife here adopted a baby girl from Romania. Now that child will never know who her real family is, will she?"

I looked over at Alex who was sitting at the bar with Ken and Ellie, watching a horse race on the small television. He was wearing a little Irish tweed cap my father had spent the morning searching Dublin's shops for.

My Irish father, his wife who wasn't my mother, my Jewish husband, my Russian son. The day before, we'd stood and listened to a soft-voiced Irish actor recite from Beckett, and I

could sense them standing around me. It had made me feel
the way you do when you discover that someone who loves
you has been watching you sleep.

I folded my copy of the Harford database, and put it away. I
could feel no real connection to the Richard Harford who was
married in 1870, or the Christy Harford who manufactured
bombs in his basement. Real family was not found in Heritage
databases or carved on headstones. It was found in the man
heading to the bar to get Monica another vodka and white
lemonade, the woman explaining what that thing on the
jockey's head was to Alex, the little boy dropping a plastic
hippopotamus into a glass of Guinness.

When lunch was over, we stood in front of the Mile Stone
and Ken took pictures of us with Monica. Then we walked
back to the rented car, Alex and my father up ahead, moving
past Balbriggan's used furniture stores and ladies' dress shops in
their matching Irish tweed caps.

*Janis Cooke Newman is a writer who lives in Northern California
with her husband and their son Alex, who has recently added Mexico,
Italy, and the New Jersey shore to his list of travels. Janis is currently
working on a memoir about Alex's adoption from Russia.*

✳

Recently, my American family got together to celebrate Mom's 80th
birthday. All of us were there, sons and their wives, daughter and husband, grandkids. It was a rare event because we don't all get together
anymore, as we did during our college days. Now we live in different
parts of the world. Jobs, children, and varying vacation schedules prevent family gatherings.

As we toasted Mom with French Champagne, indulged in Russian
caviar, and took bites of King salmon, I reflected upon the fact that this
American family was in some ways closer to me than my biological
one in Nepal. I had now known them for more than twenty years.

When my college friend John first invited me to spend a holiday with his parents, I declined. I confessed that having grown up in an extended clan, I was not fond of families and their Byzantine politics of control and manipulation. Besides, I had just left my home in Nepal and was enjoying freedom, such as staying up all night and getting up at noon. But John said I would be free to do as I pleased.

And so I spent my first American summer with them—and have been forever grateful. Since that first visit years ago, I have come and gone like one of the family. Thanksgiving, Christmas, spring break, any long weekend.

I was present the day Dad died, he who called me "Son Number Four" and introduced me to the joys of Bloody Mary before dinner, before brunch, and after a game of tennis on a Sunday afternoon.

I was the Best Man at John's wedding.

And it has often struck me that I have shared the most fundamental aspects of life—birth, marriage, death—more with my American family than with my own.

As we ate and drank, took photos and video, and celebrated Mom, I secretly celebrated my own terrific luck on having found a family that continues to cherish me despite my idiosyncrasies and perhaps even disgraceful behavior. I never send birthday cards, seldom buy Christmas gifts, don't recall specific anniversaries, and go long periods without responding to their phone calls inquiring about my whereabouts and health, but in retrospect, isn't that exactly how a wayward son or daughter behaves?

—Rajendra S. Khadka, "The Hovering Hindu:
An Education on Two Continents"

PART TWO

Some Things to Do

★ ★ ★

Honolulu Mamas

*The author put off taking his elderly mother
on a trip as long as possible—and then
wondered why he had waited.*

THEY SAID IT COULDN'T BE DONE. THAT GOING ON VACATION
with my mother in Hawai'i would be a big mistake. Cooped
up together there would be a good chance that the hard
fought calm between us would explode into corrosive flows of
emotional lava.

I wasn't concerned. I didn't think we'd actually get to
Hawai'i. For the last few years, as Mom closes in on 80, she
has repeatedly voiced her interest in a series of improbable
adventures that never came off.

"I'm thinking of studying Icelandic," she'll say to me on
the phone from the East Coast. "Their epic story-telling fas-
cinates me."

Or, she'll say, "You know what I'd like to do? I'd like to rent
an RV and drive across the country."

I used to challenge her cruelly whenever she mentioned
what I considered another preposterous notion. "What are
you talking about?" I would counter. "You fall asleep behind
the wheel on the way to the corner market. Now you're

going to drive across the country in a Mini-Winnie?"

"Well, I'd like to," she'd say, her enthusiasm dampened. "If I could find someone to go with me."

Invariably, Mom begins our weekly telephone conversation with, "Oh! You know who died?" It's her way of reminding me she's not going to be around forever, and that maybe I should pay more attention to her.

So when she said, for the sixth time, "You know what I'd really like to do?! I'd like to see Hawai'i," I realized that this was not another passing fancy.

Traveling anywhere with Mom is no carefree outing to the park. After 45 years in the frozen Northeast, she doesn't venture outside unless she has several layers of clothing, emergency food, and a snow shovel.

"What do you think the weather will be like in Hawai'i?" she asked. A decade ago I spent a summer in Hawai'i. That made me an expert on island life.

"Snowy and cold," I told her, reverting to form.

"No, I'm serious," she said. "I want to know what clothes to bring."

"It'll be tropical and balmy," I told her.

"Tropical and balmy? What does that mean? Will I need a sweater?" she asked. "What about a raincoat?" As we discussed wardrobes, I saw storm clouds building off Waikiki. I made a final attempt to discourage her.

"Mom," I said. "You don't like the sun. You don't like the beach. I can't see you taking up windsurfing. You don't even like swimming. I mean, you haven't gotten your hair wet since FDR was in office. Why do you want to go to Hawai'i?"

"I don't know why I want to go," she said, a tinge of anger rising in her voice. "I just know I want to see Hawai'i—while I'm alive!"

Cheap airline tickets and a free place to stay in Honolulu

joined forces to make Mom's dream a reality. After half a dozen telephone calls about the exact nature of "balmy and tropical weather," we were set to leave.

"Guess what?" my wife said to me. "I mentioned the trip to my mother. She didn't exactly ask to be included, but I think she'd really like to go."

My wife and I had been married two years. Our mothers were conspiring to test our marriage.

"Would you like a peanut butter sandwich?" my mother asked a few minutes after take-off. She had been carrying them from the East Coast. "Just in case," as she likes to say. The jelly had already soaked through the bread and was clotting on the inside of the Ziploc bag.

"No thanks," I told her. "They're going to be serving lunch in a few minutes." Besides, we had finished breakfast only 90 minutes earlier.

"I know," she said, "but I have to have something right now. I'm starved."

My mother has the metabolism of a lemming. If she doesn't eat continuously, she's likely to pass out. Her purse is always bursting with crackers, candy, gum, a few vintage sandwiches, and at least half a loaf of bread. In an ocean liner disaster, she will be the last one alive in the lifeboats.

Probably like everyone's mother, mine has a number of idiosyncrasies. To the outside world, they are endearing. "Your mother is just great," people say after having spent five minutes with Mom. But we were about to spend five days together. Five days of listening to Mom read all the street signs in Hawai'i out loud. Five days of watching her write mental notes in the air with her index finger and then erase them with a wipe of her hand. Five days of listening to her hum while she eats, watches television, and reads the paper. I had no idea how this would work out. We hadn't lived under the same roof for more than twenty years. I heard myself concocting justifiable homicide strategies to the judge. "Your Honor, I was becoming just like her," I would plead. But she was my mother. She wasn't getting any younger, as she often reminded me.

Five days. It was the least I could do.

I had no idea what we would do for five days. More importantly, I had no idea if our mothers would get along. My mother-in-law is a firebrand who marched through the streets of Berkeley in the sixties. At the slightest hint of any injustice done to anyone anywhere in the world, her first comment is likely to be, "The bastards!" A piece of plastic litter blowing down the street will start her off on a crusade against the multinational petroleum companies ("The bastards!"). On the plane to Hawai'i she insisted that we hang on to the sandwich bags and other plastic items for recycling on the mainland. I still haven't found the courage to tell her that, on occasion, I have voted Republican.

My mother, on the other hand, can't stand confrontation. "It's a shame" or "Isn't that awful" or "Someone ought to look into that" are about the strongest comments she can muster about something like, for example, the Chernobyl disaster.

Mom has spent thousands of hours in the beauty salon. My wife's mother washes her own hair and leaves styling to the wind. She grew up eating spicy Middle-Eastern food. Anything more daring than a boiled chicken breast sends my mother to the gastroenterologist. As the plane approached Honolulu, this family vacation in Hawai'i was looking more and more like a tsunami about to wash ashore.

The balmy and tropical weather I promised my mother turned out to be a tropical depression. Mom's hair was under assault before we left the airport. She quickly produced one of those hair protectors that begins about the size of a stick of gum and unfolds into a protective shield of hideously unattractive plastic. I'm told stores will not sell these to women under 65 years of age.

To escape the slashing, cold rain, we went to the IMAX theater in Waikiki.

Circle of Fire, a film about the movement of the tectonic plates of the Pacific Rim, was playing. On the enormous screen, mountaintops were exploding, earthquakes were reducing cities to rubble, rivers of lava flowed from red hot fissures into the ocean which erupted into scalding columns of steam. The theater rumbled with SurroundSound. I looked over at Mom. Her head was thrown back. Her mouth wide open. She was dead asleep.

"Wasn't that something?" she said as the credits came up. "I've never seen anything like that. That was great."

"You know why they let seniors into the movies two-for-one?" I said to my wife. "Because they figure that together two of them might see the entire movie."

The next day the weather at last turned balmy and tropical. "What would you like to do?" I asked. I had told our mothers and my wife to get some travel books and research Oahu's many sights. I didn't want to be responsible for everyone's entertainment. "I don't know," they each said. "What do you recommend?" We began our first of several circumnavigations of Oahu.

Since our mothers come from the opposite ends of the political activism spectrum, spelling and pronunciation were items they could discuss right away without much potential for rancor. Every street sign, every advertisement, became a pronunciation challenge. It was a reverse spelling bee—in Hawai'ian.

"K-a-l-a-k-a-o-u-a," Mom would spell out. "How do you say that?" she would ask from the back seat as though I were the Magnum P.I. of Hawai'ian pronunciation.

"I think these names are very musical," my mother-in-law added.

"Ka-me-ha-me-ha," she sang out with the trill of a tropical song bird.

"Kai-lu-ah-oo-ah," my mother chirped back.

My wife and I exchanged sideways glances at each other. This back and forth tweet-tweeting went on for the next four days.

Food was another area of non-controversial common ground. One day we passed a store that had dried beans on sale. After spelling out and pronouncing the name of the shopping center (Ha-wa-eee-Ka-ee," my mother-in-law yodeled), my mother commented, "We really don't have enough beans in our diet."

Reacting as though my mom had just come up with the formula for world peace, my mother-in-law said, "You're right! And why not? They're delicious."

"And easy to fix."

"And inexpensive."

My mother then lowered her voice, as though she were about to reveal the details of a particularly sinister conspiracy, and said, "What I don't understand is why people don't eat more lentils. I love lentils."

"Yes, they have been ignored."

I looked at my wife. She was clenching her stomach, squeezing her eyes, her face frozen in a pained grimace beyond laughter. She either had to let go or we would have to come up with a good explanation for Avis.

"What about lima beans?" I asked of the back seat. "Why don't they get more attention? Or fava beans?"

"I've never understood that either," my mother said.

"There ought to be equal opportunity for beans," my mother-in-law said. A shriek sliced through the car. Tears streamed down my wife's face.

We did just about everything one could do in Hawai'i without getting wet or having one's hair blown out of place. Bit by bit Mom loosened up. At a roadside stand she tried some papaya. We went out for Japanese food. I ordered the chicken with *udon* noodles in *miso* for her, thinking that was about as close to boiled chicken breast as the Japanese get. It wasn't close enough.

The next morning she was at our bedroom door. "Robert," she said, clutching her stomach with one hand and the door with the other, "I need some bread."

"Now?" I asked. "It's quarter to seven."

"Now," she told me.

At Safeway, she tore into a loaf of Italian white bread. The color came back to her face. She was restored.

As we drove around Oahu, my mother-in-law exclaimed over every flowering shrub and tree. "Oh, look at that one," she said. "And that one. Oh my goodness, who can imagine such colors?" Like a frenzied Hollywood fan at the Oscars, she tapped my mother on the shoulder at every new sighting. "Did you see that?" she would say having spotted another banyan or plumeria. "Did you see that?"— tap, tap, tap.

When I was young my dad bought me a boogie board and taught me to ride the waves. Our summer fun always took him back to his youth in Honolulu. Every Sunday the family would go to their favorite beach, Barber's Point, for endless hours of bodysurfing. Whenever I return home at the holidays, he still uses his pidgin—greeting me with a "Howzit?!"

◆

—Jennifer L. Leo,
"Missing Pidgin"

"Lovely," my mother answered. "Robert, can you find a store? I'd like to get some bread."

"Mom, what is it with you and bread? Are you worried that Hawai'i is going to run out of flour? We've got three loaves at the house."

"I'd just like to have some bread in the car," she would say, her voice a bit more forceful.

"But Mom," I'd begin again before feeling my wife poke me in the ribs, a reminder that it was easier to stop for bread than to uncover my mother's incessant need for it.

One day, driving along Oahu's North Shore, I spotted a fisherman poised with his net on the rocks just above the surf. There is tremendous skill involved in tossing a net out in a perfect circle. I thought "the ladies," as we had begun to call our mothers, might like to see it.

For half an hour the fisherman didn't move. He peered into the surf and waited. And waited. And we waited. I don't ex-actly recall how the following conversation got started, but it went something like this.

"It's very sad," my twice-widowed mother said.

"What's that?" my divorced mother-in-law asked.

"When people are alone."

"Yes, it is sad."

"You know who it's particularly sad for? Gay men."

"Yes, you're right. And also for fishermen."

"That's true. Fishermen do have lonely lives."

"Do you suppose a lot of fishermen are gay?"

"Yes, I've heard that also."

"Isn't it terrible? They spend all that time by themselves, on the boat, and then they can't find anyone."

"It's sad to be alone. But to be a gay fisherman and alone, that is really very sad."

"You're right. Oh look!"

A pick-up truck had pulled up on the side of the road. A single man got out. He went down on the rocks to confer with the fisherman. He stood there waiting, and watching, with the fisherman.

"Do you think that's his boyfriend?"

"I hope so. He looks very nice."

"And he's so patient. I think they're very happy together."

"Me too."

I looked at my wife. For the umpteenth time she was about to pee in her pants. I turned to the back seat.

"You know," I said, "I don't think that people really appreciate just how difficult life is for gay Hawaiian fisherman."

"No, they don't," the ladies chimed in from the back seat. There was a squeal

*G*arbage collectors in Honolulu, Oahu, have a clause in their contract that allows them to go fishing as soon as they're done with their route, which is usually just before dawn. This is part of what Hawaiians used to call the *ukapau* (go fast and be done) system of receiving payment for work done instead of time spent.

◆

—Richard Saul Wurman, *Hawaii Access*

from the seat next to me. The passenger door flew open and my wife raced out of the car holding her belly.

It took a bit of persuasion, but a day later I got the ladies out to Hanauma Bay, Oahu's marine park and popular snorkeling spot. I don't think either had had her face in salt water for many, many years.

"No way my mom is going to do this," I told my wife.

"You're always underestimating her," she said.

"Well, she's not getting her hair wet, I'll tell you that."

"Wanna bet?"

We led the ladies out into the water by the hand.

"Now don't let go of my hand," Mom said. Although she was

very careful not to get her hair wet she did stick her mask in the water to look around. We were lucky. Moorish idols, coronet fish, all kinds of wrasses and puffers swam right up to the ladies. It wasn't clear who was more enchanted—the ladies or the fish.

I was surprised by my mother's adventurousness. But after four days of wind, rain, and sun, her hair was a mess. The Aqua-Net force field that has protected her hair for as long as I can remember had failed her.

"I really should get a touch-up," she said, looking in the car mirror.

"Don't worry, dear," my mother-in-law said. "We'll fix it at home." I sensed a smirk growing across my wife's face.

"You think so, dear?" my mother responded. On day four, the ladies had taken to calling each other "dear."

We dropped them at the house and went to the store for more bread. Mom wanted two loaves even though we had only 24 hours left in Hawai'i.

When we returned to the house, I heard light-hearted humming coming from the bathroom.

"That looks lovely, dear," I heard my mother say.

"What's going on?" I asked.

"Nina's mom washed and set my hair," my mother said, her hair up in rollers.

"You washed your hair?!"

"Sure, why not?" my mother-in-law said. "You think she's allergic to shampoo?"

"Ha!" my wife shrieked. "You owe me a hundred dollars."

"A hundred dollars? For what?" my mother asked.

"He bet me a hundred dollars you wouldn't wash your own hair."

"A hundred dollars! I don't believe it."

"Oh yes," my wife said, her hand opening and closing in my direction. "Pay up."

Hearing about our wager, my mother broke up completely. She reached out for the sink, afraid she might topple off the toilet she was laughing so hard.

Tears began to fall. In my 40 years, I had never seen this. "A hundred dollars. Oh my, oh my." The moment her hysteria began to fall to a girlish giggle she would look at me and break up again. "A hundred dollars." I couldn't believe it. She couldn't believe it.

The next day we set out for the airport three hours ahead of departure. Mom wanted to get there in plenty of time. Having spent most of her life traveling in and out of the Northeast, she must have been worried about a freak snowstorm.

"Well, I just want you all to know I had a wonderful time," she said. "Thank you."

"Me too," my mother-in-law added. "This was great."

"I'm glad you enjoyed it," I told them. "Only two more hours till we leave."

The trip I had dreaded and now found myself enjoying was about to end.

Neither of the ladies had learned to hula or surf, but my wife and I had been hysterical most of the time. Turns out our aging mothers were stand-up comediennes. We were their straight men.

"Anyone hungry?" Mom asked, as she puttered around in her purse. "I've still got a few peanut butter sandwiches. Let's not waste them."

We chewed our way through the week-old PB&Js in silence. My mother-in-law gathered up the plastic sandwich bags for recycling on the mainland.

"You know what I'm thinking, dear?" Mom finally said. "I've been thinking about a trip to Sicily next year."

"Ooohhh," my mother-in-law said. "That could be lovely, dear. You know the Italians have the most wonderful bread."

"I've heard that, too," my mother responded. "And some lovely trees."

My wife put her lips next to my ear. "Think they have any gay fishermen in Sicily?" she whispered.

"I don't know," I told her. "But it might be fun to find out."

Robert Strauss is the author of more than three dozen television documentaries and has worked as a management consultant in over fifty countries. His articles have appeared in the Chicago Tribune, Saveur, *the* Los Angeles Times, *and* Salon. *This Hawaiian piece recently won a Lowell Thomas award. When not traveling, he is likely to be at home spending a quiet evening with his wife and daughter. One of his favorite moments in life is when the doors to the airplane are closed for take-off and everything is out of his hands.*

★

On our first day we were tucked into a canary-yellow kayak slowly meandering up a jungle-like stretch of the Huleia River, on Kauai. My daughter Kate was on the lookout for Tarzan, gorillas, and killer ants, none of which exist in the islands, but how was I to dampen the enthusiasm of a chirpy, blue-eyed blonde in heavy sunscreen? After all, one of her favorite films, *Raiders of the Lost Ark*, was filmed in Kauai. She thought my job was to find Harrison Ford—although Tom Selleck would certainly do.

We were with a small group of other kayakers. As the band of boats wound up the river, we marveled at the explosion of emerald-green vegetation nearby, and plucked at floating flowers on the water's surface. Later, Kate and I struggled up a mud-slicked hill to swim together in a mountain-fed pool sliced by a ribbony waterfall. It was one of the most dazzling afternoons of Kate's young life. *Keiki* means "kid" in Hawai'ian and she decided that it should mean "Kate" instead.

"Call me Keiki," she told our kayak leader. "I'm Hawai'ian."

—Karen Horton, "The Other Side of Paradise," *Child*

* * *

Shaping the Clay

An art lover wanted to make a connection
with a Zapotec artisan, but it was his
son who provided the key.

A MAN IN A COWBOY HAT CRACKED OPEN A WALNUT WITH A
machete. An old, thin woman in a nearby stall was selling
beeswax candles—and perhaps dispensing curses and spells,
too, judging by the crowd around her. The "balloon man,"
the Pied Piper of vendors, had a pack of kids trailing him as
he yelled, *"¡Globos! ¡Un mil!"*

It was Friday market in Ocotlán, in the southern state of
Oaxaca, Mexico, and my wife Laurie and I felt a familiar gid-
diness. We were back in Mexico for a vacation. It didn't matter
whether we were climbing a pyramid or snorkeling off the
Yucatán or watching a man crack walnuts with a machete—we
were once again intoxicated by a swig of life south of the border.

But was Noah, our six-year-old making his first visit to
Mexico, feeling a similar excitement? Seated on a bench, he
stared without expression at the swirl of activity.

"What if he hates Mexico?" Laurie whispered.

It was an interesting question, or at least the underlying
issue was. How do children discover the pleasures of travel?

How can parents help kids appreciate other peoples and places? Or is the process too mysterious and complicated for a simple tutorial?

Moments later, we headed out of the market and I had started to think about my own reasons for our trip to Ocotlán. A dusty fanning enclave about twenty miles south of the city of Oaxaca, it was the home of Josefina Aguilar, a ceramist. Several years ago, I'd bought two of her clay sculptures at a Seattle folk-art store.

The first piece, smooth and radiant, is a curvy mermaid floating through a bright array of fish and seashells. The second, a big-busted streetwalker prowling the night with a cigarette dangling from red lips, is comic, jaunty, subversive. These colorful figures, set in my kitchen, bloom with whimsical charm and chase away the Seattle grayness.

My idea was simple: find this source of alchemy and relay my thanks.

Perhaps I allowed myself a fantasy: Josefina, happy to see distant travelers, would invite my family to dine on tamales, beg us to stay in her home, help us move to Mexico, allow me to sip margaritas beneath a *palapa* for the rest of my life...who knows what I was thinking.

In any event, after obtaining directions to Josefina's house at

> *My* daughter Natasha and I have wandered together all over the world on what we like to call our "girl trips." But a getaway to Mexico gave me pause—when I needed a notarized consent from her father, my husband, in order for Natasha to enter the country. Any minor (under eighteen) going to Mexico alone or with an adult, even if that companion is the parent, needs such a statement that indicates both parents are in agreement about this south-of-the-border travel.
>
> ◆
>
> —LM

the market, we walked along the town's main street for about a mile until we found ourselves outside her gate. Atop a brick archway, a line of two-foot-tall ceramic figures—among them, a religious saint and a farmer—formed a welcome party. We walked through the open gate into a courtyard set inside a two-story, stucco home.

Nearby, a woman in a simple white blouse and loose skirt knelt on the ground and rolled out a sheet of moist, brown clay. She was a big Buddha of a woman—heavy-set, brown-skinned, impassive. She appeared to be about forty years old.

When I announced that I wanted to meet Josefina, she flicked a glance at me, then returned her attention to the clay.

"That's Josefina," said a man in the courtyard, pointing to her.

I introduced myself, and in awkward Spanish, I told her that I loved her work, that I had two of her sculptures in my house, that I had come to see her "all the way from Seattle."

"Gracias," she responded, politely. She told me in Spanish that she had made pottery all her life, learned ceramics from her mother, and had traveled to the U.S. to exhibit her work— "all the way to Texas and Chicago and Boston."

She spoke in short sentences. She did not smile. Unnerved, I tried to talk of the special spirit of her work. I blathered on that it "breathed of Mexico," that it was transcendent, that it spoke from the heart yet was rooted to the earth, until soon I began to sound like a lunatic combination of Shirley MacLaine and Ricardo Montalban from *Fantasy Island.*

She gave me a long look, then resumed her work. She wasn't hostile, but I didn't think we'd be sharing a plate of tamales soon.

To be truthful, I was feeling miffed. I had half-expected to be mobbed by children hawking ceramics, but there was just the silence of this square-jawed Zapotec woman, solid as the earth, working the clay with such smooth, natural movements that her hands seemed to rise up from the ground.

Rebuffed, I felt my eyes begin to canvass the courtyard, ferreting out corners and peeking into alcoves. I knew the symptoms: I was transforming into The American Shopper, looking for something to buy.

At the far end of the courtyard, a girl about twelve years old applied glitter to a mermaid sculpture. I wandered over and when I discovered the price—about $10—I gulped hard. I'd paid eight times that much in Seattle for a similar piece. Now I was in for another shock: neither this sculpture nor any others were for sale. All were on order for U.S. shops.

I cursed my luck, thundered at "greedy *gringo* gallery-owners," and contemplated ransacking the garbage for "seconds." Just as shopper's lust threatened to overwhelm me, I happened to look back at Josefina.

There she was, still seated in the dirt, but beside her was Noah. Cross-legged, he sat transfixed, his eyes locked on her movements.

The "glitter girl" was advising me when to return for better shopping opportunities, but now my attention was on Noah. He held a piece of clay in his hands. Moistening it with water, he rolled it in his palms and tried to shape it as Josefina directed him.

I watched as she brought out a primitive tool, a foot-long wooden stick with a metal hook on it. With a baker's hands—strong, thick wrists, and fingers that fluttered like butterflies—she pushed and poked the clay as if it were a ball of *masa*, or tortilla dough. She shaped it into a human figure, then continued to mold it until it grew into a village woman with a sliced watermelon on her head. She returned the clay to a formless mass, then rolled the ball into a cherub's face, with big cheeks.

Shy and private, Noah said nothing, but he did not take his eyes off the clay. When Josefina offered it to him, he accepted it eagerly. Ignoring us, he kneaded the clay into an oval shape, using the tool to make fine marks. Every so often, he looked up to study Josefina's human figures, then plunged back into work.

When I got close, I saw that he had composed something quite lovely: a woman's face—long and majestic, even noble. When he finished, he held it out and deposited it in Josefina's hands. Her eyes lit up. Muscles in her face moved.

"El niño es un buen artesano," she said to the man painting candleholders nearby. He joked about hiring Noah and she laughed. Her seeming dispassion melted away. She was buoyant.

For the next half-hour, this unlikely pair—a woman/spirit from the Zapotec world and my 50-pound blond kindergartner—were at each other's side. Without speaking, she used her hands to instruct him, teaching him how to hold the clay, how to touch it, how to feel it.

Finally, Noah finished working and stood up. He placed his ceramic face atop one of Josefina's human torsos that were drying in the sun.

"Tell her it's a present, Dad."

"Un regálo," I said.

She fastened her eyes on my son and nodded her head. A word formed slowly: *"Gracias."*

Amid this wonderfulness, I confess I held out hope: would Josefina save my failed shopping excursion and make us a present of a prized sculpture?

She did not. But we had our gift: the look of wonder on my son's face. It announced the birth of a traveler, the first step to citizenry of the world.

Nick Gallo is a Seattle freelance writer, who specializes in travel to Mexico.

✳

I am often asked by nervous parents if it is safe to take their children to Mexico. It's not only safe, but can actually make parts of the trip much easier for everyone.

Children are natural icebreakers; when you enter a small village, just send the kid out into the street and within minutes your welcome will be assured. Mexicans lavish attention on their children and are very considerate to *gringo* kids, especially if the child is timid or just plain scared.

A friend of ours recently made a long trip to Mexico with his eight-year-old daughter, the first time he'd ever tried traveling with a child. When I asked him how things worked out, he answered, "It was like having a diplomatic passport." He explained that all the people he normally expected to be cool toward him (he is tall, with a fierce black beard and long hair) completely ignored his appearance and treated him like a loyal and devoted parent. He and his daughter were given special attention in restaurants, escorted to the head of the line in the train station, and generally treated like VIPs.

"I even got a better deal on souvenirs," he laughed. "I just let her do the bartering."

—Carl Franz, *The People's Guide to Mexico*

CYNTHIA GORNEY

⋆ ⋆ ⋆

Keno Kids?

*Las Vegas is trying hard to convince
Americans that it's a great family town.*

ON OUR FIRST MORNING IN LAS VEGAS, WE WOKE UP ON THE
ninth floor of a black glass pyramid and my twelve-year-old
son Aaron lifted our room's window shade, which tilted back
over his head at a diagonal, as one might expect a pyramid
shade to do. We had a view of a castle. Then we rode in an elevator at a 39 degree angle that descended along one corner of
the hotel, walked past a bank of slot machines, and went to
breakfast in a restaurant with hieroglyphics on the upholstery
and Nubian sculpture on the walls.

My husband, Bill, read from the menu. "Cairo Lox and
Onions," he said. "Eggs Benedict a la Cheops."

A restaurant patron walked by in very tiny star-spangled
shorts, her midriff oiled, a golden crucifix shining from deep
within her cleavage.

"Pass me a Keno card," said our nine-year-old daughter,
Joanna. Keno is like Bingo, except that in Las Vegas it is
arranged for your personal convenience so that you can play it
while eating your breakfast. The Keno ladies will just walk

117

right up to your breakfast table in amazing little outfits and take your cards and money while you work out pencil calculations on the place mat.

As parents, we were somewhat unclear on the concept. Was wagering together at the breakfast table meant to be one of the family attractions in Las Vegas? "Come on, Dad," coaxed Aaron, nudging his father for a fiver to put down on the next round. But Bill gave him one of those not-in-this-lifetime looks, and Aaron adroitly changed tack.

"So okay, let's talk about video games," Aaron said. "We'll need a lot of money for video games."

I ate my toast and considered the language of a press release I'd read describing Las Vegas. "A world of dreams and fantasy for people of all ages. A one-stop, multidimensional resort destination," it promised. "A nongaming fantasy world of imagination designed to attract a spectrum of domestic and international travelers spanning all ages and economic status."

Since "people of all ages" is the time-honored public relations code phrase for "bring your children," we had. And thus it was that having slept inside a pyramid and eaten our pyramid breakfast and finished our pyramid coffee, we considered our first Las Vegas day.

We were more or less at the southern end of the Strip, where the big buildings line up in hysterical growths of peculiar architecture—Roman temples and 30-foot gladiators and golden lions the size of the Supreme Court building, and, of course, our pyramid guarded by a Sphinx with lasers in its eyeballs.

We started at the Forum shops, an indoor mall with expensive stores and vase-bearing maiden statues, because we'd heard that's where all the cool video games and something interesting involving 3-D were housed. We proceeded down the length of the grand faux-Roman street, growing more disori-

ented by the minute, until it came to an abrupt dead end at
something called CINEMA RIDE, all in capitals, just like that.
After we paid the $5-per-person admission, uniformed atten-
dants handed us 3-D glasses and placed the four of us in a small
movie-viewing room, where the seats flung us about while
rocks and sharks and nasty-looking watercraft (atomic-pow-
ered submarines, I think) roared out at us in Technicolor.

When my husband and I emerged, we both had the momentary sensation that all of our clothing had been ripped off and
put back on the wrong way. Aaron waved his hand dismissively
and said, "Oh, I've been in better ones." He took his sister and
vanished into the video arcade. Bill and I stood in the shopping mall and watched as a large statue of Bacchus began
laughing unpleasantly and heaving his wine cup around. Aaron
and Joanna reemerged after they had used up all their arcade
tokens. Aaron pronounced the video arcade "pretty good."
Then we went for lunch.

"MGM Theme Park next," I said briskly, consulting our
itinerary. I read aloud from our press release: "The 33-acre
movie-lot theme park features ten food and beverage loca-
tions, twelve major attractions, theme streets, four theaters,
and other attractions that feature a Cotton Blossom Riverboat,
Ghost Coaster, Journey to the Center of the Earth, which is a
motion machine, French Bumper Cars, a haunted silver mine,
and more."

To get there, we walked along the sidewalks of the Strip,
which is an experience that other urban parents might wish to
duplicate by choosing an afternoon of particularly glaring sunshine and taking their children on a stroll through the local
red-light district. Every twenty feet or so, men who looked in
deep need of a bath offered my husband small flyers that I
gather were supposed to be folded for discretion but usually
weren't. My husband was holding hands with a nine-year-old

girl with a Dutch-boy haircut, but that appeared to make no serious impression on any of these men. They would sort of insinuate the flyers at Bill, as if to say, "Here, buddy, just stick it in your back pocket and the kid won't notice."

"What's in the papers?" Joanna asked.

"Naked ladies," I said.

"Oh," Joanna said. She gave me a sideways look. "They get paid for sex," I said helpfully, and she rolled her eyes, as if, for God's sake, anybody could figure that out.

We walked through the giant golden lion's mouth into the MGM Grand. We discovered that the park was behind the casino but situated so that you had to walk past a room filled with thousands of slot machines and past the blackjack tables and past the men and women bent over the craps tables to the very end of the hall, where MGM has plunked its all-ages amusements into a wing with a truly formidable decibel level.

Our children are desperate to reach Las Vegas. In his innocence, my husband, Dan, planned two nights for us there. The lobby of the Mirage greets us with garish parrots and walls of animated sea life. We note, especially, the tank of circling sharks.

"Dad," our daughter Lydia asks, "is this really bad good taste or really great bad taste?"

♦

—Rebecca Okrent, "Oh Beautiful, for, Like Wow, Spacious Skies," Travel & Leisure

A large sign explained that it cost $15 to enjoy the park's many fine attractions—children were discounted to $10 apiece—but you could check it out for free. "We'll be checking it out for free," Bill announced firmly, so we did. We bought cotton candy and walked around in the sunshine. Bill pointed out that from where we stood there were no visible slot machines and the air had stopped smelling of Marlboros. We sat on a bench and drank Coca-Colas, feeling temporarily at peace. Aaron and Joanna spent $5 at a shooting arcade and said it was "hella fun."

By amusement-park standards, it was a nice little effort and reminded me of a place we once found in the middle of some fields outside Coeur d'Alene, Idaho. Actually, the Coeur d'Alene park had more things to do, but then, in Coeur d'Alene it was not possible to dispose of one's kids while disappearing inside a hotel to gamble.

The MGM Grand had gone to all the trouble of providing a pay-by-the-hour "youth center," a sort of indoor parking lot with supervisors and Nintendo games. The center's telephone-information recording, however, advises that due to certain licensing regulations, each five-hour stay at the center must be followed by a "two-hour mandatory break with parents."

Aaron leaned up beside me on the flume-ride fence. "I'm hungry," he said, so we went back to our pyramid. On the way, we passed tiki gods and a rock that played music at us. The naked-lady-magazine men had stationed themselves at regular intervals all the way down to the hotel. My son's face was beginning to look faintly gray. "This is like taking your kids to a crack house for vacation," he said. "Could we go hiking or something?"

The next morning we went for a terrific hike. We drove half an hour out of town to a place called Red Rock Canyon, where the desert wildflowers were in bloom and fabulous scarlet rock formations piled up weirdly one on top of the other. The kids put their heads in a waterfall, and we breathed sweet dry air, and I finally learned what a Joshua tree looks like (gnarled and splendid, with cream-colored plumes in the springtime). Then we drove back into town, past Reliable Bail Bonds, Oasis Motel Adult Movies, Private Lingerie Modeling

Naughty But Nice, Graceland Wedding Chapel, Silver Bell Wedding Chapel, Wee Kirk o' the Heather Wedding Chapel, and Ray's Beaver Bag.

"What are bail bonds?" Joanna asked.

Her father, who is a lawyer, explained bail bonds. At least she hadn't inquired about Ray's.

We went to a show that night, a big brain-numbing Las Vegas production with Andrew Lloyd Webber music and a lot of people roller-skating furiously all over the theater. When the show was over, we walked several blocks to the Treasure Island Hotel and watched pirates shoot Englishmen who then plummeted into the water; and when the English ship had sunk, we stood outside the Mirage Hotel and watched the volcano blow up and set fire to the hotel fountains; and when the fountain water had stopped flaming, we stood outside our hotel and watched the lasers come out of the Sphinx's eyeballs.

We went swimming in the hotel pool, too, which was only three feet deep, so you probably couldn't drown in it even after finishing off several of the alcohol-filled obelisks that sell for $9 apiece in the lobby. Then we sat through some arresting-looking 3-D and special-effects movies with entirely unfathomable plots. Aaron and Joanna spent a great deal of time playing two video games, which included, and here I quote directly from my son, "ladies in bikinis dancing in cages and guys running around that you blew up, and when you blew them up, all these chunks of red blood flew pppfffttt all over and all these skulls and blood and stuff splattered."

During our stay, three separate taxi drivers told us that most of the gamblers in Las Vegas didn't want children there in the first place, that the children kept walking around looking like children and giving all the gamblers the creeps. By the time the third cab driver was telling us these stories, we were on our way back to the Las Vegas airport.

"Sorry, we have to detour here," the driver said cheerfully, swinging his taxi away from the Strip. "Some kind of hostage situation near the Aladdin. Jeez, there was an incident in front of Caesar's about a month ago—one guy shot another guy six times, and then danced around the body for a while."

The sun beat down through the taxicab window. All the other traffic was detouring with us, so we sat without moving with the Funtazmic on one side and the In-N-Out Burger on the other, but you could still see the black glass pyramid in the distance.

"What's a hostage situation?" Joanna asked.

Cynthia Gorney was a staff writer for The Washington Post *for seventeen years. She is the author of* Articles of Faith: A Frontline History of the Abortion Wars. *Now living in California, Gorney avoids all things on vacation that light up, go whir, and promise jackpots.*

✳

The classic travel paradox begins with responsible, caring parents not wanting to put their kids through the discomforts of travel. On the other hand, those discomforting travel experiences are filled with valuable lessons. Thank goodness my parents opted for the valuable lessons.

As a seven-year-old, I vividly remember a hot and humid August day in St. Louis. We were in the middle of a family vacation that had had its ups and downs. The ups included a spellbinding miniature golf course and the St. Louis Zoo. The downs centered on the obligatory visit to some distant relatives. The day, however, was going to be the pinnacle of our vacation. We were going to see our first major league baseball game. The St. Louis Cardinals with Stan "The Man" Musial were playing some other team. Who cared? We had tickets to a game. That's all that mattered.

The valuable lesson began on the way to the ball park when our car made a terrible thumping noise that was followed by a symphony of horn honking. We were stopped in the middle of a very busy St. Louis intersection with our car's drive shaft lying on the asphalt. The valuable lessons were coming fast and furious now.

I learned that universal joints are to drive shafts what knees are to legs. I also learned, if you're going to have problems with a U-joint in the middle of a busy intersection, it's best to also have a gas station on a nearby corner.

The next batch of lessons hit all at once. I learned that those events you look forward to the most, like a major league baseball game, can evaporate into thin air. The gas station mechanic then taught me that public transportation can solve a host of U-joint problems and get you to Busch Stadium in time to join in singing the National Anthem. By the way, Stan Musial did hit a home run that day, and I saw it.

Now, should caring, responsible parents subject their kids to the discomforts of travel? You bet. My St. Louis U-joint memory is nearly 40 years old, and I still remember boarding the city bus with renewed hope.

—Scott Ahlsmith, *The Complete Idiot's Guide to the Perfect Vacation*

JOYCE WILSON

✦ ✦ ✦

Lessons of the Nile

Mother and daughter travel to Egypt
and learn about the unexpected.

I LET MY DAUGHTER PACK HER OWN SUITCASE FOR OUR TRIP to Egypt, biting my tongue while I watched her bring all the wrong things, those over-sized men's boxer shorts that all the girls her age were wearing with logo t-shirts, the cotton sweater that reached her knees, the visor hat. Then I folded what I was sure she'd need—a dress for dinner, her first high-heeled shoes, a cardigan—into the corners of my own suitcase.

She was in the throes of adolescence; I was trying to culti-vate rather than smother her growth. On a daily basis, I prac-ticed benign neglect. I had watched her grow from a darling armful of delicate joy to a girl-with-a-lisp-while-her-front-teeth-were-missing who held my hand when we walked from the car to the supermarket, the dentist, the flute lessons. I tried not to suffer the pain when she needed her first stitches after falling across the kitchen floor; I took deep breaths and counted to one hundred when I saw her smash her finger against the soccer ball during tryouts. Yet every time she saw the worry in my face, my daughter concealed whatever physical hardship these experiences brought her, internalized them, and, in fact, turned them to pearl.

The night flight across the Atlantic, the Alps, the Mediterranean was a long ordeal. A cloud of smoke from the cigarette and cigar smokers hung just below the cabin ceiling; the dining facilities did not carry vegetarian alternatives; it was impossible to sleep. The flight crew made it clear they did not like to be asked questions. The male nurse on board was very stern with me when I told him that my daughter was vomiting in the toilet compartment. "You have to give her phenobarbital before she leaves the ground," he said. "There is nothing I can do for her now. But tea. Get her to drink black tea."

But she would drink nothing. So I spent the rest of the flight drinking black tea for her, hoping that I might persuade her by example. It was difficult to get excited about the city of Cairo from the air or the ground, where it exhibited little of the excesses of electric power that we were accustomed to. Our hotel room was comfortable and spare, clearly free from the influence of former colonial indulgences. Yet this disappointed my daughter more deeply than I had foreseen. It was to my surprise that, as soon as the porter left, she threw herself down on the bed and sobbed.

"Oh, my darling," I said. "What is it? What is wrong?"

"I just thought it would be different," she mumbled between gulps.

"You mean the hotel? Or the city? In what way?"

"I thought it would be more English!"

It was then that I reminded her that her father was half Lebanese, therefore closely related to all Arab people.

"You always say that," she said. "But I don't feel it. I don't see anything to have in common with anyone here."

"I had no idea you loved the English culture so much."

"Neither did I!"

✳

After a helping of chicken on a kabob and rice pilaf, sleep, and then rice pudding for breakfast, she was greatly improved in spirit. We met the others who would join us on our tour, a group representing all the English-speaking countries, and I was encouraged to meet two families with girls her age. After visiting the pyramids, a noisy disorganized tourist trap and not the best introduction to Egypt, we climbed back on board our roomy air-conditioned bus to go back to our hotel. On the way we were forced to take a detour. It was fascinating to see camels at an auction block, an open air meat market where the skinned carcasses hung in the sun amidst swarms of flies, a cow standing quietly beside an old Ford, small houses without foundations that extended for acres. On the narrow thoroughfare, we exchanged places with a local bus where occupants were packed in like sardines. I exchanged glances with a professorial-looking man in a brown suit and wire-rimmed spectacles and felt all the ambivalence of privilege.

"I saw that little boy go to the bathroom in the street!" my daughter whispered in horror.

"Well, this is the city we're not supposed to see," I repeated. The bus driver later admitted that he had never visited that section of the city before. I told her excitedly. "This is the real Cairo!"

The next day our bus took us to Luxor, where we moved onto the cruise ship, an old paddle-steamer, much like the steamers on the Mississippi. It was delightful to be on the water, and the wooden boat creaked through the currents with a reassuring nineteenth-century stateliness. I hoped this setting would be more agreeable to our expectations.

One afternoon, relaxing on the deck, my daughter read aloud from a guidebook:

The concept that is essential for the traveler to understand about Egypt is that of the Nile, for the River Nile is the very life blood of Egypt. It runs from south to north and therefore, the southern portion of the country is known as Upper Egypt and the northern part, Lower Egypt.

She put the book down and sighed. "This is the source of confusion," she said. "The people are completely messed up. They're all upside down!" She reread the guidebook and looked up at the horizon. "The real Egypt," she said. "And all I see is desert, desert, and more desert."

I could see that this might be boring for her, but for me it was a perfect setting. To watch the banks of the desert go by in measured tranquillity was just what I needed to prepare for my spring semester teaching load. I had to digest and annotate *King Lear* and *The Heart of Darkness* by the time we returned. I also liked the sense of confinement aboard ship, the assurance that my daughter would be close by. My recurring nightmare pictured her running away ahead of me. I heard my feet pounding on the earth's surface, crushing generations of microscopic civilizations as I chased after her. I woke in a sweat.

When we visited the temple at Karnac, she asked to borrow my camera and spent over a half hour photographing the rams heads that lined the ancient walkway. It was gratifying to see her smile as she returned from the temple remains, as if she understood what they were all about.

> *Y*our children are not your children.
>
> They are the sons and daughters of Life's longing for itself.
>
> They come through you but not from you.
>
> And though they are with you yet they belong not to you.
>
> ♦
>
> —Kahlil Gibran, *The Prophet*

It didn't take me long to realize that the men in the Middle East, especially the men on the street, favored her upon first sight. All ages of male were drawn to her immediately, and most of them did little to conceal their interest. It seemed they knew a virgin when they saw one. As they took in the luster of her face, her hair, the flesh on the limbs of her barely developed body, they nearly smacked their lips in gustatory approval. At the temple of Hatshepsut, a group of students asked to be photographed with her. I felt my blood boil as I watched them gather around her and smile at the camera without removing their sun glasses. I shooed them away like gnats. Our guide related the story of Hathor, goddess of love who slew armies of men in a rage and then drank their blood from the sand like barley water. I'll show you what it's like to see a woman drink the blood of her victims, I wanted to say. The Egyptian male showed no interest for an attractive unmarried woman of twenty-five on the cruise with us. For those of us who clearly were married and fit and attractive, even youthful in appearance, not a glimmer. But for a fourteen-year-old girl, he salivated as if in the presence of baby lamb ready for the spit.

At the village of Edfu we visited a temple dedicated to the goddess Nut. The mural of her long figure covered the walls and ceiling, so encompassing was her influence on daily life, in which she ate the moon every night and gave birth to the sun every day. Afterward we walked along a dusty road between rickety stands and shops, where hawkers called out to us to buy something. I thought I might buy a *gelaba*, or long flowing robe, and my daughter was interested in some jewelry. We approached a shop where a young boy sat on the steps. Inside the shop, I was looking at the long cotton robes, some white, some black, one electric blue with birds and flowers printed in broad borders on the sleeves and skirt.

"Excuse me, I heard you speaking English, but I could not hear your accent. Are you English or American?" I looked up to identify the speaker and realized that he was addressing my daughter, not me.

"American," she said.

"Ah, good, good. The English, they are so stiff, but you Americans, you are filthy rich! Come with me and see my jewelry. Do you like silver?"

I peered through the hanging garments to watch. My daughter was laughing gaily. I could only hear their voices. "So how do you like Egypt? How long will you stay?"

"Until our tour ends."

"When you leave, I would like you to take me with you to America, so I can get rich too!"

"I don't know, do you really want to leave?"

"I am small. I will fit in your suitcase!"

"What about your shop?"

I suddenly became involved in a serious conversation with Mrs. Smythe about our plans to go to Abu Simbel so that I lost track of the rest of the conversation. My daughter joined us by the time we boarded the bus. She sat behind me and burrowed into another guidebook. I turned around and asked: "No stow-away in your suit case?"

"Mom, he was only practicing his English."

"Did he sell you anything?"

"No."

"No?"

"Mom, he was only a kid!"

"Your age."

"Mother," she said, leaning toward me. "What will happen to him? Do you think he'd like living in the States? Do you think he could make it there, with his family?"

"Oh, yes, I'm sure they could."

"He asked me what my life was like, and I told him I lived in a beautiful town with shade from trees and gardens with beautiful flowers, and a house for one family and two cars! I said I thought he'd be happy there. But would he? Should I have told him that?"

"I think it's fine."

"But his life here is beautiful, don't you think? I hate that American dream stuff. But I told him about it." She leaned back in the reclining seat. "He told me what those words mean, Salaam Aleikum. It means peace be with you. And the way you reverse the words to answer, Aleikum Salaam, means the same thing in return! He gave me this." She held out a large metal Egyptian cross.

"You didn't pay him for it?"

"He wouldn't take any money. Really, he said it was a gift. It's the Egyptian symbol *ankh*, the hieroglyphic that means everlasting life. It is also the shape of the Nile. He showed me how this piece is the river running south to north, and the cross piece is the delta, where the river splits and loops and comes back again. It's the river of life."

"You should probably return it."

"But Mom, it was a gift!"

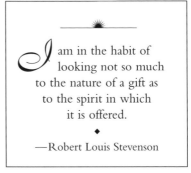

I am in the habit of looking not so much to the nature of a gift as to the spirit in which it is offered.

—Robert Louis Stevenson

That night she wore the dinner dress, clearly relieved that it happened to be among my things. As we walked into the dining hall, I realized she was making an impression on others and thriving on the results. "The family from New Zealand thinks she's a first year student in college," said Mrs. Smythe. "Not high school."

I looked again at the long-sleeved, knee-length black knit dress, the knit ruffles at the wrists and hem, her shoulder-length hair brushed under, and the poise with which she walked in the high heels, and marveled at her sudden sophistication. Clearly she was a daughter to be proud of. But she seldom spoke during dinner conversations. Silent and observant, she contributed only when asked a question. "Sometimes, it is rude to stare at people," I had chided her.

We sat with our guide Ibrahim. His role as travel agent and native Egyptian secured him a high degree of popularity with all of us. It seemed there was no question he could not answer. "And why do you live in America, Ibrahim?" I began. "Will you ever come back here to stay?"

"I doubt it! I love America. But I also love Egypt. The city of Thebes is where I was born, the ancient city, the cradle of civilization. When we go to Aswan you will see the new university in the desert. The buildings are magnificent and modern. That is the Egypt for me. But it's coming too slowly. When you look at the Egyptian man, any man, age eight or eighty-eight, look closely. You will see an old man in every one. It's the poverty and hunger. That is Egypt."

"But you have the Nile," my daughter interjected. "The river of life." Ibrahim threw back his head and laughed. "Yes, the Nile has always been the central part of Egypt's economy. It is our river of life." He looked at her and continued more soberly. "So much was accomplished in ancient Egypt," he said. "And what was accomplished then has brought us around again. Every day, parts of Egypt are beginning again, after three thousand years!" He smiled at her.

"And what about religious differences? How do you tell a Muslim from, say, a Christian?" I asked.

"Only by the name! That is the only difference! Because more and more, the mixtures abound. I was raised in a Muslim family, but my name is from the Old Testament, because of my father. It is better to grow up with two religions in one family. More realistic. A Muslim name is from the sixty names for God: the strong one, the all-knowing one, the courageous one. El Abdul is pure Muslim. But aside from the name, the people are the same inside!"

"My mother's always interested in the Christian view," my daughter said.

"Well, that's all right, isn't it?" He laughed. "I believe that all religious difference is political. In Egypt today, politicians are capitalizing on religion, promising Christians a church steeple higher than the neighboring mosque. It's a carnival."

"Like you, we have poverty in our country," she said, and I felt my spine quicken. "It's not the same as your situation, but it is a problem."

Ibrahim said, "Yes, democracy's little secret! Of course, I live in Washington, D.C., where you walk through a courtyard of a government building one minute, then turn the corner, and look out! Yes, there is poverty everywhere. It is the same," he smiled. "But not the same!"

I asked him later if she should return the piece of jewelry, which she had gotten from a shopkeeper for nothing. "What, a metal *ankh*? Nah! It's worth so little. Let her keep it. Something to remember the trip!"

Later that week we arrived at Pullman Cataract, the hotel where the film *Death on the Nile* was made. It was an enclave of European taste as well as an escape into the past. The Victorian wooden structure, painted red with white trim, was a rare vision after villages of stucco and sandstone. We walked through the courtyard, a formal garden with pruned roses, clipped herbs, and a trellis covered with orange blossoms, and out onto a beautiful terrace overlooking the steep inlet of water. Brightly printed fabric hung in softly draped scallops and was illuminated by the afternoon sun. We sat on the terrace and watched the rushing water till the water became a soft muted gray, nearly lavender. Soon, night would override these visual pleasures with its own laws and sense of order.

Many on the tour exclaimed their delight with this hotel. We were held in the sway of its fantasy. "When we come back, this is where we might stay," I suggested to my daughter.

But she was fingering the *ankh*, her mind on other things. She looked down at the cross in her hand. She held it delicately in her palm and traced the loop with her index finger. It was perfect in shape, the symbol of continuity and everlasting life. She wrapped her third and fourth fingers around the base of the cross and felt its thickness and density, the strong basin of Egypt. She rubbed her thumb over the crosspiece and felt the depression of the hieroglyphics, the creative and innovative writing etched into the metal, a symbolic entity of an ancient people, of a struggling civilization.

Later that evening, she began to talk about her plans for school, the courses she would take, and how she hoped to run for the track team as soon as we returned. It was thrilling to hear her talk about her future and the rest of her life. She talked and talked. There was no stopping her.

Joyce Wilson is the editor of a Web page of poets, The Poetry Porch *(http://www.world.std.com/~jpwilson/). She lives in Massachusetts.*

★

Moreover, in this country it could be said that a heart beats in all things, even in the sun which was named, blessed, and implored like a god and tenderly loved like a human father, and even in the dark stone of the tombs...you will contemplate the indefinable reality and will finally understand the words of André Malraux: "The Egypt which first invented eternity is also the most powerful actress in life."

So do not set out with the intention of discovering this country. It is Egypt which, by your good fortune, will take possession of you.

—Henri Gougaud and Colette Gouvion, *Egypt Observed*

Through the Eyes of a Little Girl

Gogo's imagination sends this
family on far-flung outings.

RIPPLING CURTAINS OF RAIN. SUDDEN SHAFTS OF SHARPENING air. We're on holiday in London—me, my wife, Maggie, and two daughters, Gogo, eight, and Daisy, five. Gogo seems oblivious to the theatrical British weather. Absorbed in a fragile trance, she studies a brown beetle crawling up her hand. "This bug's head is so small," she says. "I bet its brain can only hold one idea."

Gogo, who plots our vacations with the world view of Alexander the Great, lives in her own ether. She has pre-Raphaelite features, wide brown eyes that seem to be off on a secret, faraway trip, and a quirky, private smile. Her mind is a pinball machine: She has a gift for making associations that even a Joycean might admire. Which is what I like about traveling with my kids. I'm enchanted not so much by their innocence as their skewed perceptions, their undiscriminating appetite for scraps of knowledge. Because everything in their experience is equally weighted, they see things whole, untainted, in clear air.

A few years ago, we took a family outing to Philadelphia's science museum, the Franklin Institute. We spent an afternoon among exhibits that elucidated the physical laws of nature. On our way out, I bought Gogo a soft pretzel. She took a bite, dropped the wax paper into a trash can, and began to giggle. "What's so funny?" I asked.

"Gravity," she replied.

Our vacations have followed Gogo's pretzel logic. Wherever her imagination wanders, we follow. She so loved *The Diary of Anne Frank* that we went to Amsterdam. She wanted to walk up the hidden staircase, tiptoe around the attic, and peek into the water closet to check out Anne's chain toilet. And Gogo did. Still, the secret annex perplexed her. "There's something I can't figure out," she said. "How did Anne keep so quiet in wooden shoes?"

Gogo was more contemplative than confused on our odyssey to Greece last winter. The Rock of the Sibyl at Delphi enchanted her. The place of Minos in Knossos enthralled her. The Acropolis Museum's statue of Cerberus, the multi-headed mutt that watched over the underworld of the dead, left her agog. Yet when we got to the sacred spot she most wanted to visit—the Cave of Hades in Eleusis—she shuffled along silently, head down, shoes scraping the ancient stones. "Are you okay, Gogo?" I asked. "Sure," she said, without lifting her eyes. "I'm having fun just kicking the gods' dust."

It was a Greek connection, sort of, that piqued Gogo's interest in England last July.

"You'll like it there," said her mother. "Londoners travel underground."

"That sounds cool," Gogo said. "But are you allowed to pet Cerberus?" That question dogged us the entire trip.

If our tour of Great Britain had a theme, it was a mystery. We began at 221B Baker Street, home to the new Sherlock

Holmes Museum. All spring I'd been reading his adventures aloud to Gogo and Daisy. But they weren't really hooked until they saw Jeremy Brett's sublimely over-the-top performance as Holmes on PBS. Days after watching an episode, they'd still be reciting lines of dialogue: "To the curious incident of the dog in the nighttime."

"The dog did nothing in the nighttime."

"That was the curious incident."

Curiously, 221B falls between 237, a real estate office, and 241, a charted accountant firm. We climbed the 17 steps to the sitting room, which was crammed with enough Victorian nostalgia to make the master exclaim in his high, strident tones: "Entirely meretriculous." Gogo inspected every alleged artifact: the severed digit from *The Engineer's Thumb,* the stuffed swamp adder from *The Speckled Band,* the locket of hair from *The Beeches.*

"Whoever cut this hair didn't use scissors," she deduced. "It must have been done with a dull knife."

Daisy raised a slightly heretical question: "Was there a real Sherlock Holmes, or was he just paper?"

Gogo pulled on the brims of her own deerstalker and drew deeply on her plastic calabash. "That," she said at last, "is a three-pipe problem." We repaired to the Sherlock Holmes Hotel to puzzle this out over bowls of Great British Pudding (cook's homemade pudding with lashings of custard). "Sherlock Holmes was alive and paper," Gogo said between lashings. "It's like Bloody Mary: she was a queen and a drink."

Appropriately enough, our next stop was Buckingham Palace. The joint was open to paying tourists for the first time, and as Gogo said, "I always wanted to see the queen's place."

We were funneled through eighteen exceedingly formal rooms redolent of majesty. William IV called the place "hideous." Edward VIII complained of its "curious musty odor." A TV pundit compared it to a tandoori curry house.

Gogo offered her own detailed critique. "The red carpets are really ugly," she said of the newly laid Axminster. "They're the same ones at the Marriott."

The girls dashed off through the Green, Blue, and White Drawing Rooms. We lost sight of them in the crimson Throne Room, where they paused briefly to check out the squat monogrammed chairs. Gogo eventually resurfaced in the Picture Gallery.

"Where's Daisy?" I asked.

"Who?"

"Your sister?"

"Oh, her. I don't know, where?"

We alerted a warden, who alerted other wardens. Pretty soon there's an all-points palace bulletin for a "three-foot-ten American in a Betty Boop t-shirt." Gogo found her in the royal loo.

Our final conundrum unraveled in Portmeirion, a tiny, Italianate dream-town boldly planted amid the slaty cliffs and wide, sandy estuaries of North Wales. Planned and built by Welsh eccentric Sir Clough Williams-Ellis in the 1920s and '30s, this architectural fantasia of columns, cornices, and campaniles was the setting for the '60s TV series *The Prisoner*. The show told the story of a British secret agent who, after resigning his post, was abducted and held captive by powers unknown in a timeless hamlet called The Village. Everyone in *The Prisoner* is under surveillance; no one has a name, only a number; and there is no knowing who is a friend and who is a spy.

It's been more than a quarter of a century since the series first aired. And yet, since 1977 "Prisoner" devotees have pilgrimmed to Portmeirion for an annual two-day synod. They cavort as Villagers, re-enact scenes from the show, and paw over its ambiguities. Everything is accomplished with scrupulous and impeccable seriousness.

Gogo and Daisy are big fans themselves. They've watched videos of all seventeen episodes and have memorized the mantra of Number 6, the show's hero. "I will not be pushed, filed, stamped, indexed, briefed, debriefed, or numbered! My life is my own."

I, on the other hand, am easily coaxed, wheedled, blandished, buttered, and cajoled. Gogo and Daisy chorused: "Can we go to the 'Prisoner' convention?"

"It's a five-hour drive from London!" I protested.

"But Daddy, we love to ride in the car with you."

My resolve crumbled after all of two minutes.

The sun was going down when we finally checked into the Portmeirion Hotel. "I'll need some information," said the desk clerk.

"You won't get it," snapped Gogo.

"Ha! So you're here for the convention."

The next morning we padded past the pillared porticoes, splashing fountains and numerous pastel-colored villas to Number 6's house, now a shop that sells souvenir "Prisoner" maps and bumper stickers. We rambled up a cobblestone path to a green Florentine dome, where the arch-interrogator, Number 2, once plotted to break Number 6's will. We rambled down to the pink Gloriette, the speaker's platform, where Number 6 once tried to rouse the Villagers to rebellion. We ambled around the green, with its fanciful statuary and elaborate topiary, where scores of middle-aged "Prisoner" wannabes mill about in striped blazers, straw boaters, and flowing capes. They were restaging the human chess game from Episode 11.

Later in the day, Gogo stumbled into a discussion group near the piazza. A bunch of earnest Villagers were mulling the meaning of a short film made by Patrick McGoohan, who played "The Prisoner." In it, he is seen strolling under a pier in Santa Monica, where he pauses to fish a coat hanger out of the surf. He keeps sketching hangers in the sand, only to have them rubbed out by the sea.

"The hanger stands for the Great Pyramid of Cheops," insisted a woman whose badge identifies her as 52.

"To me," said someone numbered 39, "it looks like a question mark on a pedestal. McGoohan wants us to keep questioning our beliefs."

It's Gogo's turn. "Young lady," said 43. "What do you think McGoohan means?"

"I think he means it's time to hang it up."

Franz Lidz is the author of Unsung Heroes: My Improbable Life with Four Impossible Uncles, *which was made into a movie, directed by Diane Keaton, starring Andie McDowell, John Turturro, and Michael Richards. He is also a senior writer at* Sports Illustrated *and a film essayist for* The New York Times.

✳

Belgians can be a stuffy lot, so I thought we might have gone too far in bringing the baby into Comme Chez Soi, the Michelin three-star restaurant they say is the best in Brussels. It was lunchtime on a rainy Sunday, and we had taken the express train up from Paris for a day of antiquing and flea-marketing. At the restaurant we used our usual tactic: divide and conquer. I didn't mention my baby when I made the reservation, and my wife went in first so she would be on her way to a table when I suddenly appeared with the child. Various people in charge gathered around me, their expressions changing from shock to helpless welcome. By the time they looked up and around, my wife had been safely seated on a banquette next to a portly old burgher wearing a pince-nez who clearly hadn't planned on being next to a five-month-old girl. But he loved it. We are always welcome back at Comme Chez Soi—as long as we bring *la petite*, Fiona.

—Richard Reeves, "Bringing Up Bébé," *Travel & Leisure*

PETER RICHMOND

⋆ ⋆ ⋆

Shake, Paddle, and Roll

Two days on a raft changes everything.

IT'S A FEW MINUTES BEFORE SUNRISE, AND WE ARE WINDING our way through the hills outside Placerville, California, 130 miles northeast of San Francisco. As I slow at each bend to negotiate the hairpin turns, my wife, Melissa, and I delight at the sight of the strange flora, the fresh scent of eucalyptus, the distinctly wild feel of the place. To a pair of chauvinistic Easterners, the crisp beauty and sharp contrasts of the Sierra Nevada foothills are unexpected and striking. Our eight-year-old son, however, is oblivious to it all. Maxfield sits in the back seat, surrounded by glacier-like piles of comic books. His face is buried in an *Archie*. Or a *Jughead*. Or he's somewhere in Riverdale High. It's his natural state, this oblivion. We could be driving through a lava slide. The car could sprout wings and fly. Max would hardly notice.

This time, though, I'm determined to shake him from his reverie. We have flown more than 3,000 miles to spend two days navigating the white-water rapids of the South Fork of the American River—something he's never done before and may never do again at least not until Super Nintendo comes out with White-Water Wilderness Mario—and right now, I don't want him to miss a thing.

"Look, Max, look out the window," I say, as we pass an orchard in bloom. "Pear trees."

"Yeah," Max says, looking up from his comic books for a millisecond. "With real pears."

My son, the Thoreau of the third grade.

Fast forward, two hours later. Our raft is hurtling toward a wall of white water about 50 yards downstream. It appears as if the raft will fall right off the edge, like a bowling ball rolling off the top of a refrigerator. I'm sitting on the left side of the boat, paddling furiously. Melissa is opposite me, doing the same. Max is standing in front, holding on to a towrope, leaning into the spray like one of those mermaids on the bow of a clipper ship. Dave, our

*T*he size of the rapid is not the only factor in determining whether to take a child river rafting. Other factors are water temperature, time of year, river topography, and the child's strength as a swimmer.

◆

—LM

guide, is in the stern, screaming madly for us to pull left, left—*left*—to avoid the boulder that sits at the top of the ledge, and then we drop into the boiling lap of Troublemaker, one of the hoariest of the river's dozens of rapids. It is angry. It is primal. For a moment, we are airborne, then—*whap*—the rubber raft bellies into the middle of the rapid. Waves cascade over us. The sound surrounds us. We're encased in a huge, wet roar. Melissa and I are tossed into the bottom of the raft. Max? He's standing tall, shouting in glee—Ahab, defiant in nature's maw.

As a rule, our family doesn't do outdoor adventure. Our lack of love for the wilderness starts with Melissa. When we were dating, I took her on an overnight canoe trip in Virginia, and she brought along a jar of asparagus tips and a nice cabernet sauvignon and refused to pee for two days. That was thirteen years ago, and she hasn't spent a night outdoors since. Me, I did my wilderness thing years ago; these days, I commune with nature by searching the meadow behind our upstate New York home for errant golf balls while I'm waiting for the coals to heat. Max sits in his tire swing and surveys the wildlife—in his *Far Side* anthologies.

And still, when I raised the idea of a family vacation out West, Melissa had to admit that white-water rafting held definite allure. She only admitted it, it's true, after I assured her that I'd found a white-water rafting outfit, known for the beauty of its trips, its safety record, and, most importantly, its gourmet cuisine.

With the brushy canyon walls framing our descent, we pulled the raft forward and—buoyed by the good, honest feel of hardworking muscles—we were instantly reminded of one of the oldest truths known to the species: that there is no sensation on earth as rewarding as man testing nature.

That afternoon we barreled our way through Triple Threat, Rock Garden, Old Scary, and half a dozen other rapids. It was in the middle of Triple Threat that something unexpected happened: I glanced over at the other side of the raft and saw Melissa—in short sleeves, paddling like a madwoman, her hair flying, water cascading around her, her biceps thick and strong—in a completely new light. Well, not completely new light. She was the woman I first saw on a racquetball court fourteen years ago, wearing a Danskin top and shorts, and whaling the tar out of her opponent. Now she was back—fit, laughing, paddling hard and steadily, propelling her family through Triple Threat. I couldn't keep my eyes off her. Where had this woman been? Well, right here, of course. All along. I just hadn't bothered to notice. Not lately, anyway. Funny how easy it is, once you've got kids, to stop thinking of you and your spouse, the two of you, as a family.

Not long after dark, we laid out our sleeping bags on the beach, and Max began to look for constellations. We had time to find three—the wheelbarrow, the rhinoceros, and the kite—before he was snoring. Melissa and I stayed up and gazed at the stars. It was quiet. Then she said, "You know, when I was young, I hated this instant karma crap. Now I kind of like it."

She always had a way with words.

At dawn the next morning, Dave was already making pancakes. I found Max standing at the water, up to his ankles, the rising sun turning his hair the color of fire. He was holding a shoelace from his boot, and this is what he was doing: he was dipping the lace into the water and swinging it over his head so that the water would stitch a fan of droplets across the surface of the shallows. I watched him do it again and again and again.

Perhaps he was taken by the randomness of the patterns: never the same, never predictable. Perhaps, I realized, I hadn't noticed a pattern myself: that when you let your son board the same school bus on the same corner each day, and read the same comic books, and follow the same electronic hedgehog through the same electronic video maze, that you're giving him very little chance at experiencing anything original.

I noticed something else about Max that morning. He wasn't bouncing, as is his usual habit. He wasn't fidgeting. His natural metabolism—that of a hummingbird on amphetamines—had downshifted. He even sat with me for a solid hour, sifting through silt in the river, panning for bits of gold. He sifted gently, carefully. I watched his fingers dip into the crystal-clear water and run through the sand and rocks on the river floor. For years he has talked about becoming a paleontologist, and right then I could envision those fingers sifting through the sands of the Gobi desert for dinosaur fossils, or searching for saber-toothed tiger bones in the steppes of Mongolia. Of course, *Calvin and Hobbes* is probably the closest he'll ever really get to a tiger, but this morning it felt as if this were a different Max—as if he'd caught the river's rhythm and let its waters scrub some of the plastic away.

Day two called for another eight miles of rapids—Elevator Shaft, Pinball, Lost Lunch, Headbanger, Bouncing Rock, Hospital Bar, Recovery Room—punctuated by diversions on the banks of the river: blackberry picking, more gold panning, and regular dives into the water.

Near the end of the day, Dave had us paddle to one side of the river and then anchored the raft at the base of an enormous boulder. Carefully, we climbed to the top. I thought we were up there for the view, until Dave pointed out something in the rock: three depressions in the stone, as deep as cereal bowls. Dave explained that the Miwok Indians who once lived on the banks of the river used the rock as a mortar to grind acorns and grains. They had done so for thousands of years—until they'd ground down the stone. Max was amazed, but the people who used to live here, I told him, got along with nature. Stone would give way to them. They had an understanding.

We did a lot less talking the rest of the day. The trip was winding down, and no one wanted to miss a detail. The final rapid was called Last Chance, and as we glided out of it, Max turned to Dave.

"That's the last one?" he asked.

"Afraid so."

"Next year," Max said, "we can do Class IV."

Dave explained that you have to be at least twelve years old to try a Class IV rapid, up on the North Fork.

"That's okay," Max said, smiling.

Maybe he figured he'd be twelve by the time next summer rolled around. He'd grown so much in two days that anything seemed possible.

Peter Richmond is a special correspondent at GQ *magazine and the author of* My Father's War. *A graduate of Yale and a former Neiman fellow at Harvard, Richmond lives in upstate New York with his wife, Melissa Davis, and children Hillary and Maxfield. His writing, often about sports, has appeared in* Rolling Stone, The New York Times Magazine, Architecture, Glamour, *and* TV Guide. *He collects antique Lionel trains and now limits his outdoor adventures to quiet paddling on a lake.*

✳

Travel companions develop a level of trust that is unrivaled. A father related the moving story of his family's summer vacation:

"For the first six hours in the cab of the camper we were all at each other's throats. The girls were fighting. My wife and I kept arguing about where to go or how to get there. Both of us bickered at our daughters, and they yelled back at us as well.

"Then, as the hours went by, something miraculous happened. I don't think we ever felt so close as a family, nor will we ever again. It was so wonderful to be together in that way. We talked and talked. The girls told us things about themselves we never imagined. In this same spirit of openness, my wife and I confided in them as we never had before.

"The trip changed us. It really did. Years from now we won't remember exactly where we went, but each of us will always remember the closeness we felt to one another.

"That summer also meant so much to me because it was the summer before our eldest daughter went away to college. It was the last time we will ever be together like that again. And it was the best time."

—Jeffrey A. Kottler, Ph.D., *Travel That Can Change Your Life*

Rounding the
Horn First

*Father and son sail a tiny boat
17,000 miles to the bottom
of the world and back.*

DANIEL: DAWN, THREE HUNDRED MILES WEST OF CAPE HORN. Full moon and angry oceans. When you think of these waves, imagine a big, green Mack truck skidding at you sideways, with 50 bathtub loads of shaving cream on top. [Our 25-foot boat] *Sparrow* bobs right over them. Last night, in a three-hour Force 8, a big wave whomped us, filling the cockpit and finding leaks not yet tested. We've screwed boards over the portholes and have all sorts of lids, caps, and cloths lashed-to, stuffed-in, and wadded-around vents, chimneys, and deck fittings.

Icebergs! Hitting an iceberg in a gale is what I fear. One reason Cape Horn is so feared is that the gales are usually westerly. If you want to go west, against them, you must fight for every mile. Captain Bligh spent 31 days in a gale, going just 85 miles, said, "Forget this!"

Force 8 winds gush to Force 9. In the afternoon, I went on deck and besides seeing that Dad was working hard at the tiller, the seas and sky looked furious. White streaks were smeared along the waves, the wind almost visible! Seas built and grew until it was necessary for us to look aft and steer down each wave, keeping the stern toward the following seas. Some waves were bigger than others—foaming and looking really mean. Graybeards. The automatic steering wouldn't work—the paddle was spending too much time out of the water. (The whole boat seemed to be spending too much time out of the water.) We took two-hour watches.

It's hard to see a wave (in photos, impossible). You see the mass of it—not much height—then you rise slowly as the water floods beneath you and you're on top. I was on the helm watching this really big one and suddenly I knew *Sparrow* hadn't risen and twenty feet of wave was straight up over us.

We surfed for a moment and fell off it to starboard, flat into the water. The boat didn't seem to tip over but the port rail rose up suddenly above me as I slid down. What I'd been standing on was above my shoulder level. I was in the ocean! The foaming waves I'd been looking at were at my chin. My tether was yanked tight as *Sparrow* came up level, surfed again, and fell over to port, the starboard deck and tail shooting up over my head. I kicked my legs and paddled for a moment in free water, then *Sparrow* righted and I was scooped on deck.

By the time all this happened, it had been 36 hours since I'd had a fix on the sun to establish our position. My dead reckoning put us near Diego Ramirez (50 miles southwest of Cape Horn). But you can't steer accurately in a gale, so I was jumpy.

The gale broke up and, with the moon full, there it was: a frozen wave at the end of the continent. A featureless gray hump. The Horn.

David: My Horn passage started at 0700 on January 7. The

sunrise had been ominous. The paddle that goes down into the water to work the self-steerer was jumping out as the stern lifted high. I jibbed and the main sheer looped under the paddle, threatening to snap it off. I called for Dan and he held me by the heel like Achilles's mother as I went in head-first for the line and cleared it. Dan was angry because I un-clipped my tether, but it didn't stretch that far and I didn't want to take time to reclip it. "But we're not moving, Dan," I said weakly. I was glad he was angry because that meant he'd use the tether himself. We dismantled the Navik and steered by hand for the first time on this passage. Seas and wind built and it was a proper gale, going with us. We took in the jib; she flew with only a spot of mainsail exposed. Slocum's phrase re-peated in my head. "Even while the storm raged at its worst, my ship was wholesome and noble." And *Sparrow* was mag-nificent: delicate but steady, swift and airy on the foam crest, strong and driving through the great valleys. She seemed born for this day.

At noon, Dan shifted course, visibility was down to a few hundred yards. Forget Diego Ramirez. If we didn't hit it we wouldn't see it. And in the slop of this gale we wouldn't see The Horn either. The Horn is three things: the rock itself, Drake Passage (the water in which you sail around it), and the whole idea of the passage. We were in the Passage, and surely we'd survive for the third. I settled for two out of three. At one that afternoon I asked Dan when we'd be off (if not crashed onto) The Horn and he said, "0100 tomorrow morning." The gale picked up and Dan steered, howling "Aaayippeeeeeee!" as we surfed down the long gray waves with their tops torn off and the spray racing us. It was quiet and dry below. I realized that Dan had hardly ever steered by tiller, but his skill was marvelous, undoubtedly honed by hours of handling the joy-stick in video-game parlors. He looked possessed. Horsemen have their centaurs, why don't we sailors have a name for the half-man, half-boat that Dan was at that moment?

Because we were hand-steering, we changed to two-hour stints. During my early evening watch, the gale started to fly apart, moderating. This is the most dangerous time of a gale, because the puffs can be fierce after random lulls, and the wind can shoot at you suddenly from a different direction. At 8:30 at night, I was below making tea and lighting the evening lamp when *Sparrow* went down hard to starboard. Then bam! down to port. Without a horizon below, hanging on and standing not upright but with the angle of the boat, I only knew that we were down because the water covering the porthole was not wave froth but solid green—I was looking straight down into the ocean. A felt bootliner that was drying knocked the lamp out of my hand and onto the bunk. The water roared, like a train running over us.

"Okay, Dan?"

"I'm fine, Dad." His voice sounded subdued.

My eye was taken during this by the blue plastic cat pan, which was secured by cord on two sides. It jumped up, did a 180 degree turn and landed upside down, then leaped again and did a full 360 degree flip and landed face down again. It looked like a little girl in a blue dress, skipping rope. I thought of that calmly. The binoculars were in my berth with the oil lamp; their teak box had broken. It was the only thing we hadn't built ourselves. Everything else was in place. I didn't learn until he told me the next day that Dan had gone overboard.

The gale broke on my ten-to-midnight watch, and the moon, almost full, showed through the racing clouds as they tore apart: a slow film flicker. After my watch I was below, again making tea, and Dan called, "Dad, I think I see The Horn," and I was up on deck at ejection speed and there it was.

"How did you see it, Dan?"

"One wave didn't go down."

I'd never seen it, but of course it was The Horn; its form must have been in my genes. The great rock sphinx, the crouching lion at the bottom of the world. The sea and the sky and the faintly outlined huge rock were all the same color—indigo, graded like the first three pulls of the same ink on a Japanese woodblock print. We embraced, then stood entranced....

The Horn bore north and I stepped behind Dan. Few had rounded The Horn in a boat this small, and he was ahead of me.

David and Daniel Hays, father and son, co-authored My Old Man and the Sea: A Father and Son Sail Around Cape Horn, *from which this story was excerpted. David is founding Artistic Director of the National Theatre of the Deaf. He graduated from Harvard, holds honorary doctorates from Connecticut College, Gallauder University, and Wesleyan University. He lives in Connecticut. Daniel works as a supervisor at a therapeutic wilderness program for troubled teenagers in Idaho. He holds a second degree black belt in Tae Kwon Do and a masters degree in environmental science. He and his father are the first Americans to sail around Cape Horn in a boat under 30 feet in length.*

★

By the time we reached Hong Kong, each of my daughters had celebrated a birthday somewhere on the road, and so we would return home officially one year older. For nearly five months they had put up with eating whatever there was to eat and sleeping whenever they got the chance. They did not complain or demand to go home. They did adapt quite happily to any sort of travel, and never once got seriously lost. They asked a lot of questions, listened to many long-winded explanations, and looked at everything with the calm, open eyes of children. We had lived in each other's pockets, spent weeks at a time in cramped train compartments, and had eaten almost every meal *en famille*. This is a great deal more togetherness than the average Australian family is accustomed to putting up with, and I'm pleased to report that we enjoyed it very much. The sense of looking after each other, forgiving each other's little eccentricities, and a common eagerness to see what was around the next bend made bonds that are still with us today.

—Paul Cullen, *Cook's Tour: A Haphazard Journey from Guangzhou to Dublin and Back Again*

WILLIAM STEPHEN CROSS

✦ ✦ ✦

The Land of My
Adopted Daughters

*A trip to China with three young
children becomes an epiphany.*

WE KNEW IT WOULD NOT BE A VACATION, BUT WE DECIDED
to try it anyway: my wife, Carole, was flying to Hong Kong
and Taiwan to interview agents in the Far East for her company, and I needed some firsthand research for an article on
Asian business trends. But what to do with our three small
children? Why, take them along, of course.

A strikingly large group of our otherwise worldly friends
thought we'd gone simply bonkers. But perhaps the idea of
volunteering for a fifteen-hour trans-Pacific flight with three
young travelers (ages six, five, and two) will seem less insane if
you know that both of my daughters were adopted from
Taiwan and that all three children speak Chinese and English.

We convinced ourselves that this trip would do the kids at
least a partial world of good. I thought the two weeks in Asia
would make the kids' Chinese classes seem less arbitrary. We realized they were too young to appreciate the experience fully,
but hoped to sow some seeds for later in life.

By the time we landed in Hong Kong, we were physically

drained and mentally exhausted, but the little ones zipped right back to full speed once they saw the kaleidoscope of Christmas lights illuminating the city. Few Chinese are Christian, but that hasn't stopped them from embracing Santa Claus, reindeer, artificial evergreens, and gift-giving.

By the next morning the long flight seemed worth it. For one thing, we kept our plans modest, relying on Hong Kong's cornucopia of transportation possibilities for sightseeing as well as entertainment. Exotic Asian scenery didn't cut it with our gang, but a sign in Chinese with the picture of a large tooth advertising a dentist (spied from atop a double-decker tram) got a big laugh even from the baby. We took a whole day to visit Ocean Park, Hong Kong's version of Disney World, and while it isn't in the same league as the Magic Kingdom, the simple rides were just the right speed for three young children.

One night we chose a slightly scroungy dumpling shop, where the staff only smiled when the baby overturned a bowl of noodles on her head. We weren't worried about being shown the door at nicer places, since the Chinese always bring their kids along when they go out.

At first I was too busy juggling three oranges to notice much around me, but gradually I realized that one of the benefits of traveling with children is the implicit broadening it brings to parents. Having seen Hong Kong through the eyes of my five-year-old son, Peter, it will literally never look the same.

As do most little boys, he loves anything that runs. He reveled in the buses festooned with giant Chinese characters, the electric trams, and the helicopters hovering over the harbor. But mostly he loved the Star Ferry connecting Hong Kong Island with Kowloon. As soon as we boarded he was in his element, yelling out to the police boats he assumed were prowling for "bad guys" or clucking with indignation at the naughty people whose garbage makes the Fragrant Harbor "fragrant."

At night, while his sisters dozed or watched Japanese cartoons in Mandarin on the Star channel, he and I would gaze with shared wonder at the lights across the harbor and the boats passing below. A room with a harbor view means something altogether different to me now.

Although boys and their fathers often do bond through a mutual attraction to things that run, my six-year-old daughter, Casey, proved more of a challenge. I hoped for a better chance to connect in Taiwan, where she and her sister, Sara, were born. On the fifth day of our trip, we packed our luggage and toys and flew to Taipei.

An unpleasant disarray of high-rise buildings interspersed with squalid two-story storefronts, Taipei belies its role as one of Asia's most dynamic economic centers. Buildings go up, are never quite finished, then age horribly in the awful air pollution, making the city look permanently temporary.

Still, because of the half-dozen trips we made to Taiwan when we adopted the girls, the city is almost a second home for us. It was an understandably emotional experience entering Mackay Hospital's maternity ward, where we'd first seen Casey six years before. Naturally, Casey, when she peered in at a room crammed with newborns, wanted to hear yet again about that first time we'd held her. She smiled with pride at all the babies who looked like Sara and her while I held her up to the window, remembering how tiny and vulnerable she'd felt in my arms then—and how right it had seemed four years later when I first held her sister.

Then one afternoon a small parental epiphany struck me.

I announced to Carole that I was going to a favorite bookstore on Chungching Road to buy a copy of *Shui Hu Zhuan*

(*Outlaws of the Marsh*), the story of Wu Song, China's Robin Hood. Peter and the baby were worn out from the city's chaos, but Casey asked to come along. At first I said no. An inquisitive six-year-old doesn't make for an intellectually stimulating companion amid the rarefied recesses of classical Chinese, but leaving a spouse cooped up in a hotel room with three kids on a rainy afternoon is grounds for divorce. So I relented.

Casey and I strolled along Nanking Street, carefully avoiding the occasional motorcycle cruising the sidewalks. Our short walk gradually turned into an exploration as I pointed out seal carvers and ink brushes, paper fans, and even jars of traditional Chinese medicinal herbs. Next door to the herbalist was one of the many branches of Ten Ren, a tea chain with outlets on virtually every corner of Taipei. In addition to selling superb Chinese tea, they also display the Yixing teapots I collect. Earthenware vessels made from a clay so fine and dense it requires no glazing. Mixing pots are esteemed among connoisseurs because tea, while it steeps, gradually imparts its flavor, seasoning the unglazed interior. Over time, Chinese creativity has transformed the vessels themselves into works of art: there are pots shaped like wheelbarrows loaded with rice, frogs on fallen logs, or ancient religious urns. Prices vary from $10 to $50,000 depending on the fame of the potter. The ones in my modest collection are simple and cost less than $100.

We slipped into the shop and I asked the saleswoman to show me the pots made in Taiwan. Then I let Casey choose one while we sipped our tea and I chatted with the owner in Chinese. I knew my daughter was shyly glad when the woman took it for granted she could speak Chinese, though Casey did nothing more than smile at all the attention.

I realized then that we had reached a silent understanding; I no longer needed to say, "This is important to me and it will be important to you someday because it's your heritage." Our squat little mud-brown pot packed securely for the trip home the next day, we strolled on to the bookstore, purchased some stickers and my classics, then flagged a cab back to the hotel. Most fathers dream of taking their sons to opening day at Yankee Stadium, but I've always schemed to impart to my oldest daughter my love of Chinese culture, her heritage. And in those two hours, I did.

William Stephen Cross speaks Chinese and is an expert on Asia.
He writes for many national magazines and lives in Upper Montclair,
New Jersey. He plays ice hockey when not shuffling his three children
to activities.

★

My brother Guangyuan and his family and I wandered through a few of Suzhou's fabled gardens, past grotesque rock sculptures and lofty pavilions, as he told me anecdotes of our family. At one point, we paused by a circular moon gate and asked a passerby to take a family snapshot. In it, we posed awkwardly—Guangyuan, his wife, their two young daughters, and me—all bundled up in drab, lumpy clothing against the chill.

The awkwardness was not surprising. I had met Guangyuan, my eldest brother, for the first time just a few days earlier. He had been born in China, I in America, and at that very instant we were still getting to know each other, strangers trying to become siblings.

My parents left China for university studies in the United States after World War II, when Guangyuan was just a toddler. He was left behind in Suzhou, in a house he remembers as having endless court-yards and halls; shortly afterward the Communist Red Army claimed victory in China, isolating it from the West for decades. My two other brothers and I were born in the United States. But Guangyuan was raised by my grandparents and lived in Suzhou until he was 40.

For decades he was my mythical brother, known only through family lore. My parents talked of Guangyuan with sadness, and with guilt over their failure to foresee the Communist takeover and the personal tragedy that would follow. When I traveled to China, the first from our family to visit Guangyuan after 1949, I'd expected our meeting to be awkward. After all, we had been raised in different cultures, indoctrinated in different ideologies. My brother was a lowly worker in a silk factory, earning less than 26 dollars a month. The family of five—Guangyuan, his wife, their two daughters, and his mother-in-law—lived in a single rectangular room divided in two by a bulky wardrobe, with a shared kitchen and no toilet facilities.

But what I had not expected was the depth of my own guilt. I was the lucky one. I'd escaped the hardship and misfortune of living in China.

—Melinda Liu, "The China I Never Knew,"
Condé Nast Traveler

✦ ✦ ✦

Team Spirit

*He never knew he'd raised
a travel buddy.*

I WAS SITTING IN A CAFÉ ON THE CENTRAL SQUARE OF
Veracruz with my older daughter, Abigail, when I revealed to
her my principal theory on Mexican music. That sort of
thing—unloading theories—is a father's role. I told her that
when I first went to Mexico, many years ago, I would offer ten
pesos to anyone who had heard an entire Mexican song that
didn't contain the word *corazón* at least once. Since the exchange rate as Abigail and I spoke was something like 3,000
pesos to the dollar, I decided against adding, "And I'm talking
about the days when ten pesos was ten pesos."

The central square—the *zócalo*, as it's known in Mexico—
of Veracruz happens to be the perfect place to propound
theories on Mexican music. Even on the quietest of evenings,
a visitor who is at all alert to his surroundings can count on
hearing, at the same time, three or four marimba bands, a
couple of Mexican cowboy combos, at least one traditional
Veracruzano trio with two guitarists and a harpist, an itinerant
whistle salesman demonstrating his wares, a band playing to

accompany the couples who are doing the stately *danzón* in front of city hall, and what seem to be several thousand birds in the trees of the park in the middle of the square. The combination can reach a level of what I consider truly creative cacophony, although I have never seen it mentioned in guidebooks as a tourist attraction of the city.

In fact, I hadn't seen much mentioned by way of tourist attractions in Veracruz, except for the annual pre-Lenten carnival. Still, I had wanted to go there for years. From somewhere, maybe a movie whose title I mixed up with another movie, I had formed a picture of what Veracruz would be like: in a bar with peeling paint, next to the docks, a man who shaves at night so he'll look tough all the next day is talking to an equally sinister-looking man about arranging a shipment of something that doesn't bear talking about to a country where the customs officials tend to be grateful for small gifts. Above them, a rusty ceiling fan goes pahCHUCKetuh, pahCHUCKetuh, pahCHUCKetuh...

Although this may not sound like a vision likely to attract the average tourist, Abigail had said she'd love to go along on a trip that took in Veracruz and some Mayan ruins in the Yucatán. Abigail shares my taste for sitting in squares, although, as it happens, she also shares my wife's taste for making a close inspection of, say, the Palladian villas in the Veneto. My wife and I traveled a lot with our daughter during what I determined as the family-trip window of opportunity—the years when the kids are old enough to accompany their parents with reasonable comfort but not so old that they have better things to do—and I suppose it never occurred to me that they would be available again in the years just after college, willing to indulge a father's daydreams and listen to his theories and, most miraculous of all, speak to the waiter confidently in Spanish. I realized that in rearing children we had also been training traveling companions.

I think of it as training because every itinerant family has a style that is absorbed naturally by the children. On any trip, for instance, our family is easily diverted, a characteristic I'm not always able to justify to people who get a certain amount of fulfillment from completing the day's schedule. When, on the evening before we flew to Veracruz, some friends in Mexico City remarked that we would be arriving during a well-known Candlemas celebration in Tlacotalpan, a pleasant river town only an hour or so down the coast, Abigail took it for granted that we would be heading for Tlacotalpan straight from the airport.

> *M*y dad and I once went down to Taxco, Mexico, for the purpose of reading aloud to each other G. K. Chesterton's *Orthodoxy*.
>
> ◆
>
> —Christopher Buckley, quoted in *Fathers* edited by Jon Winokur

We did in fact spend most of a sunny Sunday at the celebration—an enormous blowout at which people were so busy drinking beer, eating great mounds of river shrimp, gambling, buying trinkets, and listening to strolling musicians that a lot of them didn't seem to notice when several hundred of the faithful pushed through the crowds in solemn procession, carrying a statue of the Virgin Mary onto a barge in the river—but we managed to get to Veracruz by nightfall. We had heard Sunday was one of the brightest evenings on the *zócalo*, which had the reputation of being perhaps the liveliest square in Mexico. What we discovered when we got there, of course, is that the image of the city I had carried around in my head all those years was completely wrong, confirming a lesson of travel we used to express the way Yogi Berra might: "Never expect to find what you expected."

I had imagined Veracruz in black and white, but it's in color. Not colorized, either; in real color. Though we could indeed see freighters, as well as shrimp boats, from our hotel windows, the meeting of downtown Veracruz and the harbor occurs not along a seedy waterfront but at an attractive seawall, *el malecón*, that is a favorite spot for evening strollers. The cafes under the portals on one side of the *zócalo* do have ceiling fans, but in working order, and the paint on the graceful arches looks as if it were freshened almost daily.

The *zócalo* itself struck me as just about a perfect square, with a beautifully maintained park, a splendid 18th-century cathedral, and a plentiful supply of the ornate iron benches (painted green, with the crest of the republic in the middle) that I have always considered one of Mexico's great gifts to civilized living. Sitting in one of the cafes under the portals on a Sunday evening amounts to watching a show—that, of course, includes yourself—with some of the players stopping at your table to offer peanuts or hammocks or wooden statuary or earrings or model ships or a serenade or, rather to my surprise, an electric shock that, according to a man carrying equipment that looked alarmingly like jumper cables, will pretty much take care of whatever ails you. If you're still feeling poorly after the shock, we had been informed, the harpist of the Veracruzano trio will sing a song he makes up on the spot to your specifications.

Abigail and I spent some time in such cafes speculating as to what sort of song we might ask the harpist to create, although Abigail suspected that his personalized lyrics didn't go much beyond inserting "Maria" or "Juan" into well-worn slots. In the mornings, still seated, we continued the conversation at the Gran Café de la Parroquia, a cavernous tiled room in a corner of the *zócalo*, across from the cathedral. At the Parroquia, which is said to serve as the de facto office for any number of local businessmen, about an inch of coffee is served in a glass. You then tap on the glass with your spoon to attract one of the *lecherones*, or milkmen, who circulate through the place carrying a kettle for refills in one hand and, in the other, a kettle of steaming milk, which they pour into your coffee from two or three feet on high in a stream that stops abruptly a millimeter from the top of your cup.

We did not spend all our Parroquia time discussing musical compositions. We speculated a bit on the deals going on around us. In a query that reassured me that we had instilled in our daughters a healthy sense of curiosity, Abigail wondered aloud whether the pourers ever fell victim to what she called *codo de lecherón*, milkmen's elbow. I, in turn, raised the question whether residents of the Veracruz state capital—Jalapa, a hill city that has an almost European feeling—are called jalapeños.

I hasten to say that, despite the attraction of the Parroquia in the morning and the *zócalo* cafes in the evening, we were occasionally ambulatory. We strolled through the city markets, which offer, among their many other attractions, seafood cocktails constructed before your eyes with the panache of a bartender putting together one of those rum concoctions that are meant to taste like cherry soda pop while blotting out the rest of your afternoon.

We drove to Jalapa, mainly to see the anthropology museum, which turned out to be as exquisite a museum as either one of us had ever visited—a spare, sunny building set on a grassy hill that visitors gradually descend as they make their way past the exhibits, particularly strong in Olmec sculpture. We drove to the village near Veracruz called Mandinga to eat oysters and red snapper on the terrace of a restaurant next to an idyllic lagoon. It was there that Abigail had a breakthrough about the song we might request of the Veracruzano harpist in the *zócalo*.

"How about asking him to do a song about a Mexican songwriter trying to write a song that does not have the word *corazón* in it?" she suggested.

"Whoever brought you up did a terrific job," I said.

When Abigail, in careful Spanish, announced our request to the harpist that evening, he looked puzzled, although I thought I detected a knowing sparkle in the eye of one guitarist. "I am a poet of the region," the harpist said with solemnity. Ignoring the *corazón* frippery, he asked rather formally what our first names were, and where we came from, and what we did for a living.

"I don't think we're dealing with a Stephen Sondheim range," I said to Abigail. She reminded me that Sondheim would probably charge more than three dollars to write and perform a song. We answered the harpist's questions, and he rewarded us with a dozen or so verses. They said, among other things, that I was a fortunate man to have come to Veracruz with my daughter, who was adorable. His song lacked those clever internal rhymes I so admire in Sondheim's lyrics, but I have to say that he caught the spirit of the occasion. I paid up cheerfully.

Before leaving home, I was informed by my wife, who'd accompanied me on a trip to the Yucatán maybe fifteen years before, what a great advantage of being with Abigail at the Mayan ruins was: she could represent the family in climbing to the top of each pyramid, leaving me on the ground like a bushed relay runner who is grateful for having just passed on the baton. Climbing the steep steps on the outside of, say, the Pyramid of the Magician at Uxmal is a matter less of stamina than of how you feel about standing on the upper rungs of a tall, steep ladder. The pyramid gets its name from the legend that one person built it in a single night, but once we were at the top I raised the possibility that a night is the amount of time he spent right where we were, trying to work up the nerve to go back down.

Abigail's presence did more than simply guarantee that I could descend without having to summon the ski patrol. She'd proved to be her mother's child in her perusal of the literature on the ruins—a perusal that confirmed the impossibility of ascertaining how the Maya used places like Uxmal and Chichén Itzá. We spent part of our time at the ruins imagining the conversation of two returned Mayan ghosts, small but tough men with names unsullied by vowels, who would howl with laughter at the guides' descriptions of sites. ("Did you hear that one, Xchlmtl, about the old swimming hole being a place where they sacrifice virgins?" "Where do they get these ideas?")

She also confirmed my feeling that anyone who has time for only one day at the ruins should go to Uxmal, even though Chichén Itzá is many times more extensive. Partly because of the many visitors it attracts, Chichén Itzá feels much more a part of the modern world. Uxmal is a place where you can stand on top of a pyramid, with a view of nothing but other Mayan buildings and the surrounding forest, and imagine the sort of life Xchlmtl and his friend Cxtlx once lived. In Abigail's view, Uxmal was to Chichén Itzá what the anthropological museum in Jalapa was to the magnificent but almost overwhelming National Museum of Anthropology in Mexico City. I thought about that for a while, and decided not to say, "Well, Abigail, I couldn't have put it better myself."

Mérida, the traditional jumping-off place for visiting the ruins, has a fine market and a grand boulevard, Paseo de Montejo, that is lined with the Rococo mansions inhabited by the old henequen barons in the days before synthetic fiber and other problems began to shrink the industry. It is not, though, nearly as good a sitting city as Veracruz—a shame, since sitting is pretty much what you're up to in the evening after a day at Uxmal or Chichén Itzá. The *zócalo* is too vast to feel enclosed, and the cafes seem too crowded with tourists. Still, when we were thinking about switching hotels, Abigail wasn't interested in leaving the center of the city.

"In Mexico, I just think you should be within walking distance of the *zócalo*," she said.

"I don't remember that as a family rule," I said.

"It's not," she announced. "It's my rule."

She has travel rules of her own? I had to think that one over. "Maybe you're right," I finally said. "Let's just stay where we are."

Calvin Trillin is the author of many books, including Family Man, American Fried, Travels with Alice*, and* Messages from My Father. *A long-time writer for* The New Yorker, *he also writes a column for* Time *and poems for* The Nation. *He lives in New York City.*

✳

Climbing down those Mayan pyramids is completely terrifying. Unfortunately, you are not going to find this out (and even if you're warned, you won't really believe it) until you are standing on top of one. So there we were at Chichén Itzá, and Larry was up on top of the biggest pyramid, and Perri was down at the bottom reading to three-year-old Benjamin from a favorite book, *The Cow Who Fell in the Canal.* After she had read it through for the seventh time, she realized that Larry was not down yet. Meanwhile, Larry had arrived at a new appreciation of Mayan culture. These magnificent pyramids, which are a breeze to climb, at a brisk pace, no hands, scare the life out of you once you start thinking about going down. Benjamin finally looked up. "Stand up, papa, stand up!" he yelled to Larry, who was inching down the pyramid in an extremely undignified sitting position. "Faster, papa, faster!"

—Perri Klass and Larry Wolff, "Temples and Tortillas
on a Mexican Tour," *The New York Times*

* * *

Mike's Cane

How does one explain the
nitty-gritty of lovemaking
to a nine-year-old?

I WAS PREPARED TO BE IMPRESSED WITH THE MUSEUM OF Anthropology and Archeology in Lima, Peru. One guidebook described it as "easily the most interesting museum in Peru," while another called it "the best in the Andean countries."

What I wasn't prepared for was the extensive collection of erotica. There was no sign saying, "Parental Discretion Advised." So when my husband, Gene, his brother, Mike, my nine-year-old son, Gino, and I stepped in front of a glass case and looked in to see a pottery figure of a man lying on his back with an erection larger than his leg, I was taken aback. A female figure knelt beside him, her lips on the tip of his mighty member.

"That reminds me of a joke," said Mike. He placed his cane behind him and sat back on it a bit, using it like a makeshift chair. "What has two thumbs, speaks Spanish, and loves blow jobs?"

No one answered.

I grimaced, glancing at Gino.

Mike pointed toward himself with both thumbs and said, "¡Yo!"

Gino's eyes narrowed, scrutinizing the figures. The female was blowing on the penis.

Maybe Gino really didn't get it, I assured myself. Should I explain this infamous misnomer? I decided that this was one time that I wasn't going to seize the educational moment that had popped up. If he asked me any questions, I'd answer him.

He didn't ask.

Next, we discovered that Mochica men had greatly enjoyed masturbation. A statue of a man, wearing only an elaborate head dress, is seated. His right hand holds a piece of work half as tall as his total height. His eyes are slightly wild. And he's smiling.

"That reminds me of another joke," says Mike.

"Zip it up," I whispered. All three guys checked their zippers.

"You know what I mean," I said to Mike.

Gino glanced at the figure again and said, "He'd have a hard time finding pants that would fit him."

I'm not sure if Gene was reassuring himself or our son when he said to Gino, "The size of it is really exaggerated."

"Speak for yourself," said Mike. He'd slipped his walking cane inside his trousers and was wiggling the end around his knee. We all laughed as he took it back out and started to walk on. Parts of Mike's arthritic body were as stiff as the male appendages of the Mochica pottery figures before us, so his cane was an important aid to him in getting around. He also waved it to flag down taxis, and once I'd seen him swing it as a weapon. But he would always relinquish it to Gino as he did now when his young nephew held his hand out for the cane.

During the months our family of four traveled around South America together, Mike's cane had served as Gino's main plaything. We'd brought dice, cards, and books for him, but no toys. Mike's cane had served as Gino's charging black stallion, his silver spear, his trusty musket. He twirled it like a majorette's baton. He conducted orchestras and led parades with it. That silver tube with a crook in one end was a pretend hockey stick, baseball bat, fishing pole, and more.

Gino played with the cane, while we adults viewed the remaining copulating clay couples and confirmed that all the positions of intercourse had been discovered before the birth of Christ, at least along the north coast of South America where these sculptures were found. They date from 100 to 500 B.C. I wondered what the original purpose or purposes of the pottery had been. Erotic? Educational? Utilitarian? The pieces, all about eight inches tall, were hollow, so they might have held a liquid. It was hard to imagine a family dinner using this pottery. If someone asked you to pass the olive oil, you might reach for the vessel that featured a woman on her hands and knees, a man standing behind her with obvious intentions. Perhaps that's exactly what they did, and in that manner they demystified sex. Perhaps we were doing the same thing now for Gino, however unintentionally?

"Cool!" said Gino from across the room. "Can we take a picture of that?"

I turned around slowly, not sure what we'd uncover next.

Gino was pointing the cane at a mummy who was sitting, with his knees pulled up to his chest, his open hands on either side of his face, captured forever in his final fear. Mesmerized by the mummy, Gino let the metal cane slip from his hand. It clattered to the floor, the sound reverberating off the tile and glass surfaces. It was a noisy climax to the silent sex.

An anxious guard came running.

"Sorry," said Gino in a contrite tone. He picked up the cane and handed it to Mike. He looked embarrassed from the unwanted attention.

The look on Gino's face changed instantly to excitement at

the next display: a case full of skulls. There were a variety of shapes. One of them was much smaller than the others, obviously a child's. Another head was bashed in on top.

"This museum is great!" said Gino. "Can we take a picture of this, too?"

Each member of the family reacted to the same museum in a different way. Mike went for laughs, without any concern for what was proper. Gene looked out for his son's emerging self-image as a male. I worried about how much impromptu sex education I should offer. And Gino?

Nine-year-old boys are much more interested in mummies than sex.

Mary Gaffney's stories have appeared in Travelers' Tales Love & Romance, Brazil, *and* A Mother's World. *She lives in Sebastopol, California.*

*

I think it was last summer, when I was coerced into spending too many minutes next to a glass case containing the skull of a seventeenth-century Englishman to whom something really nasty had happened, that I realized our annual tour to Europe with the children had lurched off into directions I never foresaw when I was single.

"What about the guillotine? I want to see it. And the Bastille. And the waxworks. Maybe they have heads."

This is from a little girl in a sailor dress, delicately mopping her mouth with her table linen. And I realize we are in for it again, the Chamber of Horrors tour of Europe. For, after years of towing Kate and Zara through the obligatory museums and pigeon-thronged squares, I know they'd give it all up for a really informative trip through the sewers. What they're after are the thrills and chills, the things that make Europe one big ghost story, that EEEWW GROSS moment that makes it all worthwhile.

— Catherine Calvert, "Grand Guignol on the
Grand Tour," *The New York Times*

ANN BANKS

A Storybook Adventure

Let a children's tale lead you around Paris.

WHEN I WAS A CHILD, MY MOST VIVID AND ENDURING DAY-dream was this: I'd open a favorite storybook to the liveliest page and jump in. Once inside, I'd still be me, but I'd get to roam the setting at will—conversing with the characters, petting their dogs, sleeping in their rooms. By the time this dream came true, the book was one belonging to my nine-year-old daughter, Kate. The place was Paris.

Our storybook adventure began quite by accident. I had set aside three days on the tail end of an overseas business trip so Kate and I could explore Paris together. Upon arriving in the city, we discovered that the only room available in our highly recommended residence hotel was grim, gloomy, and so small we could barely turn around. We wanted out—but where could we go? I hadn't been to Paris in years, didn't know any hotels, and don't speak French. But I recall a reference to "the loveliest hotel in the whole city of Paris" in the book I'd brought along for Kate to read, *Linnea in Monet's Garden*, by Christina Bjork.

Published in 1987 and now something of a classic, *Linnea* tells the story of a delightful Swedish girl who falls in love with the flower paintings of the French Impressionist Claude Monet. Wanting to learn more, she travels to Paris with her neighbor, a retired gardener named Mr. Bloom. They stay at a hotel called the Esmeralda, "Right on the River Seine, which flows through all of Paris," says Linnea. "From my window, I could see all of Notre Dame Cathedral. That is the city's most famous church."

As Linnea explains, the Esmeralda is named after the beautiful gypsy in Victor Hugo's *The Hunchback of Notre Dame.*

Kate and I were entranced by Linnea's story. Suddenly it came to me: Linnea could be our guide to the city. We had merely to enter her book. In no time, we had checked out of our dismal hotel, made our way across town in a taxi, and were standing in the Esmeralda.

The tiny lobby looked just as it does in the book. On the rough stone wall by the stair hung the painting of the gypsy Esmeralda dancing with her pet goat, Djali. On the red velvet couch lounged the hotel's

*M*y wife, Ann, and I brought our two sons, Willie and Nicky, then eight and six, to France. We were thrilled that they learned to enjoy fish and duck (we told them it was chicken before the first meal, but after Nick said, "This is the best chicken I ever tasted!" we fessed up). Most of all, I loved the sight of them sailing their model boats in the famous pond at the Luxembourg Gardens like *deux petits garçons Français*, and playing with the French children at the wonderful playground nearby. And in so doing, of course, they learned some French, notably *arrete!* and *Je suis Americain*!

◆

—Peter Herbst, editor-in-chief, *Family Life*

dog, Canelle, over whom Linnea makes such a fuss. ("In Paris, lots of dogs go out by themselves, particularly on our little street. Canelle knows them all," Linnea reports.) After making friends with Canelle, Kate and I settled into a room just like the one in the book, "ancient beams in the ceiling" and all. The view from our window was exactly as Linnea describes: Notre Dame Cathedral, of course, but also, directly below, a park containing the second oldest tree in Paris. (This, according to Linnea, "came all the way from America in a basket, and was planted there in 1681.") The amenities were modest, but the nightly rate was reasonable.

Like Linnea, Kate and I took the Metro to see the Monets. As we traveled around Paris from the Musee d'Orsay to the Orangerie to the Marmottan, I thanked my luck that the engaging Linnea had preceded us. Without her lively running commentary on the art, it's doubtful I'd have gotten away with dragging my daughter through so many museums. Kate, like Linnea, favored the water lily paintings, even taking out her colored pencils and copying one at the Orangerie. "You can put any color you want in the water and it looks okay," she observed.

Having done the museums, we decided to spend a day at Giverny (as Linnea and Mr. Bloom had done), the village where Monet lived and worked. We wanted to see for ourselves his famous pink house with the green shutters and the lily pond that so inspired his painting. Standing on the lovely Japanese bridge, we looked hard at the water below and tried to see all the colors that Monet had seen.

Back in Paris again, we sought guidance from the "More Things to Do in Paris" page at the close of the book. Despite her passion for Monet, Linnea recognizes that the soul isn't nourished exclusively by art. There's also chocolate — especially in Paris, a city of unabashed chocolate-lovers. Linnea satisfies her craving with a chocolate africaine with whipped cream at Angelina's on the rue de Rivoli. Our search led Kate and me to the very elegant La Maison du Chocolat, where the hushed ambiance befitted a place that charges $8 for a cup of cocoa. ("Worth every penny!" wrote Kate in her journal.)

We also mastered the art of toy sailboat sailing at the Luxembourg Gardens. We claimed the Notre Dame bell tower and chose our favorites from among the gargoyles. At least once a day we dropped in Shakespeare & Co., the eccentric English-language bookshop just around the corner from the Esmeralda.

I'm sure Kate and I would have had a nice time in Paris without Linnea's guidance. But following her happy adventures made it magical. On our last day, Kate wrote in her journal, "I love this city so much!"

Once in a while, when the planets are lined up just right, a parent and child can enter the same daydream, side by side.

Ann Banks' articles about family travel have appeared in Condé Nast Traveler, The New York Times, Travel Holiday, Parents, Parenting, *and* Family Life. *She is the author of eight books for children, including* The Children's Travel Journal. *She collects old travel books.*

✳

The prospect of Pisa excited the children enormously. Like the Little Mermaid, the Eiffel Tower, and Legoland, it was something they knew of as legendary, and they reckoned a visit to it scored them several useful points on the classroom argonaut scale. Although neither of us had ever been there, my husband, Tom, and I were less enthusiastic. We could already imagine the *charabancs* and crowds, the snapping cameras and whiffs of hotdogs. We even suggested giving it a miss, but the girls were having none of that.

"Don't you realize it's leaning, Mummy?" said Ellie, scathingly. "Any day now it could fall down, and we would miss it. You took us to Venice because it was sinking, and Holland because it was nearly flooded. We must go to Pisa."

I rather liked this Near Disaster Tour Theme. How close to death had Ellie felt we'd been? And how often? Had she taken the "Danger—Wild Boar" signs seriously at Sababurg?

"Why is it leaning?" asked Tilly. I looked at my husband Tom hopefully. He looked back.

"Well, there are lots of theories. Some people think it happened halfway up, when it was being built. Sort of slipped, you know. But they decided to go on just the same. Some people think it happened after it was finished—subsidence. Those people are still waiting for it to go on slipping. Then some people say that it was a challenge—to actually build a leaning tower from scratch—an interesting exercise."

"But why is it leaning?"

I gave up. "I don't know."

—Christina Hardyment, *Heidi's Alp: One Family's*
Search for Storybook Europe

MARC JACOBSON

✦ ✦ ✦

The Thrill of the Ride

The neon's still glowing, the ice cream's
still flowing, and the bumper cars
are still a scream.

I NEVER UNDERSTOOD HOW MUCH MY GRANDFATHER LOVED
me until that day last summer, more than fifteen years after his
death, when I, with Rae, my eight-year-old daughter, at my
side, nearly blew my cookies on the Coney Island Cyclone.
The 'Clone is probably the most horrific roller coaster in cre-
ation. Its appalling first drop is legendary, but even more
bloodcurdling is the rickety appearance of the ride, the splin-
tered wood scaffolding, the faint veneer of rust on the rails.
No doubt the same unsettling conditions prevailed in my
grandfather's day. Yet, past seventy, with diabetes and a stooped
back, for no other reason than to please me, he more than
once endured the 'Clone's lightning nightmare, not to mention the summer heat, the humidity, the crowds, and that
equally stomach-lurching ride, the Parachute Jump.

The old man's sacrifice was a mighty one, and it made a
great impression on this adoring grandson. Ever since those
Coney Island days, for me seaside amusement parks have
evoked summer's magic: walking barefoot on wooden-slatted

piers, wide-eyed children running ahead of their parents, the gear-gnash of machines bearing tender names like Hell Hole, the smell of fatty carcinogens frying on a flat steel plate. Yes, summer's magic and a lifetime's worth of memories....

With that in mind, I snapped off the television, had Rae and her friend, Gen, throw some clothes in a duffel bag, and hustled them into the car for a four-day tour of Atlantic Coast boardwalks. I would extend boardwalk lust through another generation of Jacobsons. I piloted our funmobile to a spot called Seaside Heights, a half hour south of the once-great boardwalk at Asbury Park, New Jersey—the scene of my first kiss, obtained in a true tunnel-of-love during a summer-camp field trip.

You can always tell when you've encountered a world-class boardwalk by the sheer concentration of screaming neon (kustard-Kustard-KUSTARD, games-Games-GAMES, golf-Golf-GOLF), swirling rides, carny booths, and, perhaps most important, a plethora of intestine-braiding fragrances. Seaside Heights scored high on all counts.

"Hey!" Rae and Gen exploded with sudden fervor. "This is cool!"

Cool, indeed.

How rewarding it was to see my charges, these former prisoners of two-dimensional, cathode narcolepsy, shriek in abject terror on the Astrorocket, have their weight guessed by men wearing bowler hats and door-knocker earrings, listen to mysterious gypsies tell their fortunes. Into the mirror house they went, down the water slide, around the corner in the coaster, cotton candy rotting their teeth all the while.

Fudge. Pizza. Doughnuts. Hot dogs. Licorice. Popsicles. On our boardwalk odyssey, we scarcely saw a child without some glowing foodstuff in his hands. On the boardwalk, though, you don't just eat ice cream, you eat Kohr's FAMOUS soft ice cream custard. Likewise, saltwater taffy cannot be generic. It must be Dolle's FAMOUS saltwater taffy. Why eat a regular French fry when you can eat a Thrasher's FAMOUS French fry? On the boardwalk, all the food is FAMOUS.

"Famous with who?" the girls asked, skeptically. To them, Cap'n Crunch is a celebrity. Mrs. Fields is a deity, but who was this scraggly-haired Mike guy who sold FAMOUS funnel cakes on the boardwalk in Rehoboth Beach, Delaware?

Gen, a budding food-faddist, looked on the regional delicacy with a hard eye. "Is this meat fresh or frozen?" she inquired of a seventeen-year-old culinary engineer with a distressed complexion. The boy reached below the counter, pulled out a stiff, red thing, and threw it onto the grill. Clang, it went. "I dunno, you tell me," he said.

No matter. We ate it all, and as we committed each celebrated item to our gullets, we walked around feeling quite FAMOUS indeed.

After a family ingests mounds of food, seaside

I couldn't understand why anyone would want to go into a dark hall that smelled of manure to look at cows, when just around the corner was The Midway! It was a place where you could shoot mechanical ducks, knock down lead milk bottles with baseballs, pick up treasures with a steam shovel, and spin until you puked on the "tilt-o-whirl." But my child's mind was most enchanted by the grotesque signs at The Freak Show. Just inside, for the mere price of 50 cents, lay unimaginable depravities: the bearded lady, the amazing reptile man, the shocking donkey man with the body of an ass. I never had the nerve to ask my parents for the money, but one day my brother came home to say he'd gone in.

"What was it like?"
I needed to know.
"Unbelievable."

◆

—Larry Habegger,
"It All Ends on Labor Day"

amusement parks offer a convenient method to lose that lunch: the rides. Just looking at some of those swooping, swirling hunks of churning metal would be enough to dekilter even Sir Isaac Newton's compass.

Weighing the options, we decided to spend the bulk of our time on the more earthbound electric bumper cars. In fact, finding those candy-apple-colored, rubber-rimmed roadsters became our central quest. Searching for the perfect ride, the girls and I compared and contrasted, and found wide qualitative disparity along the boardwalks. Funland in Rehoboth Beach offered a cramped floor crowded with cars, which led to L.A. freeway-type pileups that surly attendants were slow to untangle. Tiny, crash-course facilities also plagued Wonderland Pier in Ocean City, New Jersey. Conversely, in Ocean City, Maryland, the vintage bumper cars sped around a veritable ten-lane highway ready-made for cruising.

The best of the tracks was probably the one in Seaside Heights, which, although small and unassuming, does not enforce a one-way rule, thereby encouraging abrupt U-turns, anarchic frenzy, and whiplash. The girls went wild here, as did every other child on the ride. Gen proved especially adept at the old "my car won't start" ruse; she'd appear to be stuck, but then, as I came around the corner, she'd suddenly spin around to launch a broadside hit. Rae preferred Terminator-style, serial rear-end bashing. Sometimes, they'd team up and really get happy. "Coming at you!" they'd shout, and blast into my car from either side simultaneously.

At each park, after a few rides, we'd usually head into the game parlors and begin to waste money in earnest. Unthinkable as it sounds, the girls had never played Skee-ball before, so they dropped quarter after quarter (quarters! whatever happened to dimes?) into these yawning slots, surrounded on all sides by Skee-hurling kids and parents dispensing sage advice.

"It's like bowling without gutters," Rae said, getting the hang of rolling Skee.

"But we've never been bowling," Gen pointed out.

"We've seen 'Bowling for Dollars,'" Rae countered.

After a while they began amassing the tickets that the arcade dispenses for good scores. You redeem the tickets for "prizes." It takes something like 200 tickets, which translates to about $25 worth of Skee-ball to obtain a six-ounce container of Play-Doh ($1.99 in the stores). Rae and Gen kept rolling, but there was no way either kid was ever going to get enough tickets to trade for anything even remotely worth carting around.

Perhaps the best thing about the boardwalk amusement park is that it allows children like Rae and Gen, who have spent their entire lives surrounded by the pretty world of My Little Pony and the Baby Sitters Club books, to be exposed, in a relatively safe environment, to a darker side of human nature.

In fact, I was in the middle of some long-winded explanation about why being fleeced into playing crooked games by overbearing barkers (they get more aggressive as you head south; by Maryland, they all spit when they talk) is an essential part of the boardwalk experience, when Rae, on her very first try, rolled a big white ball over a hundred red goblets right into the only silver one.

"Oh my God, you won!" Gen screamed out.

"I thought nobody ever won these stupid games!" Rae shouted, completely beside herself. The old carny was obviously of the same opinion. Disgruntled, he trudged into the back room to dig out what must have been the biggest, ugliest stuffed baboon ever to roll off a Korean assembly line. The creature is currently taking up half our apartment.

By nightfall, the teenage date crowd starts to come out. This is something to be aware of on the boardwalks. After sunset, the tawdry fun gets a tad tawdrier; the pulsating lights and the callow laughter of barkers take on a slightly sinister tone. This ambience is definitely not for everyone, and most families actually head for the parking lot come eight p.m. or so, but for two girls closing in on adolescence, the garish allure was irresistible.

In this spirit, the barker's banter did not seem out of place.

"Come on, pus-brain, you're not gonna let that cute little daughter of yours see what a cockroach sniffer you really are, are you?" he sneered, sitting on his perch above the tank of water, dressed as Bozo.

The only way to quiet the creep is to dunk him in the tank, and the only way to do that is to hit a distant, tiny target with a tennis ball. The tennis ball costs 50 cents a throw. I thought I'd quit after about twenty unsuccessful tries, but Rae spurred me on.

"You've got to get him, Dad. He's saying terrible things."

Then, with one lucky toss, I managed to dump the big-mouth in the drink.

Rae and Gen ran over to the tank yelling, "That'll shut you up!" to which Bozo, some poor college student, could only smile sheepishly.

Later, as the moon rose high over New Jersey, we were topping the arc on a giant Ferris wheel. Nearly 200 feet into the sky, the summer breezes blew fresh against our faces, the moonlight spread across the ocean behind us.

"So," I asked, "are we having fun, or what?"

The girls agreed that we were, as I knew they would. For just as my grandfather had hooked me, the girls were now in the grip of the seaside amusement park. Once bitten by the boardwalk bug, they could have stayed forever, riding the Zipper and Dipper and Flipper one more time. Our trip was already being committed to the best kind of memory. I suggested that it might be time to get in the car and drive home.

No, they protested, there must be a FAMOUS French fry they hadn't tasted yet, some impossible game they hadn't played.

"One more, please," came the cry.

What else was there to do but give in? My grandfather would have. That's another thing he taught me about the boardwalks—how they get you to miss dinner, stay out late, take one last ride.

Mark Jacobson, a FAMOUS freelance writer, is the author of the novels Everyone *and* Noone *and* Goiro. *He has been a contributing editor at* Esquire, The Village Voice, Natural History, *and is currently a staff writer and contributing editor at* New York *magazine. He has three children and lives in Brooklyn, New York.*

✳

I remember Riverview. This vast amusement park was located on Chicago's North Side. It was magnificent, dangerous, and thrilling. There were freak shows, illicit gambling, the place reeked of sex. It was a dangerous dream adventure for the children and for their parents. My father took me up in the Parachute Jump. We were slowly hoisted ten stories in the air, seated on a rickety board, and held in place by a frayed rope. We reached the top of the scaffold, the parachute dropped, the seat dropped out from under us, and my father said under his breath: "Jesus Christ, we're both going to die here." I remember wondering why I was not terrified by his fear. I think I was proud to be sharing such a grown-up experience with him.

—David Mamet, quoted in *Fathers*,
edited by Jon Winokur

✦

Into the Woods

Like father, like daughter—portaging through
the Boundary Waters.

FROM THE FIRST, KATE'S PACK HAD GIVEN US TROUBLE. IT WAS one of mine. We'd tried it on at home, loaded with 30 pounds of gear, nearly half her own weight. It sagged on her shoulders, and the belt encircled her skinny waist like a ring around Saturn. Some angular part of the payload gouged her back. Even the short hike down to the end of the driveway and back seemed to stagger her.

So now, it is with some trepidation that my nine-year-old daughter steps from the canoe to begin the first portage of our three-day trip through northern Minnesota's canoe country wilderness. I want Kate to take part in portaging—carrying canoe and camping gear from lake to lake, a necessary ritual of traveling these waterways. At the same time, I want her to enjoy herself.

I've saved the heaviest items for my own pack, leaving Kate with soft, bulky gear that will rest more easily on her back. I hold her pack as she slides her thin arms into the straps.

"Stop and rest whenever you want," I say.

Then I watch her set out down the well-worn path. I shoulder my own pack and the canoe and follow her into the dark shadows of the woods.

Kate has canoed with me since she was seven months old. She was a year and a half when we took our first long outing. Since then we have spent many days on the water, but never have we paddled and camped together in an area this remote. I don't doubt Kate will take to the paddling and camping. She'll even tolerate the mosquitoes.

No, my main concern is the portages, which range in length from a few feet to more than a mile. True, we could put in on a big lake, where islands and miles of water would give us plenty to explore without ever having to leave the lake. But I want to give Kate the true North Woods experience. And that means following the portage trails deep into the wilderness.

My worries evaporate once I reach the end of the portage. Kate stands smiling by the next lake, waiting for me to load her pack into the canoe. "I didn't get sore at all," she says brightly. "It was pretty easy." We load the canoe, Kate jumps into the bow seat, and we push off onto a long, island-studded lake rimmed by a rocky shore.

The two of us are traveling the Boundary Waters Canoe Area, a federal wilderness hard against the Canadian border. In bygone days, according to one explorer's map, it was called only "region of rocks and water."

It is these things and more. It is a land of 1.1 million acres of unbroken forest and some 2,500 lakes. It is a place where loons call and wolves howl. With few exceptions, it is a land where motors are not allowed and progress is measured by the firm bite of a paddle in clear water and the weight of a canoe and pack on your shoulders.

It is a natural place for kids, with freedom to hike, canoe, swim, fish, and explore, following the trails used by Ojibwa

Indians and French-Canadian voyagers hundreds of years ago. The challenge is to get kids involved in the paddling, portaging, and routine chores of camping while keeping the trip easy enough—for parent and child—to be fun. That requires being prepared and knowing how to make adjustments in your plans.

After our portage, Kate and I face a long paddle across the lake. Here, I know Kate will excel. She seems to love the feel of the paddle and the quiet glide of the hull through the water. We stop on an island for a quick lunch of pita bread, cheese, and sausage. I spread our map across my knees for Kate to see. We trace our route so far—down the light blue fetch of Sawbill Lake, across the black dotted lines of our first portage and Alton Lake, to the red dot representing the island campsite where we now sit. After lunch, we make two more portages…then pick a campsite on a rocky point that slopes into the lake.…

Kate leaps to the tasks at hand. She helps unload the canoe and carry gear up from shore. Together we pick a tent site, set the tent, and spread out sleeping pads and bags. As I start dinner, Kate forages for clusters of ripe blueberries.…

Low clouds settle in. Gray sky, gray water, hills of dark green spruce. The scene makes me ache with a melancholy I can't identify. I feel as though I sit on the cold, hard heart of the continent. The Ojibwa Indians saw spirits in every rock, wave, and tree. Floating on this lake with Kate, I feel the company of other spirits.

I had first come to this country when I was twelve, on a canoe trip with my dad and younger brother. We'd paddled and portaged across several lakes before setting up camp, much as Kate and I have done. We spent the next three days canoeing, fishing, searching for turtles and beavers along the shore, hiking the portage trails, cooking and lounging about camp. "We could do the same thing," I tell Kate over breakfast. As I study the map, she munches a strawberry Pop-Tart, which is the perfect trail food: compact, packable, loaded with calories, hermetically sealed, and absolutely immune to spoilage. "We can stay on this lake and take short trips into other lakes today and tomorrow," I say. "We can swim and fish and paddle during the day and camp here at night. Or…we can do a loop."

A loop. Kate seems to come fully awake with this information. A loop! Why sit still when you can be on the move, ready to see something completely different….

"Let's do a loop!" she says without hesitation.

I trace the route on the map: northwest through a chain of a half-dozen lakes and scattered unnamed ponds and more than a dozen portages. Then east along something called the Louse River. From there, we'd puddle-jump through a knot of lakes, ponds, and portages back to our starting point. In all, about 35 miles and 35 portages, including a monster carry of one and a half miles near the end. The problem is this: if we get tired halfway through, we have to finish the loop—or retrace our steps—to get home….

"It might be a lot of work," I say.

"Let's do it."…

As the canoe glides toward the landing, I step into the shallow water with my rubber boots to protect the lightweight hull from rocks. I help Kate to shore, hold her pack, and watch as she disappears down the trail. I stow our two paddles and the spare in the stern of the canoe, secure them with a bungee cord, tuck the map in the pocket of the pack, and sling the pack onto my back. Then, making sure my footing is solid, I lift the canoe, cradle it overhead until it rests comfortably on my shoulders. Then I, too, set off down the path—no loose ends, nothing left behind. As much as anything in the Boundary Waters, I enjoy this efficiency of travel, the existential ease of moving through the country, like a salmon up-river or a vagabond on the highway. But what I remember most is the sight of Kate's blue back bouncing through the green woods, as her long, springy legs stride down the portage trail....

Clouds gather through the afternoon. A thunderstorm catches us on the portage to Malberg Lake. Drenched, we begin to search for a campsite. The first we find is second-rate, low, and marshy. The next several are taken by other canoeists. Finally, we paddle into a back bay just as another canoe emerges, occupied by three young men in rain gear. That can only mean that the site is already claimed, by them or someone else.

"Is that campsite taken?" I ask without much hope.

"Yeah, by a big black bear," one man says.

I laugh.

"We're not kidding."

I've run into bears many times in the Boundary Waters. They can be relentless in their quest for food. And they have always frightened me a bit. Too many *Outdoor Life* "true adventures" and tall tales from my dad.

"Let's go somewhere else," I say to Kate.

"Can we see the bear?" she asks.

---

*J*ean was gratefully breathing in the fresh mysterious scents and trying, eager as a pup, to catch those elusive thumping rabbits through the subarctic summer nights. In the Peace River, Jean was getting the chance to be young out in nature, and it was helping her grow into some kind of real person.... How glad I was that the children could have these experiences.... Robert Louis Stevenson said, "Seek out where joy resides, and give it a voice. For to miss joy, is to miss all."

◆

—Constance Helmericks,
Down the Wild River North

Her curiosity and lack of fear surprise me. "Okay."

The site comes into view. No bear.... Should we camp? Why not? These are black bears, not grizzlies, after all. For that matter, the bear could be headed toward any campsite on the lake by now. Besides, it's getting late....

We pitch the tent and spread our sleeping pads and bags inside. Then we paddle out into the lake to dip a big cooking pot for drinking water. When we turn the canoe toward shore, the bear stands on the broad outcrop, about 100 feet from camp.

"Paddle hard," I tell Kate. We speed toward the bear and begin to yell. The bear runs off a few feet. It turns, sees that we're still coming, and flees into the brush. At the very least, I want the bear to think twice about coming back.

Kate carries water.... Dinner that night is pasta Parmesan—eaten as we look over our shoulders at the dark woods behind. We wash the dishes scrupulously and patrol the site for crumbs that would give the bear a reason to visit camp. We stash the garbage in a

What to do when you see a bear:

1. Never feed a bear. Once a bear gets food from a human, it associates all humans with food.

2. Do not approach a bear. Quietly observe the bear if it keeps its distance.

3. If a bear comes too close, make loud noises such as clanging pots and pans together, yelling and whistling.

4. If noise fails, throw small rocks toward a bear's rump. Be bold, but keep a safe distance and use good judgement. Do not turn and run.

5. If attacked, fight back. Although there are no guaranteed methods of fending off an attacking bear, fighting back works most of the time.

◆

—California Department of Fish and Game

backpack with our food. Using a 100-foot length of strong rope, I suspend the pack between two widely spaced trees, a full 15 feet off the ground. I stack the pots and pans by the fire grate. We build a fire. Thick smoke rolls from the wet wood, barely rising in the damp air....

Through the night I hear noises. Surely a mouse, I tell myself. Too noisy for a bear, which can pad through the forest with surprising stealth.

Suddenly the pots and pans scatter. I shout and think I hear the bear run off. Kate stirs groggily.

"Don't worry, honey, he's gone," I say....

The next day we strike camp and enter the Louse River. A portage appears where it doesn't belong. Is our map in error? Or am I? Have I simply lost track? Or worse, have we strayed off onto a different route? It's amazing how easily panic rises, how quickly you think of spending the night in the woods, location unknown, hacking out a makeshift camp in a stand of birch and balsam.

"Are we lost, Dad?"...

"A little, but we'll find our way."

And so we do. After two portages, the Louse River gives way to a wide stretch of blue. It can only be Bug Lake. The name notwithstanding, it's a relief from the claustrophobia of what Kate and I have dubbed "the accursed Louse."...

Portages here are gauged in rods, a logging measure that equals sixteen-and-a-half feet. The Portage ahead measures 480 rods. Having walked down nearly three dozen portage trails, I no longer have to run through the mathematics. No need to multiply by sixteen and divide by 5,280. As a unit of measurement, the rod has been thoroughly internalized. After three days I know how long it is, how it feels in the knees, in the thighs, along the neck where the pack straps and carrying yoke cramp your shoulders. Four hundred and eighty rods is exactly one-and-a-half miles.

By way of preparing Kate for this, I tell her we have the rest of the afternoon to take this portage, if necessary. We can rest as often as we want. She, in turn, regards The Portage with bouts of giddy anticipation and melodramatic dread. "Oh, no!" she cries as we glide to the landing. "The Portage!" But I can see she's smiling.

I help her with her pack. "If you get tired or if you're not sure of the way, just wait for me," I tell her. Then Kate, true to form, disappears down the trail before I can shoulder my load.

The trail rises from the lake, then levels. I try to turn my attention from the load on my back. I watch the forest floor for flowers, berries, and other small treasures. Suddenly, I come to a stretch of mud. Then another. Finally, a long black quagmire. No sign of Kate.

She has apparently found a way around. Or through. I take a step along the edge. Instantly, I sink to my knee. I try another step and hear a great sucking sound. It's my boot, buried deep in muck. I'm left standing on one leg like a giant flamingo, balancing precariously with only a sock on one foot and 100 pounds of pack and canoe on my back. I throw down my heavy load in disgust and dig through the mud in search of my boot.

I see Kate in the distance....

We return to the main path and portage on. The trail rises and travels along higher ground. Finally, it begins to drop, and I spot the refreshing blue of water through the dark trees. At water's edge, Kate has shed her pack and happily munches M&Ms and sunflower seeds. Her boots are caked with muck.

"What did you think?" I ask.

"Not bad."...

We load and launch. As the canoe glides along, the little

swamp river gradually widens and grows into a long, rocky lake. This place thrills me, and so does my daughter.

Greg Breining, a freelance writer living in St. Paul, Minnesota, spent the summer kayaking around Lake Superior. His stories have appeared in Sports Illustrated, Audubon, Islands, International Wildlife, Family Life, *and other magazines. One of his proudest achievements this year is teaching his daughter how to perform an Eskimo roll in a kayak.*

★

We paddled down the southern shore of Indian Lake, in the Adirondack wilderness, for a while, passing what seemed to be miles of tent campers, then hung a left and disappeared behind a promising hemlock-topped rock island, whereupon we found a group of people frolicking in the buff.

I smiled politely as my seven-year-old daughter, Maggie, and I tooled by the nudists, who much prefer to be called naturists, but is a naked person any way you care to look at them, which I tried not to do, particularly the lady with the mammoth physique wearing only a big friendly smile and water-stained Mets cap.

"Hi!" she chirped at us. "Great weather at last, huh?"

"Very nice indeed." The weather, I meant to add.

A skinny naked guy fiddling with a camera on the shore lifted his hand to wave, and several other unclothed people smiled sweetly at us as we glided past. I thought about apologizing for intruding on their private Kodak moment, but decided to just keep paddling for dear life. The second we got safely around a corner of the island, Maggie jerked her head around, blushing and grinning.

"Dad, did you see those people? They were all naked!"

"Really? I guess I failed to notice. Actually, darling girl, I think the proper, polite description is buck naked."

"Dad!"

"Okay, okay. I saw the Mets fan was missing her top.…"

I explained to her that in ancient times, there was a widespread belief that nakedness enhanced the power of a woman and reduced the power of man, which perhaps explained why the magic of men was said to dwell in their garments—the vestments of war they put on, the armor of battle, and badged uniforms that signified their position and rank in society, and so forth.

"Cool," she said, looking back to see if the naturists were still in view.

—James Dodson, *Faithful Travelers: A Father, His Daughter, A Fly-fishing Journey of the Heart*

PART THREE

GOING YOUR OWN WAY

* * *

An Eye for an Eye

A married couple takes a journey
down a tear-stained path.

PAOLO, MY HUSBAND, DECIDED HE WANTED TO SHOOT AN elephant. We had a serious argument about what appeared to me to be a futile and cruel desire I could not justify.

Had he known what we now know about elephants, their sensitivity and gentleness, their family patterns and loyalty, and most of all their uncanny intelligence, I have no doubt that Paolo would have never gone for that elephant. But he was a hunter and those were different days. Shops supplying all sorts of hunting equipment flourished in Nairobi; so did taxidermists, and curio shops offering ivory trophies and skins. Now it seems a distant and different era, but it is not twenty years ago. Decent people, respected game wardens, the rich and the famous now turned impeccable conservationists, hunted then as a matter of course, and no one raised an eyebrow. How much rarer has wildlife become and how much has man's regard for it changed.

Paolo decided to go north, and booked a hunting block around Garbatula and Isiolo. Grinding my teeth, but drawn by curiosity to see a part of the country I did not yet know, I accepted the offer to join the safari. Paolo invited Colin and Luka, our friends, as well. Colin wanted a "hundred-pounder" [an elephant with 100-pound tusks] or nothing. Even then, hundred-pounders were practically impossible to find. Now they have all been killed. Colin, in fact, never found his hundred-pounder.

Doum palms, hot dry country, dust, sand, and camels were the background to our adventure among the Somali and Boran tribes. Handsome and wild, they were still clad mostly in their traditional robes: long checkered *kikoi* and turbans for the men, long dresses and veils and shawls, or skin skirts and amber and silver jewels, for the tall proud women with eyes of dark velvet.

Our days were spent stalking through the bush on foot, with a Somali guide, looking for a large male with big ivory; going through villages and nomad camps, in the heat and flies; meeting people carrying gourds filled with sour, dense camel milk; inspecting for tracks near murky waters, where, through the footprints of camels, donkeys, goats, and cattle, one could sometimes detect the majestic, soft-wrinkled, rounded elephant spoor.

Our evenings were spent around the campfire, the men with a beer and their stories of hunting adventures, I with a glass of ouzo, feeling a bit alien, and short were the nights of deep tired sleep: I do not have especially good memories of those two long weeks after the elusive elephant, which was always ahead, invisible, and—I secretly gloated—unreachable. We met many small and large herds, and I could appreciate Luka's skills, the dexterity and suppleness with which he led us straight into the middle of a group, literally between the legs of those huge creatures, and surrounded by their pungent smell, so that we could almost touch them.

One afternoon, finally, unexpectedly, we came across three elephants feeding up-wind. One was a large male with thick if not too long tusks, the largest sighted so far; the others, his two younger companions.

The hunter nodded to Paolo. Paolo looked at Colin in offer, but he shook his head: the bull was obviously not a hundred-pounder...perhaps a seventy, eighty?

I think Paolo was growing tired of what must have seemed even to him a pointless search. He could see I was not happy. I was consciously being a pest, subverting the safari in subtle ways. Perhaps I should not have joined the party in the first place, but I wanted to be with Paolo, and, of course, I was curious about any adventure which promised to be out of the ordinary.

Paolo looked briefly to me. I shook my head vigorously. We both turned to the elephant, no more than 50 metres away, who, intermittently slapping his ears, ignored us, and kept quietly feeding from the nearby bushes.

Now and again he shook his large grey head. Then he turned towards us, undisturbed and unseeing, aware of our presence but, not being able to smell us, unbothered by it. I saw Paolo's jaw harden in determination, and my heart skipped a beat. On soft quick feet he approached the elephant, and I could only follow him closely out into the open, looking up at the grey powerful mass and feeling vulnerable. Paolo put the gun to his shoulders and aimed.

The elephant looked at him with alert ears. I protected my own ears with my hands: I knew the shattering blast of the .458.

The air exploded, dazzling the flies and lizards, and the old bull lifted his head backwards abruptly, tusks pointed to the sky, without a sound.

For a few instants there was just this stillness. Then he collapsed, a majestic tree stricken by lightning.

Nobody breathed: my heart beat wildly. Everything was suspended, as in a soundless slow-motion film. His companions, stunned and uncomprehending, searched the air for explanation with extended trunks, trumpeted furiously, opened their ears wide in a mock charge, then unexpectedly turned away in unison and disappeared, crashing through the bush.

Paolo started running towards the elephant for the *coup de grâce*, with me at his heels. When we reached him, we could see that a round dark hole had sprouted, like a small evil flower, in the middle of his forehead.

It had been an accurate brain shot: but the elephant is the largest animal to tread the earth. His big brain takes some time to die. I could see one of his eyes, so close that I could easily have touched it, brown-yellow, large and transparent, fringed with straight, dusty, very long eyelashes. The pupil was black and mobile. He was looking at me. I looked into that eye, and as in a mirror, I saw a smaller image of myself reflected, straight, in khaki shorts. I felt even smaller,

> *O*f all the African animals, the elephant is the most difficult for man to live with; yet its passing—if this must come—seems the most tragic of all. I can watch elephants (and elephants alone) for hours at a time, for sooner or later the elephant will do something very strange such as mow grass with its toenails or draw the tusks from the rotted carcass of another elephant and carry them off into the bush. There is mystery behind that masked gray visage, an ancient life force, delicate and mighty, awesome and enchanted, commanding the silence ordinarily reserved for mountain peaks, great fires, and the sea.
>
> ◆
>
> —Peter Matthiessen,
> *The Tree Where Man Was Born*

realizing with shame and shock that I was the last thing he saw. It seemed to me there was an expression of hurt surprise in his dying yellow eye, and with all of my heart, I tried to communicate to him my sorrow and my solidarity, and to ask his forgiveness.

A large white tear swelled up from the lower lid and rolled down his cheek, leaving a dark wet trail. The lid fluttered gently. He was dead.

I swung around to face Paolo, my own eyes full of tears, a knot of rage and shame blocking my throat. "What right…" He was watching me.

The hunter came up and patted his back as was the custom. "Well done. A clean brain shot. Congratulations."

Paolo kept watching me. As so often happened with us, that special link was established, and the rest of the world had receded, as if only he and I were left in it. And the elephant.

My eyes were glaring. Suddenly, his became sad and weary. He shook his head as if to cancel the scene of which we were part. "No more," he said. "No more, I promise. This is my last elephant." It was also his first.

Luka was sharpening his knife. The car was miles away, and together we went to fetch it. When we came back, we found that the two younger askaris [elephants] had destroyed bushes and small trees around their friend, and covered his body gently with green branches.

I spoke no more that day. Paolo was strangely quiet. In the dark of the night, just before sleep, I remembered that an elephant had killed his brother.

Kuki Gallmann was born near Venice and studied political sciences at the University of Padua. Fascinated by Africa since her childhood, she visited Kenya first in 1970, and returned many times, eventually living there with her husband and son. An active conservationist, she was

*awarded the Order of the Golden Ark by HRH Prince Bernhard
of the Netherlands for her major contribution to the survival of the
black rhinoceros in Kenya. This story was excerpted from her book,*
I Dreamed of Africa.

✳

Revenge is a kind of wild justice, which the more man's nature runs
to, the more ought law to weed it out.

—Francis Bacon, *Apothegms* (1624)

CHELSEA CAIN

A Room in Oaxaca

*In Mexico, a daughter relives her mom's
final days—and makes peace
with a motherless future.*

THIS IS THE ROOM WHERE MY MOTHER BEGAN TO DIE. IT IS AN unremarkable place; simple, small, and old, layered with 50 years worth of paint and heavy with the smell of long-settled dust. There is a low double-sized brass bed, a desk, a bedside table, two metal chairs with Naugahyde seats, and a blocky wooden coat tree. A watercolor of a church painted from a distance hangs in the gold frame off center above the bed and a lamp and ash-tray are placed on a neat white doily on the bedside table. The bathroom is through a thin metal door spray-painted silver. A toilet, a shower, a pedestal sink, two thin white towels on a rack.

Behind me the señorita throws open the large double windows that open out on the courtyard and then stands quietly in the doorway, waiting. She is small and stout, her black hair in a long braid. She grins and nods, *"¿Si?"* she says. She holds the key dangling between two fingers. "Ninety pesos." I smile and nod. I would pay much more. She puts the wad of pesos in a pocket of her apron and disappears into the courtyard of foliage and squawking parrots.

I unpack carefully, ritually. I sling my tattered jeans jacket on the coat hook, and stack my mother's journals and maps on the desk. I hang my own towel next to the thin white ones in the bathroom and set my toiletries on the sink. I shake each item of clothing before putting it away in the closet: pants and underthings folded on the shelf, shirts and skirts hung on metal hangers. Last, I slip a photograph of my mother out of a book and affix it to the mirror by the bathroom door. She stares over her shoulder at me with bright, grinning eyes.

At the moment of her death I remembered everything. I had been so afraid. Listening to her breaths grow shallower and further apart, waiting for the silence. I kept my head pressed against her neck, my eyes squeezed shut as if I could prevent the inevitable simply by not witnessing it. I stayed like that for a half hour after she stopped breathing. I didn't want to see my mother's corpse. I didn't want to see her face, empty of expression. When I finally sat up I braced myself for the sight of her body, and instead found that she was looking right at me smiling, as if, in that second before she died—or during it, or after—she had seen something wonderful.

I sat there a long time, five or six hours, letting her look at me. I didn't want to break that final connection. Family and friends came in and out of her bedroom, but I remained, squatting on the mattress next to her, holding her hand until her fingers curled and her body got hard with rigor mortis. I memorized everything: her pale, freckled thighs, her square hands, the mole at the base of her left ear, the way her toes bent towards each other. I went over all of it: the snapshots of our lives, every old apartment, each fight and victory, every friend and lover.

I was twenty when she was first diagnosed with melanoma, in 1992. The specialist she saw told us not to worry. He told her not to bother with chemo or radiation. The statistics, he said, pointed to a full recovery.

The thing he didn't tell us was that the statistics were worthless. Four years later on a warm summer afternoon, my mother died while Dinah Washington sang "Cry Me a River" on the stereo on the wicker table beside her bed. She died nine months after the melanoma metastasized, after radiation and hospitalizations, lung surgery, blood clots, stereotactic radio-surgery, acupuncture, therapy, *chi kung*, visualization, prayer, drugs, demons, grief, acceptance, courage, and grace. She said to me: "You have made my whole life different and I love you." She said: "The novelty of dying is wearing off on me." She said: "I have no regrets." She said: "Promise me you'll go to Oaxaca."

The first time we had traveled together in Mexico was in the winter of 1995. I don't remember who thought of it first, though later we would each give the other credit for it. I was going to be in Florida that year for a Christmas family reunion on my father's side, so I flew from there to Mérida. My mother flew down from Portland, via Mexico City. We traveled for three weeks, spending most of the time in Mérida and Isla Mujeres, a small island off Cancún, tramping over

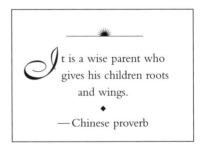

*I*t is a wise parent who gives his children roots and wings.

♦

— Chinese proverb

many ruins in between. I left her, at the end of the three weeks, standing on the dock on Isla Mujeres, as I motored away on the ferry. She stood barefoot, wearing the long black slip she had taken to wearing as a dress, a black vest, skin slightly tan, brown hair a long, unrestrained tangle. I can see the image perfectly in my mind, because even then it struck me. She stood completely at ease, fearless, as I left her in this distant world. It was as if she were preparing herself for some next thing. And I remember feeling, even then, as if it were the last of something.

She stayed in the Yucatán for three more weeks after that, mailing me a postcard every week that I would affix to the fridge, as I mapped her progress further down the south side of the coast. I missed her. I was used to talking to her on the telephone every couple of days and I longed for her counsel and humor and wisdom.

When she returned to Portland in February—in time to mail me off a box for my twenty-third birthday—she made clear to all of us that it was only to tie up loose ends before returning to Mexico. She had decided to fly back for an undetermined amount of time, to travel without an itinerary for as long as it suited her. "I have to be there," she said to me, and I don't think she could explain it any more than that.

"What about a job?" her pragmatic sister asked. "Can you afford to put off a job?"

"Oh, I'll be dead in three years anyway," my mother answered matter-of-factly. She laughed then, and her sister, utterly disturbed by the whole exchange, would remember thinking she seemed relieved.

It had been, at this point, three years since the original melanoma diagnosis, and she had stopped going for her check-ups. "I just don't feel the need to know," she explained. "I don't want to live my life obsessing." I encouraged her to resume her six-month appointments, but eventually let it go. She had to choose how she wanted to live, and, to be honest, the concept of the cancer returning seemed so remote and frightening a notion that I could not even begin to address it as a possibility. But my mother had. She would tell me later that she knew, even then, that she was dying. She knew in her body, silently, the way that you know you are pregnant, before any symptoms or pain or tests, somehow she simply knew that the cancer had metastasized and would eventually take her.

That March she returned south and began, in earnest this time, the serious business of vanishing. She traveled from Mexico City to the Yucatán, down the Peninsula, through Belize and Guatemala and then, over the next few months, back up into the mountains. Eventually she ended up here, in room 12 of the Casa Arnel on Calle Alameda in Oaxaca, Mexico.

Oaxaca. Three thousand miles from my apartment in New York City and all the expectations of my twenty-something life. I have come to this city of a quarter million people in the mountains of central Mexico to understand what it is she found here. It is a trip I have thought about a thousand times in the twelve months since her death. I have walked the city in my mind's eye—sat on a cement bench in the *zócalo*, bought bread in the market, stood on the crest of an Aztec temple a thousand feet above the earth. I have been telling myself that I would make this journey, without ever considering, for a moment, that it would happen this soon.

Oaxaca is a city rich with sounds and smells, at once nothing and everything like what I had imagined. The buildings are old Spanish colonial stucco, two stories, with tall shuttered windows that open out on to the street. It is a place that has endured—from the original Spanish construction on an Aztec settlement, through two major earthquakes and countless political tensions. It is like an old woman who has seen too much and lived too long to become distressed over trifles.

I came here thinking about Chiapas and the Zapatista insurrection, but that's twelve hours away by bus and I've yet to see signs of unrest here. I have yet to see poverty and graffiti;

only a middle-class city that wears its Catholicism like a scapula, dressing its little girls in white ankle socks and selling crucifixes on the street, 50 pesos apiece.

I sit in cafes here scribbling in my journal, asking Big Questions and wondering what it is she wanted me to find here. I retrace her steps, visiting the spots she marked on her map with small black "x's," taking the day trips to ruins she wrote about in postcards.

After checking into the Casa Arnel, I head to the *zócalo*. Old men shine black shoes. A dog sleeps on her side, then wakes, walks a few steps, urinates. The ornate iron benches and gates are painted shiny kelly green. Men wear straw cowboy hats. Mothers carry little girls dressed in party dresses and white anklets. In the center of the *zócalo* there is a large gazebo where the young men lean and watch from. The garbage cans are oil drums painted bright orange. A couple chatters away in Spanish next to me. She throws up her hands. He shakes his head. Music drifts from somewhere. Dishes clank at the cafe across the street. A middle-aged mustached man watches me write in my notebook. Another *turista* scribbling away. What is it, he must wonder, that Americans are always writing?

The dog appears again, wandering up and laying down next to where I'm sitting, resting her old head on my foot.

I turn to the man.

"*¿Señor?*" I say. "*¿Su perro?*"

"*Sí. Sí, mi perro.*"

In a few minutes he gets up and, with an affable nod in my direction, wanders on. Soon he is replaced by another old man. He is half my size, with whiskers, leathery skin, and bad teeth. He attempts to engage me in conversation. At first I think he wants money and I am about to turn away, but I stop. My mother would have listened.

The old man tells me his name is Antonio. He speaks no

English, but he is very expressive, his small square hands flutter in the air like dying birds.

He is a witch doctor, he explains. He heals with herbs. He has never been to the States but he has heard that some doctors there charge twenty dollars a day. He laughs. So much money and they can't even diagnose the right illness. He can tell what's wrong with someone without even touching them. By pouring a glass of water. By listening. He prescribes herbs his patients can buy in the market. Cheap. In the United States they use too much surgery, too many drugs, too many tests. He leans forward. In California, he says, he's heard they use tarot cards. He shakes his head. He's not so sure about that.

After an hour I get up to leave. Antonio tells me that he will teach me witch doctoring someday. He says that a lock of my hair would be very powerful.

The second week I am in Oaxaca my Spanish begins to improve, thanks in part to the class I am taking, and in part to my struggle to talk with native speakers. I have met several friends. I go to the same cafe every morning for coffee where my mother did, exchanging words with the same gruff proprietor she spoke of. I have climbed Monte Albán, the ruin that overlooks the city, and visited the holy cypress tree at Tule. I have swum in the pool at the Hotel Victoria and ducked through the tents at the Central Market. I walk by myself everywhere here, day and night, and I am not afraid. I know enough Spanish that I can ask for directions if I get lost, so I begin to wander farther from the central part of the city, embarking on day trips and explorations. I walk miles and miles everyday. I talk to cab drivers. I eat in local restaurants.

The day before I am to leave I run into Antonio again in another square in the city. I am sitting on a bench in the sun, and he comes and sits down next to me. He is wearing the

same clothes and hat and sandals as before. We talk some
more and he asks me why I am traveling alone. I explain that
I am on a journey.

Aren't I lonely? he wants to know.

A little, I tell him.

"Where are your parents now?" he asks.

I tell him my mother is dead. That she died last year and
that she came here while she was ill. That's why I'm here, I
tell him. This is the reason behind everything.

He is thoughtful. "Your mother is dead?" he repeats, to make
sure he's understood.

Yes, I say.

"She died?"

I think he is about to offer me condolences, comfort, a kind
word. Instead, he smiles and speaks the first English I have
heard him utter: "Ah, you and your father must be very rich."

Mexico. May 28, 1995

Dear Chelsea—After talking with you, I felt your
sadness at my absence. And a fear that our relationship
would change. So I am thinking in terms of my responsibility towards you. In the midst of so much thought, I
realized something profound. And it is—through this
trip I have come to terms with my death. Death is everywhere here. Caskets are sold by the sidewalk. Meat coun-
ters display the head of the meat of the day, complete
with soft furry ears. Over half of the Indian children die
before the age of five. It is difficult to deny death is waiting for all of us. And given my melanoma diagnosis, it
may be closer for me. Odd to realize, given how incredibly alive I feel as the result of my adventures. I don't say
this to further sadden you, but simply to admit it aloud
to both of us. So I feel better knowing you are perhaps

reshuffling relationships and becoming able to imagine a life for yourself without my physical presence. You might also recall that it is very Buddhist to live with death. It's a part of many cultures—unfortunately not ours. Denial has been too long a part of my life. In order to begin anew, I want to be completely honest with myself and that includes you. Admitting to death is to open one's heart to real life.

Love, Mom

Sartre said that the only moment we are truly free is when we are faced with our own death. The example he gave was a resistance fighter in the hands of the Nazis, who must surrender his comrades' names or die. The choice to live or die, betray or stay true—that choice is made alone in a room. Everything else—relationships, social pressures—they fade away until all that exists is your final private voice.

My mother said that cancer is like one long existential moment. Because when you are dying, everything is different. Everything looks different. Everything feels different. Because you are different. All at once you are stripped down to what you really are: mortal. And one of the first things you realize is that everyone is dying.

Your parents are dying. Your children are dying. Your friends are dying. And the really amazing thing is that none of them seem to know. They are all so concerned with your well being because you might die that night or in a year or two, when they are all in the same imminent danger. And you want to scream at them: don't you see? Your house could burn down tonight. You could fall down the stairs and snap your spine. A small plane could crash on the freeway, taking your Volvo with it in a hail of fire. Your cells are, at this very moment, breaking down and disintegrating and aging one by one. You're sick.

You need to take stock of your life. You need to follow your bliss. You need to save your soul.

That's when you catch yourself, and slowly you begin to realize that you are completely on your own.

This is the key.

I came here, to this mountain town, to look for what my mother wanted me to find here, but the longer I am here the more I think what she wanted me to understand had less to do with me than her. I think she wanted me to understand why she had to go; why she had to make the journey on her own.

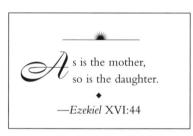

*A*s is the mother, so is the daughter.

—*Ezekiel* XVI:44

In the winter of 1995, when we were traveling for the last time together, we stumbled across a humble ruin called the Temple of the Seven Dolls. We hired a guide to show us the way, a Mayan man whose English name was Willie, and who was studying with a witch doctor in Mérida. Willie was very wise and thoughtful and he and my mother immediately fell into an easy rapport. He taught us a lot about Mayan culture that day and told us stories and sayings his village had passed down for generations.

Fear, he said, is a phantom. If you believe there are snakes in the jungle then you will see many, but if you believe you will make your way safely, you can walk many miles without seeing any.

My mother understood.

In Mexico, she found a culture that does not fear death, a culture that, like old Antonio, celebrates dying as one of life's essentials, a loss and a windfall. In bringing me here she let me taste a little of her experience. She let me glimpse the culture that allowed her to find peace with her own mortality. She allowed me to, as much as I can, see and feel what she did. In a strange way, she allowed me to let her go.

In doing so she has left me with the uneasy knowledge that, like her, I am not afraid to be alone.

Chelsea Cain is the author of Dharma Girl. *She lives in New York.*

✳

Dia de los Muertos, the Day of the Dead, is the tourist event of the year here; it's the only time the Patzcuaro, Mexico, tourism office gets it together to print maps.

Intellectually, we knew open discussion about death is healthy, but since we didn't know how to do that with a three-year-old, it was a bizarre relief to know that the local school, where we had enrolled our daughter, Annalena, was taking the lead educating her about the subject. The kids painted skeletons and marigolds and wrote (or dictated) poems about death. Annalena's homework included talking with us about the people in our family who have passed away and what foods they liked to eat. A blue-bellied lizard drowned that week in our wash basin, and choking with tears she sobbed, "I really, really miss my friend, Mr. Lizard! He's d-e-a-d!"

Each class made their own pretend grave in the garden, carefully decorating it with flowers, candy skulls, photos, poems, drawings, *muertos* bread people, and favorite foods of the departed. Parents were invited at eight p.m. to assemble by the candle-lit graves, drink hot chocolate, and watch the children perform a play about death, sing a song about death, and read their poems about death. At the principal's request, my husband Dave, a jazz saxophone player, played between presentations. Kids came up to him afterwards saying his music was "*muy padre*" ("very father" meaning "way cool"). It was cheery and festive, and touching to see my grandmother Mae and Dave's brother Peter honored on the preschooler's altar.

—Gina Hyams, "Escape Artists"

ROBIN LEE GRAHAM
WITH DEREK L. T. GILL

✦ ✦ ✦

A Seaside Birth

On a boat, far from home, a labor begins.

IN MID-JUNE, PATTI'S DOCTOR TOLD HER THAT THE BABY would not be born before the end of the month, and on June 19 he said it would be okay for us to go sailing and to spend the weekend off Santa Catalina island. We sailed with friends Al and Ann to Santa Catalina island in her father's power boat, the *Jovencita*. The weather was perfect and we stocked up the boat's icebox with the last of our Galapagos lobsters, from our recent around-the-world voyage to discover adventure and love.

After a two-hour trip to the island, we moored close to shore. I was surprised when Patti refused to come skin diving with me. She loved diving. She said she was feeling a bit uncomfortable and decided to stay in the dinghy while I explored the ocean floor. It's terrific diving off Catalina, which is famous for its protected garibaldi fish.

I swam back to the dinghy. Patti was on her hands and knees doing one of the Lamaze breathing exercises. She said, "I've got a rather peculiar backache."

I splashed her with water. "What you need," I replied, "is to loosen up with a swim."

But she wouldn't. "No, honey, I just don't feel like it. I feel just pooped—and if you splash me again, I'll clobber you with an oar."

I still didn't suspect anything was wrong. She'd seen the doctor only a few days earlier. He'd been very pleased with her.

It was toward midafternoon. The sun was hot, the water clear as glass. I went on diving and swimming around. Next time I looked over the side of the dinghy I felt the first nag of concern. I'd grown so used to Patti looking like an advertisement for Florida oranges. But now she looked rather strained. She was still doing her breathing exercises in the bottom of the dinghy.

"It's probably nothing," she said a bit too quickly, "but I've just had quite a strong contraction."

"But the doctor told you—"

"Oh, I know he did. But—well—do you think he could be wrong?"

"He'd better not be," I laughed. "I'm all for prepared childbirth, but not in a dinghy."

She smiled. "What about on the rocks—like the iguanas in the Galapagos. Remember?"

"Not on the rocks either," I said firmly. "Maybe you should get back to the *Jovencita*."

I paddled the dinghy across to the boat and helped Patti up the ladder. When she was settled on the quarter bunk she said she was fine. I left her for a while, but when I returned I found she was having a contraction.

She didn't smile this time. "Wow, that was quite a strong one!"

Through the porthole the sun was sliding to the horizon.

"Couldn't it be false labor?" I asked.

"Probably," said Patti, "in which case what about some dinner?"

She actually did join Al, Ann, and me at the dinner table. The Galapagos lobsters looked terrific. I knew how much Patti enjoyed them, but when she ate only two small mouthfuls I knew there was something really wrong—or really right.

Al volunteered to raise the doctor on the mainland. He got through on the radiotelephone but the doctor wasn't at home. His partner came through eventually.

The partner was very professional, very bedside-manner. He said, "Now if you're worried you can bring your wife to the hospital. But I advise you to wait. First babies usually take their time. It's probably false labor. You just tell her to have a good night's rest."

The doctor didn't seem to understand that we were at least three hours from the hospital, at Huntington Beach—two hours by sea and an hour through the Saturday night traffic.

As I gave Patti the doctor's advice she was again seized with a contraction. It didn't look like false labor to me. But we thought we'd better stick to the medical advice. Al and Ann went to bed.

At two o'clock I realized that unless we acted quickly there was a chance of the baby being born in the cabin of *Jovencita*. At the Lamaze classes they had told us about the things that could go wrong. I didn't tell Patti how worried I was, but I woke up Al. There seemed to be three courses open to us. We could call the Coast Guard helicopter and fly Patti to the hospital, or we could try to sail to the mainland in the *Jovencita*, or again we could see if there was any chance of getting Patti to the tiny hospital on the island.

We eventually decided to try the Catalina hospital. On the radio Al managed to raise the doctor on duty, who said he would bring an ambulance down to the wharf at Avalon, the harbor on the other side of the island.

Al couldn't get one of the cruiser's engines started, so we

limped around the island on one engine while I returned to Patti in the cabin. The time between the contractions was shortening rapidly. Sometimes they were only minutes apart. Patti was really into her breathing exercises. All the things she had needed at the hospital were in the trunk of the car on the mainland. But she did have the stopwatch in her purse. The stopwatch is important equipment in the Lamaze method. The idea is for the husband to time the period between contractions so that he can tell more or less how far along the labor is and what exercises his wife should do. We started the full drill and I massaged Patti's back to relieve the discomfort.

The ambulance and the doctor were at the Avalon wharf. I explained to the doctor how we had been trained in the Lamaze method and that we wanted to be together at birth.

The doctor nodded. "Yes, yes," he said quickly, "that's all right."

Patti was convinced the doctor was humoring her. She told him hotly, "I'd rather have the baby on the boat than go to the hospital and you not allow Robin to stay with me."

She made the doctor promise I could stay with her right through her labor before she would get into the ambulance. She made him promise that he wouldn't give her any drugs.

We were luckier with the doctor than we had dared to hope. He was quite young and had just returned from a spell of practicing medicine in Alaska. He had seen Eskimos have babies and he was enthusiastic about natural childbirth.

We looked pretty primitive as we shuffled barefooted into the eight-room hospital. We had no spare clothes—just a couple of toothbrushes. There was a nice nurse on duty who gave us a real welcome. Births are rare on Catalina. The nurse gave me paper overshoes two sizes too big and a white coat for the delivery room. Patti put on a linen thing with tabs at the back. The adventure of childbirth was suddenly exciting again.

Patti's contractions were now separated by seconds. The

nurse was puzzled because in the book she should have been moaning and crying out. Patti never whimpered. She was totally absorbed in what she was doing. I was amazed at her courage. She didn't talk much. She sometimes held my hands very tightly. The doctor didn't even unseal his hypodermic syringe.

Quimby's birth was the most terrific experience of our lives. Actually it was quite a long labor, but whenever Patti forgot her different breathing exercises I was there to remind her what to do—slow and easy between contractions, medium breathing as the contractions moved to a climax.

I am no expert on childbirth and I know things can go wrong. But I know that Quimby's birth is how a birth is meant to be.

Somewhere along the trail of man's evolution to the electronic age the secret has been lost. For millions childbirth has become a horror of pain and fear and drugs. Most mothers in "civilized" societies are hardly aware of what should be the most fulfilling moment of their lives.

It wasn't that way for us. I was there to tell Patti the moment Quimby's head appeared. I was there to announce that our baby had ten fingers. Then, after a surge like the highest wave of a full tide upon a beach, I told Patti, "It's a Quimby!" This was a name we had once mentioned in the Galapagos.

Patti's face was wan and drawn, but she managed a marvelous smile as she reached out and touched her daughter's hand....

I left her then to rest and went out into the early morning sun, glistening off white cottages and the sea beyond. In front of one cottage there was a garden full of flowers, and near the wall a rose, pink and perfect, the dew still on the petals.

On sudden impulse I pushed open the garden gate, walked the short drive and knocked on the door. A woman, gray-haired and in a robe, appeared. She look startled.

"There's a rose in your garden, the one near the wall. May I have it? I'll buy it," I said.

The woman pursed her lips. "Oh, I don't sell roses, and the one you're pointing at is the best in my garden."

"I need it for my wife," I said, and then I told her of the events of the night and of the birth of Quimby.

She listened in silence, then disappeared into the house and returned with some scissors.

"I've got some more roses in the back," she said. "Your wife deserves more than one."

"No," I said, "just one—just that one."

The woman walked across her garden and snipped off the perfect rose. I returned to the hospital with the single bloom. They'd moved Patti into a small room filled with sunlight, and with a view of mountains and very green grass—not another building in sight. Patti was lying quietly. The color had returned to her cheeks. She looked as if she had been lying in the sun all day. She was not asleep. The nurse found a thin-stemmed vase and I put the rose on the table beside Patti's bed. She didn't say anything but her eyes followed me around the room and then settled on the rose.

That evening the doctor told us it was rare to see such an easy delivery in modern society. He questioned us closely on the techniques we had learned together.

The hospital people waived the rules and allowed me to stay in the room with Patti for the next two days. Then on Monday morning the three of us—Patti and I and the child of the isles—flew back to the mainland in a small seaplane.

Robin Lee Graham is the author of Dove, *the true story of a 16-year-old boy who sailed his 24-foot sloop around the world.*

✳

The stress from facing constant challenges is accumulative. People do things differently in various parts of the world. It is exhausting learning new customs for how to shop, communicate, or take care of your most basic needs. This isn't the case just with visiting a foreign country, but in every region of our own continent.

In addition to stressing out over differences, you must also contend with other things going wrong, such as lost reservations or baggage. Like so many of these challenges, you can think of them as disasters or opportunities for growth.

One woman recalls with a smile: "The best trip I ever had in my life was with my family. Our Jeep was packed full with bodies and baggage, including a large container full of clothes and sleeping bags mounted on the roof rack. The first day, somehow our sleeping bags blew off the roof. The second day we managed to lose everything remaining on top. Here we were on our way to a camping trip without any clothing or sleeping bags!

"What surprised me was that we found our situation hilarious. Laughing together over this 'disaster' actually brought us together in a way that couldn't have happened otherwise. Ordinarily, back at home, I would have found this so stressful I couldn't have enjoyed myself at all. This time, though, we supported one another and dealt with the situation as best we could. There is nothing we ever did as a family that created such learning and intimacy."

—Jeffrey A. Kottler, Ph.D., *Travel That
Can Change Your Life*

⋆ ⋆ ⋆

The Cheese Sandwich
that Changed My Life

On Montserrat, the taking of a job on a
whim leads to unexpected wealth.

I WAS STANDING IN THE KITCHEN OF A CARIBBEAN NIGHTCLUB, looking through the screen door, through the rain, down the potholed one-lane road, when I first laid eyes on the small boy picking through a trash can behind the rum shop next door. The boy had big bare feet and spindly legs with scabby knees showing below dirty shorts, and a wet, too-small t-shirt stuck to his skinny chest and arms. Undeterred by my presence, he made his way toward the trash can that stood just outside my door. From the other side of the screen, he looked up and smiled at me as though he were an expected guest arrived for the luncheon that would be served from my dumpster. I invited him into the kitchen for a snack.

I did not know, as we shared a sandwich I cobbled together from pizza ingredients, that I was inviting this boy, Lenox Barzey, into the rest of my days. I think of this now, years later, as the cheese sandwich that changed my life.

That was in September 1981. Just a few days earlier, I had been living a few blocks from the Chester River on Maryland's

Eastern Shore, making minimum wage as a maintenance worker for the mayor and council of the small town in which I lived. My life was going around in circles, quite literally: I told my friends that I was a necropolis engineer, while my parents told their friends that I mowed the grass around tombstones in the town graveyard. My mother, Isabelle, was a librarian and my father, Eberhard, a biochemist. They frequently remarked that I was 28 years old and should be looking for more meaningful work.

This advice had been in the back of my mind when I read in the newspaper that Paul McCartney was recording on a tiny island called Montserrat, a British colony in the West Indies. I wrote a cover letter explaining why I should be employed to keep rock stars company in the Caribbean, attached a resume that included the degree I had earned in Romantic poetry and the many interesting ways in which I had avoided hard work in the five years since my graduation, and sent the whole package to two people mentioned in the article: George Martin, who had been the Beatles' producer, and Skip Fraczek, the nightclub owner who was renting his villa to the McCartney family. Weeks later an overseas telephone operator announced a call from Skip; I assumed it was a joke until I heard the voice on the static-filled line asking if I would manage his nightclub while he returned to the States on personal business. He said he would put me up in his villa—occupied as we spoke by Paul McCartney and Stevie Wonder—show me the ropes of the bar business, and then be off for a short time while I sunbathed and supervised his operation. He wanted me there in two weeks.

When my small plane landed on the volcanic island at dusk, Skip was at the garage-size air terminal to meet me. The McCartneys, he explained, had left for London that morning and he must also fly out sooner than anticipated. He would be returning to the States in the morning, but I could call him long distance if I had any questions—like, say, how to manage a villa and a nightclub when I had never managed anything in my life.

Skip's villa was grander than I had expected. His nightclub was not. Skip had told me that locals showed up for rum and pizza in the afternoon, Canadians and American expatriates came to the club after dinner for beer and reggae, and often, after midnight, rock stars

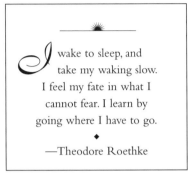

I wake to sleep, and take my waking slow. I feel my fate in what I cannot fear. I learn by going where I have to go.

—Theodore Roethke

who were recording at Martin's nearby Air Studios would pile in for cognac and play music with the house band. But when I took my first self-guided tour of the club it was as quiet as the graveyard I had left behind. The "nightclub" turned out to be a pavilion built of louvered shutters, which opened onto a black volcanic-sand beach. Fronds of banana and palm trees grew through the lattice back. Folding chairs were drawn up to rough-hewn tables. In the center of each sticky table, day-old oleander and hibiscus blossoms drooped from empty hot-sauce-bottle vases. The Montserratian staff had not yet arrived to sweep up last night's cigarette butts or to meet me, their new boss. The steady rain that drummed on the tin roof and splashed in onto the cement floor made me feel every bit as alone as I really was.

Which was why, I suppose, I took so quickly to Lenox.

Lenox was still chatting away at me as the club staff arrived later that afternoon. Accepting me as Lenox's new friend, they began to coach me in my responsibilities as their supervisor. My chief duty, it seemed, was to keep a financial account of the operation, and to take the checkbook wherever it was needed. I shopped for supplies in the afternoon before opening, and I paid the band in the early morning after closing. I learned many things by trial and error. I learned that though plantains may look like bananas, the plantain daiquiri is not a popular drink, and that Rastafarian musicians named Kitaka and Ikim prefer not to be called by their checkbook names of Clarence and Dwight. I spent many days at Air Studios drinking champagne in the company of very rich and very funny men as they reworked the lyrics of songs that the rest of the world had not yet heard. I was quite confident that I had, at last, found my life's work.

I also found that seven-year-old Lenox became a constant companion on my errands around his island. When I walked barefoot down the road to market for laundry soap or to meet a rock star for lunch, I would look back and there would be Lenox, "walking" behind me on his hands, the pale pink soles of his dirty feet pointed straight up at the sun. Then he'd tumble into cartwheels around me, race ahead, and wait for me to catch up. His front baby teeth had dropped out, so he had a big toothless grin that spread across his face and crowded the bright eyes that seemed to take in everything. I enjoyed Lenox's company and the attentions of tourists and musicians who followed my acrobatic friend as he followed me. I also enjoyed the friendships that grew as Lenox introduced me to the Montserratians and expatriates who had small businesses and few cares on the slow-moving island.

Lenox's mother, I learned, had been killed by a car when he was a baby. His father, a man whose street name was Sam Hustler, had a large legitimate family living in a nearby village. He acknowledged Lenox as his son, but assumed no responsibility for this illegitimate child. Lenox shuttled among his mother's relatives: women he called Nanna and Auntie this or

Auntie that, who lived with their extended families in one-room wooden houses on the beach or the mountainside. For all intents and purposes, he lived on the streets and supported himself with his wits.

These were well-honed. Once, when Lenox followed me into another restaurant in town, he pointed at the only pinball machine on the island and asked, "How does it work?" I explained how, gave him a quarter, and showed him how to start the machine up. He seemed reluctant. I assumed he wanted to keep the quarter for a worthier purchase. So I dropped my own quarter in the slot. When the machine exploded into action I could read the reason for his hesitation. On the screen in front of us, the game's all-time high-scorer was surrounded in lights: Lenox Barzey. The champ gave me a sheepish grin and then played on and on without having to spend the other quarter, which he had blithely pocketed.

Months passed before Skip returned to the island with his family and a houseful of musicians. I was invited to stay and work with them in the bar and band business. I moved into a bedroom over the club and Lenox often stayed there, supplied with pizza and Pepsi, when I went downstairs to work. "Work" was drinking and dancing all night and then counting profits in the early morning—making it hard to distinguish from the after-work parties that ended with breakfast at the yacht club or the recording studio. At some point the next day Lenox would always appear behind me, my grinning and tumbling shadow.

Not so often, I would follow Lenox onto the mountainside where he sometimes stayed with one of his aunties. This auntie was a large, formidable woman who kept many children for many absent parents. She was an expert at emotional extortion. On each visit, she would tell me at length about the hardship that was her life and give me a long list of things that would help her endure. When I shopped for her, I added little gifts for her many children; Lenox reported to me that most of these candies and clothes were not distributed. More often, Lenox did Auntie's shopping for her, and he was clearly afraid of shortchanging her. He told me he sometimes lost her quarters and was slapped across the face for this carelessness. I wondered how many times his face had to sting for him to become the secret pinball wizard.

Once, when I hadn't seen Lenox for a few days, I walked along to Auntie's house to ask if my friend was all right. As I climbed unannounced up her path, I saw Lenox, naked and cowering, as Auntie flailed at him with something. When I interrupted, she explained that Lenox was supposed to take care of her goats but that he must have mistreated the nanny because her kid had been delivered dead. She had been thrashing Lenox with the stillborn fetus. Dumbfounded, I asked if I could take Lenox to town. Auntie gave me a list of things that she wanted while Lenox got dressed. On our walk down the path Lenox just grinned up at me as though this was going to be another good day. There was some filmy stuff from the fetus still stuck to his dirty skin.

By this time I had grown to love Lenox in much the same way that I had long loved Paul McCartney. It was a wild, unrealistic love, a love that I had learned from the Romantic poets I had studied for so long. In short, I was in love with my idea of who Lenox might be.

I'd been away on Montserrat for seven months when my mother called, late one night, to tell me that my father had been killed in a small plane crash. I went in the dark to pick one of every kind of flower that grew in the jungle and at dawn I went to the airport to stand by for the first available flight home. I waited a long time and I will never again be able to smell those kinds of flowers without being sad. Late that afternoon, I put my bouquet in the trash can and began my trip through a succession of airports to be reunited with my family.

When my father's estate was settled, I learned that he had left me the financial resources to get started on any venture or adventure I might choose. The problem was, I hadn't a clue about what I wanted to do or who I wanted to be. My brother, Barney, suggested I work for a travel agency so that I might continue to wander aimlessly around the world while letting my mother believe I had a responsible job.

This seemed reasonable. I had been a travel consultant in Washington for about a year when my friend Susan MacLeod called from Montserrat to tell me that Lenox was adrift, too. I had thought about Lenox often and had visited him once when my travel business had taken me close to his island. On that trip, Susan had helped me negotiate with Auntie to enroll Lenox at a private day school on Montserrat. I had given Auntie a small amount of my father's legacy to pay for Lenox's first semester and had left the island feeling fine about Lenox and myself. Now Susan was calling to say that both Lenox and the tuition had disappeared for a while, and only Lenox had reappeared. Susan reported that Lenox was now seen only at night, hanging around rum shops, begging for money. She said that he looked sad and afraid.

I announced to my family that I was going to use the rest of my inheritance to adopt a Montserratian street child. My mother knew, from years of study, the algebra of my emotions. In other words, she knew that if she displayed the perfectly reasonable reservations she might have about my announcement, her concerns would be met with stubborn resolve. So she offered me her support, and I began a lazy investigation into what this whimsy might entail. Then someone—maybe one of the adoption agents or immigration officers I casually interviewed—made the mistake of telling me that my scheme was impossible. From then on, I was no longer just daydreaming, I was determined.

An unmarried woman pursuing an interracial, international adoption was not commonplace in the early 1980s, and I worked hard to understand the intricate tables of red tape. Only in retrospect did I realize that I had not expended anywhere near the same energy to look into my future and Lenox's, and to try to understand the implications that these actions would have for both of our lives.

I spent a year and a half traveling between Washington and Montserrat, taking care of logistics. On one trip I took Lenox a rough-terrain bicycle. When I returned a few months later, I met Lenox riding down the mountain on the island's sole paved road. He had one foot on the seat, the other on the handlebar, open hands flung wide in the air, his wide grin now filled with permanent teeth. His odometer showed that he had ridden more than 1,000 miles. On another trip I took him his first pair of sneakers, and on another, a waterproof watch. I always took Auntie what she had requested from the trip before. I did not tell her the purpose of my trips until the paperwork was almost completed; then I invited her to the office of my Montserratian attorney to ask her about my plan. My lawyer explained to Auntie that it would be illegal to exchange money for the child, as she proposed; he did allow, however, that I could pay to install the telephone she wanted so that she might call Lenox in his new home. This seemed to make her very happy and she agreed that Lenox should go with "Miss Pat." That is what Lenox called me, until I put the plan to him. Then he said, "Sounds good to me, Mom!"

This is how I ended up in May 1985 in Montserrat's High Colonial Court, asking a panel of her majesty's lordships in white-powdered wigs for permission to adopt Lenox Barzey. After hearing evaluations from community representatives, the magistrates queried Lenox about his future. Lenox, standing tall in the short-pants suit I'd carried from Kmart, said: "Your Lordships, I would like to go to America so that I can go to school so that I can study to be a judge."

Adoption granted.

He told the flight attendant on the plane north that he was going to America so that he could study to be a jet pilot. He flew the rest of the trip in the co-pilot's seat. As we circled Miami, Lenox announced to everyone over the PA system that "this America is sure one big island."

Lenox had accepted so many adventures with so much aplomb that I really didn't stop to think how strange everything must have seemed to him. As an airline captain escorted his new friend through the terminal to the immigration office, we walked toward an electric door that opened as we approached. Lenox stopped still, a puddle growing around his shoes, and began looking wildly about for *jumbies*, which is what the islanders call evil spirits. The captain and I stepped onto and off the rubber carpet as the door opened and shut, and soon Lenox was laughing with us. He collected his "green card" and everyone's best wishes and we continued to Washington. Lenox told the taxi driver who drove us from National Airport that he wanted to be a chauffeur one day, and when we arrived at my mother's house the driver refused to take our fare for his service.

As soon as we were inside, Lenox, like most weary travelers, asked for directions to the bathroom. I waited a long time for him to return so that I could introduce him to the rest of this family. When I finally went looking for him, I found him frantically stepping on and off the small oriental rug that my mother had placed in front of the bathroom door. When I turned the handle and pushed the door open, he just grinned up at me and rushed in.

Exhausted, I plopped down on my mother's sofa. My new son and I had traveled thousands of miles from his tiny Caribbean island to my childhood home in Chevy Chase, Maryland. I did not know that our long journey together, our exploration into the meaning of family, had only just begun.

Experienced in bartending and waitressing, Trams Hollingsworth returned to her alma mater, Washington College in Chestertown, Maryland, to be director of Alumni Affairs. She earned her advanced degree in psychology in 1995, the same year that Lenox graduated from high school. Lenox is currently a college student working toward a career in law enforcement.

*

I have always had an excellent sense of direction and my mother always trusted it. Looking back now, I think she was crazy to do so. When I was fourteen, she decided she had to see Europe, so she got me a passport and let me wander freely through the great capitals—London, Paris, and Rome. Once, as our taxicab sped through London streets, we saw a fruit vendor selling peaches and my mother said, "God, I'd love some peaches." When we got back to the hotel, she went to rest, and I made my way back through the streets.

I returned two hours later with a bag of beautiful peaches. Since then my mother has never concerned herself about my wanderings. She had never pictured me lost. I have never felt her afraid.

I never told either of my parents the truth about the places I've been. My father would write me newsy letters, photocopy them, and send copies to every American Express office in Europe or China or Central America, hoping I'd show up for my mail. And I'd write back chatty notes about going to the beach or visiting a native market. I never told them about the earthquakes in Mexico, the near-rape in Jerusalem, the searches of the Soviet border guards, the mud slides in Bolivia. They have come to assume that somehow I'll return safe. So far, I have.

—Mary Morris, *Nothing to Declare: Memoirs*
of a Woman Traveling Alone

Paddling Right

*A new awareness of shared
awe is born on the
Colorado River.*

RAFTING ON THE COLORADO RIVER THROUGH THE UPPER
half of the Grand Canyon was one of the hardest things I have
ever done. To make the journey I left behind my six-month-
old son.

The invitation to raft the Grand Canyon had come when I
was still pregnant, and at that point the decision seemed relatively easy. Who could turn down a chance to raft the
Colorado River through the magnificent Grand Canyon,
symbol of the American West? But that was before I had held
my baby Rhys, a warm bundle in my arms, and felt the world
spin to a stop. I had fallen under the spell of his sparkling blue
eyes and irresistible Mr. Joyful grin.

When we enter the river at Lees Ferry, the sun is already a
searing blade. I peer out through my sunglasses and put my
hand into the clear river, feeling the sting of cold. Our river
guide estimates it to be 45 degrees. "If the boat flips in a rapid,
swim," she lectures. "You don't have time to wait to be rescued.

231

Get yourself out of the water." Her warning fills me with excitement and fear. I know something of whitewater. In high school I competed in whitewater kayak races, but when I was seventeen I had almost drowned in a kayaking mishap. I had not been on a river since.

Now I am on the Colorado River about to ride a raft through big water and I am a new mother. When I left New York the morning before, I had woken as usual to nurse Rhys at four o'clock, but then could hardly bear to put him back in his crib. I kept staring at him curled in my arms, a grin on his sleeping face, a dribble of milk on his chin, then I was weeping at the thought of leaving him for a week.

Soon we head into our first rapid. "Tighten your lifejacket straps," our guide tells us. Our raft dives into the whitewater, then bucks up and down through a series of waves. Water smashes over the raft, rolling us like dice. Which way is forward? I can't see through my dripping sunglasses, but I don't care either. We are riding on raw power and are coming through. The thrill makes everyone, even our guide, whoop and shout.

Then as quickly as we have entered the rapid, we are out. I wipe my soaked face and see that, like me, fellow passengers are gripping the sides of the raft like children, their faces radiant. I think of Rhys, of how he clings to my arms, his face beaming, a tiny explorer as I carry him through the house. Here on the river, thousands of miles away, I feel suddenly close to him, as if I now share something of the state of awe which is his every waking moment. I am no longer a new mother, struggling to nurture her career as well as her baby, trying to do six things at once while the baby naps. My mind is no longer an overstacked tray of dishes—chores, writing projects, phone calls—all delicately balanced and about to tumble.

Each day I am pulled closer to the water. In calm stretches, when the surface of the river shimmers gossamer, I dip my paddle through the smooth surface and fight a momentary impulse to jump in. Riding the rapids, I am addicted to the feel of the river's power against my paddle, to the crash of cold water that smashes over us. And when we are through, the danger over, I sink my fingers into

*O*ne may go a long way after one is tired.

—French proverb

the boils of eddy water. At night, curled in my sleeping bag on the sand, I still feel the current's rock. When I wake, the moon rests on the canyon's rim, a slim white boat floating in blue sky.

On the fourth day, I ask the trip leader if I can try the in-flatable kayak and paddle solo on the river that day. The sky is gray and the water glass. I will have to manage several riffles, but only one major rapid named President Harding, which our guide says can be called "President Hardly" if one enters the rapid correctly. In the kayak I remove my helmet and lie back against the center cushion, closing my eyes. Left to the cur-rent's whim, the kayak spins slowly around and around. The river is so quiet I can hear the rustle of bushes on the shore. I keep my eyes shut, feeling the river's glide. This is the sound of time, moving us forward imperceptibly.

When I open my eyes, the red walls of the canyon have closed and now shoulder the river. I see the guides strapping down gear in preparation for whitewater, and I put my helmet back on, then reach for my paddle. The rapid begins as a whis-per, faint at first, then louder. The water picks up speed. I feel a rush of adrenaline. The last time I was in a kayak I was rid-ing upside down in frigid water, strapped into my spray skirt until I finally got myself free. *What am I doing here?* I suddenly think. *I'm a new mother: What if something happens to me? What about Rhys?* Yet it feels good to be alone in the kayak on the river. I feel something of my old reckless, adventuring self. Ever since Rhys was born I have begun to see the world as a series of potential hazards—a bottle cap as something he can choke on; the bed a terrible height from which he can fall; even the spoons he loves to grab pointed objects he may poke into his eyes. To be a mother, guardian of new life, is to become implicitly conservative.

I practice turning into eddies, digging my paddle in hard, then paddle forward and backward a few times. "Stay to the right, the far right," calls the guide on the oar boat I am to follow through the rapid. "There's a big boulder under the water there, so don't go over that. But don't get pulled left either. Work at paddling right. The water's big today."

I steer the yellow kayak down and into the tongue of the rapid, paddling hard to keep to the right. But as soon as I feel the force of the current I know that I am no match for the river which sweeps my small boat forward in a terrific rush. Before I know it, twin walls of water are rising up around me. The kayak is sucked forward and up then down into a cauldron of boiling whitewater. I feel the boat buckle then flip like a potato chip and I am thrown out into the river and am tumbling. The river tosses and pulls me this way and that. I am sucked down into absolute coldness, then pushed up to the surface. I gasp and sputter and cling to my paddle while jerking my arms and legs in a semblance of swimming. The river pulls me along at what seems like a fantastic rate. I don't see any boats, and the shoreline is spinning by: swim, I tell myself. Don't panic. Swim. I can see an eddy to the left and thrash toward it. Suddenly the yellow tube of a raft bobs near my face and hands reach down to grab the neck of my lifejacket. I hear people shouting, "One, two, three, pull." I am lifted out of the water and land in a heap in the bottom of the raft. Faces are peering down at me.

"I still have my paddle," I say weakly. I am so grateful to be out of the river, I smile. "She's smiling!" our guide yells to the other boats, who had watched me flip in the rapid and now wait anxiously downstream. "I want my boat back," I say, and I do. I wasn't ready to get spilled into the river and I am both astonished and enraged. Our guide throws me polypropylene underwear, rain gear, and a wool hat. I gratefully pull the warm clothing on over my wet skin.

Back in the kayak I paddle hard to get warm, weaving back and forth across the river which is once again serene, the silver water one smooth sound. I am freezing but feeling great. I've been baptized by the river, and reborn as my pre-motherhood self.

One week later I am back in New York, holding Rhys while he nurses intently, but I have only to shut my eyes to be once again in the canyon. I can see the red rock, lit with sun as if on fire from within. I can see the stars, so many it seems as if the night sky is draped in lace. I can smell the gentle tang of tamarisk, and I can hear the water, rushing like time through the canyon.

Leila Philip grew up in Manhattan and upstate New York. She did a two-year pottery apprenticeship in Japan, then went on to get a master's degree in creative writing from Columbia University. She is the author of The Road Through Miyama, *which received the 1990 PEN Martha Albrard Citation for Non-Fiction. She has received numerous awards for her writing including a National Endowment for the Arts fellowship in Literature.*

*

To see the world through Mia's eyes makes all those worn clichés about having children sound fresh. And we are really blessed to have

Mia because she does all the things we do. She's been going sea kayaking, camping, and bike riding with us since she was six weeks old. Last full moon we kayak camped on the edge of Tomales Bay. The sky was clear. No wind, and the water was like glass. Even in the middle of the bay we could see the vibrations the night bugs made on the surface. The moon was as big as a search light. We could hear the hush of owl and bat wings as they flew around us, and the roll of fish. It seemed like we were going twenty miles an hour over the water. So effortless. We were out there until 10:30, and Mia seemed as amazed as we were.

Of course, it isn't always that easy, but as parents know so very well, the lessons in that lack of ease are manifold.

—Allen Noren, "Paddling with Mia"

✦ ✦ ✦

Time Flies

*On Martha's Vineyard, a daughter
races past her father.*

I'M THE LEADER. I RIDE THE FIRST BIKE BECAUSE I AM THE father, and I will handle any of the problems that may arise. An out-of-control car? I will take the brunt of the collision. A sudden dip in the topography, a patch of sand, a stone wall? I will meet the trouble first because my daughter is only five years old and this is her first bike and the training wheels have not been removed for very long and…no, this is not exactly the truth.

My daughter is seventeen years old. She rides a bike very well. I am the leader because I don't know what else to be. I suddenly am the father of a young woman.

"Why do you keep looking back at me?" she asks.

"Just checking," I say.

"Well, I'm all right," she says. "Just watch the road."

This is the summer between her junior and senior years in high school. She was born about a week ago, and I think I remember taking her to kindergarten for the first time last Thursday. There was a nervousness about a junior high school dance just yesterday. Seventeen years old? A senior? I am the victim of some mad prank in time-lapse photography. I finished building that three-foot-tall green dollhouse only last night, wallpapering the rooms with pieces cut from a fat, sample book. Why has a covering of dust suddenly appeared on the roof?

The last time I was on Martha's Vineyard, my daughter was not born. Her brother, Leigh Alan, who now goes to college, was only a year old. There was a tidy clapboard motel on the edge of Edgartown that catered to young families. The motel featured a swimming pool and a kiddie pool and a set of big iron swings that looked very dangerous at the time. Who would let a kid ride on those swings? I remember picking up a killer sunburn in approximately 35 minutes, sitting by the kiddie pool, on guard against all danger.

"That motel we passed…" I say.

"I know, I know, you were there when my brother was a year old," she says. "You told me this three times already. You picked up a sunburn in 35 minutes. Sitting by the kiddie pool. The swings are still there. Isn't it amazing?"

Everything is amazing. Edgartown has not changed. Martha's Vineyard has not changed. A triangular-shaped island, twenty-two miles long and nearly nine miles wide, Martha's Vineyard sits off the shoulder of Cape Cod, surrounded by the Atlantic ocean, removed from the modern commerce of the mainland by a 45-minute ride on a ferryboat from Woods Hole, Massachusetts. There is still a Disney sort of perfection to the island on a summer's day. Looking for New England? Disembark from the ferry at Vineyard Haven, with the cars and the tourists and the hubbub, and disappear into the fantasy, which also is reality. The boats in the harbor are actual fishing boats, used every day by actual fisherman. The lobster pots collect actual lobsters. The various restaurants in the six Vineyard towns sell the lobsters, with actual college students waiting on tables, taking the orders with actual smiles.

I am told that in the winter the island can be a bleak outpost, the days gray and unemployment high among the 12,000 year-round residents. The summer is much different. Shutters are opened. Plywood panels are removed from storefront windows. The population is increased by a multiple of five or six. Money is spent as if it has just been invented.

"John Belushi is buried here," I say. "It seems the perfect place for him…"

"You told me this on the boat," my daughter says. "His grave is in Tisbury, right? His wife still lives here. Right? Carly Simon lives here. Walter Cronkite. Spike Lee has a place in Oak Bluffs. You gave me the entire story. I know, I know. That movie *Jaws* was filmed here. You can stop pointing out scenes, because I never saw *Jaws*. I was too young when it came out. You said I'd be scared." You never saw *Jaws*? I say to myself. Didn't it win some Academy Awards just this year?

The idea of this trip is that we ride the bikes, spend three days traveling together. The car is parked in a lot on the mainland. The only means of transportation we use are biking

> *Y*ou know that everything changes, but you're seldom prepared when it comes to your children. When your children are toddlers, change seems gradual: you know you'll have fifteen or more years together. Then suddenly they're teenagers, and the years are flying by. They're all grown up with plans of their own, plans that don't always include you, and you realize that the time together is precious—the years have shortened into months.
>
> ◆
>
> —Judy Ford, *Wonderful Ways to Love a Teen…Even When It Seems Impossible*

and walking. The weather, late in August, finally is terrific after a cool and rainy summer. We have t-shirts for the days and sweatshirts for the nights, shorts and sandals and sneakers and that's it. There is no schedule. There are no lessons for her, no assignments for me.... We can pedal and talk. We can swim and sunbathe and talk. Talk. It is a vacation luxury.

Neither of us is what you would call a cycling enthusiast. We own sturdy, fat-tired bikes with a mystifying assortment of fifteen gears. I ride maybe a dozen times a year, half of these times when my car is being serviced. My daughter rides more, out of necessity. She has no car of her own and sometimes needs a way to travel to her part-time job at a bakery or to her music lessons. That is the scope of our cycling. We have done no special training for this trip except lifting the bikes on and off the rack on the back of the car. I suppose we would be considered novices, but I would call us normal tourist riders.

We ride everywhere. Our base is Edgartown, at the Harbor View Hotel. The town is an old whaling village, the nineteenth-century homes of the captains preserved and almost venerated, the ghosts of dour women patrolling the many widow's walks in veils, eyes turned toward the sea in search of absent men. The streets are narrow, the sidewalks cobblestone. The tourist crush overwhelms the scene, well-dressed families back from the beach and in search of the perfect t-shirt or pizza.

> *M*y daughter's eyes are the sea upon which the ship of all my dreams set sail.
>
> ◆
>
> —Charles Ghigna,
> *If We'd Wanted Quiet, We Would Have Raised Goldfish*
> selected by Bruce Lansky

Our grand in-town adventure is a narrow brush with an

oncoming Ben and Jerry's truck that is delivering ice cream to the populace. We do not see the truck. The driver does not see us. There is a three-way squeal of brakes at the last possible moment. My daughter says it would have been a perfect yuppie death, the two of us hit by a Ben and Jerry's designer ice-cream truck in the midst of a yuppie town, and we would have been taken directly to yuppie heaven. I wonder how such cynicism is borne by someone so young. She says she learned it from me.

The prettiest trip is a six-mile ride along the coast to Oak Bluffs. A paved bike path takes us past the long state beach to a town of totally different character from Edgartown's. In the path is a menagerie of riders ranging from professional-looking racers who fly past with a careful warning—"Left!"—to slow-moving families with little children riding in carts attached to the backs of the bicycles. At any point there is a place to stop, spread a blanket, and enjoy the sun. On our trip we see hundreds of riders, more bicycles than we see cars on the adjacent tracks.

Oak Bluffs is Victorian and funky. It was built mainly in the 19th century by Methodists. The houses feature ornate gingerbread trim on their porches and eaves, and many are painted in pastels. The area has long been a vacation spot for affluent African-Americans, who call the local stretch of beach the Inkwell. One of the oldest merry-go-rounds in America is in town. It is a historic preservation that actually works. I tell my daughter that I remember riding on the horses with her brother when he was a baby. She says I have told her this already. I almost fell off reaching for the brass ring. That is the punch line. Hilarious.

Other trips take us to the beach at Katama, to the Wampanoag reservation at Gay Head, and to the center of the island, where only the sea air tells you that water is not far away. We also take a small ferry across a channel to Chappaquiddick Island, the site of Senator Ted Kennedy's automobile accident in 1969. This is probably the most historic spot in the area, where a presidential future died along with young Mary Jo Kopechne. I remember my last visit, not long after the accident. A wonderful beach was on the other side of the Dike Bridge, where the tragedy occurred. We would go to the beach every day, and every day tourists would gather, re-creating the accident. How did Kennedy's car go off the bridge? How did Kopechne drown in such shallow water? When my daughter and I arrive, I am surprised to see that there are three groups of tourists still asking the same questions. Will this ever stop? I also am surprised to see that the bridge has been closed. A large fence bars passage.

"You should see the beach on the other side," I tell my daughter. "It's the best on the island. At least as I remember it."

"But what are you going to do?" she says. "It's closed now. Gone. To go to the beach, we're going to have to go back to Edgartown, then on the road to Oak Bluffs."

"Right."

We have brought our towels in anticipation of the beach, and we keep them around our necks as we pedal back. This ride on top of all the other rides seems to be a bit too much for me. I feel a pain in my backside, pain in my thighs, pain in my calves. Almost without noticing, I am not the leader anymore. I am laboring, and my daughter has moved to the front.

I watch her as I clunk along. She is confident. She is strong, balanced evenly on the bike, hair flying behind her. Danger? She can handle danger. A construction truck rides past. It contains two young guys, and one of them whistles. My daughter rides straight ahead as I glare into the cab. Next summer at this time she will be busy, preparing to leave for some college, and in the summers after that, who knows what she will be doing? She will be in control. My daughter, Robin. The young woman.

How did this happen? I still am not sure. I simply keep peddling.

Leigh Montville is an editor and writer at Sports Illustrated.

✳

We've taken several exotic trips with our kids but one of my favorite adventures was a simple one—to the Amish country near Lancaster, Pennsylvania. Hunter was seven and Hayley was five. I arranged to stay on a farm and was sure that the kids would love feeding the calves and traveling around to see all the Amish in their wonderful clothes. But all my children wanted to do was to play with two little puppies. They were in heaven! It was a watershed moment for me. I realized that to enjoy a family trip you have to accept that your kids might not love what you want them to love. You will go to London and they will whine all the way through Westminster Abbey and then be ga-ga over the Tube or the black taxis.

—Kate White, editor-in-chief, *Cosmopolitan*

MICHAEL CRICHTON

_* * _*

Coming Up for Air

A brother and sister diving team
gets into trouble.

THE SETTING SUN GLOWED RED OFF THE OCEAN AS WE WADED
clumsily out from the beach with our scuba tanks and lights.
We paused, waist-deep in water, to put on our face masks and
adjust the straps. Behind us, at the Hotel Bonaire, people were
heading for the dining room to eat.

I said to my sister, "Hungry?"

She shook her head. My sister had never been night-diving
before, and she was a little apprehensive about it.

We had come to Bonaire for a two-week diving holiday.
Kim had just finished her second year of law school, and I had
completed a draft of my next novel; we both looked forward
to a good rest and a lot of superb diving.

Bonaire is a Dutch island 50 miles off the coast of
Venezuela. The island is actually a sunken mountain peak
with sheer sides; 20 yards from the sandy beach, the crystal-
clear water is 100 feet deep. This makes night-diving easy: just
walk out from the hotel beach at sunset, and drop on down
to 100 feet. You could make your night dive for an hour and

be back at the hotel dining room in time for dinner.

This was our plan.

My sister put her mouthpiece between her teeth, and I heard the hiss as she sucked air. She clutched her shoulders and pantomimed that she was cold; she wanted to get started. I bit my mouthpiece.

We sank beneath the surface.

The landscape is deep blue, small fish flicking like shadows over the sand and heads of coral. I hear the burble of my air bubbles sliding past my cheek. I look over at Kim to see how she is doing; she is fine, her body relaxed. Kim is an accomplished diver, and I have been diving more than ten years.

We go deeper, down the slope into blackness.

We turn on the lights, and immediately see a world of riotous, outrageous color. The corals and sponges are all vivid greens, yellows, reds.

We move deeper, through black water, seeing only what is illuminated in the glowing cone of light from the flashlights. We find large fish sleeping beneath overhanging shelves of coral. We can touch them, something you can never do during the day. The night animals are active, a black-and-white-spotted moray eel comes out of its hole to

*T*he underwater landscape of Bonaire is what's so spectacular, so inviting. I float effortlessly, as I imagine the baby inside me floats, without volition, moved by outside forces. As I drift and watch the fish, I narrate what I see, at times mumbling into my snorkel, which releases strange sounds into the water, but silently for the most part, as if, being in there, in me, he or she can hear and know and see.

◆

—Sue Halpern,
"Island of Good Omens,"
Condé Nast Traveler

flex its powerful jaws and peer at us with beady black eyes. An octopus scurries through my beam, and turns bright red in irritation. In a niche of coral we find a tiny red-striped crab no larger than my little finger.

On this dive I plan to take photographs, and so I have my camera around my neck. I take a few shots, and then my sister taps me on the shoulder and gestures she wants the camera. I take the strap from around my neck and hold it out to her. I'm moving slowly; with a flashlight dangling from my wrist, things seem awkward. Kim pulls the camera away.

Suddenly I feel a sharp yank at my jaw, and my mouthpiece is torn from my lips. My air is gone.

I know at once what has happened. The camera strap has caught on the air hose. My sister, in pulling the camera away, has also pulled out my mouthpiece.

I have no air. I am hanging in ink-black water at night and I have no air.

I remain calm.

Whenever you lose your mouthpiece, it invariably drops down the right side of your body. It can always be found hanging in the water alongside your right hipbone. I reach down for it.

The mouthpiece isn't there.

I remain calm.

I keep feeling for it. I know it is down there somewhere near my hip. It has to be. I feel my tank. I feel my weight belt. I feel my backpack. My fingers run over the contours of my equipment moving faster and faster.

The mouthpiece isn't there. I am sure now: it isn't there. The mouthpiece isn't there.

I remain calm.

I know the mouthpiece hasn't been ripped from the air hose, because if it had I would be hearing a great blast of air.

Instead, I am in eerie black silence. So the mouthpiece is around me, somewhere. If it hasn't fallen to my right side, it must be behind my neck, near the top of the air tank. This is a little more awkward to reach for, but I put my hand behind my neck and feel around for the air hose. I can feel the top of the tank, the vertical metal valve. I feel a number of hoses. I can't tell which is my air hose. I feel some more.

I can't find it.

I remain calm.

How deep am I? I check my gauges. I am in 60 feet of water now. That's okay, if I can blow out my air in a slow, steady stream and make it to the surface. I am sure I can. At least, I am pretty sure I can.

But it would be better to find the mouthpiece now. Down here.

My sister is hanging in the water five feet above me, her fins kicking gently near my face. I move up alongside her, and she looks at me. I point to my mouth. Look: something's missing. No mouthpiece, Kim.

She waves at me, and gives me the high sign that everything is all right with her. She busies herself with putting the camera around her neck. I realize that in the darkness she probably can't see me very well.

I grab her arm. I point to my mouth. No mouthpiece! No air!

She shakes her head, shrugs. She doesn't get it. What is my problem? What am I trying to tell her?

My lungs are starting to burn now. I blow a few air bubbles at her, and point again to my mouth. Look: no mouthpiece. For God's sake!

Kim nods, slowly. I can't see her eyes, because light reflects off her glass face mask. But she understands. At least, I think she understands.

My lungs are burning badly now. Soon I am going to have to bolt for the surface.

I am no longer calm.

In the darkness, she swings slowly behind me. Her light is behind my head, casting my shadow on the coral below. She is picking around my air hoses, near my neck. Sorting things out. Now she is over on my left side. Not my left side, Kim! It's got to be somewhere on the right! She moves slowly. She is so deliberate.

> *O*ne of the first things you learn to do in scuba certification class is to share your air with a companion in trouble by passing your regulator back and forth.
>
> ◆
>
> —LM

My lungs are burning.

I know I am going to have to bolt for the surface.

I am telling myself, over and over: remember to breath out, remember to breathe out. If I forget to exhale on the way up I will burst my lungs. I can't afford to panic.

Kim takes my hand. She gives me something in her slow, deliberate way. This is not the time to be giving me something! My fingers close on rubber: she has put the mouthpiece into my hand! I jam it between my teeth and blow out.

Water gurgles, then I suck cold air. Kim looks at me tentatively. I suck air, and cough a couple of times. Hanging in the water beside me, she watches me. Am I all right?

I suck air. My heart is pounding. I feel dizzy. Now that everything's okay, I feel all the panic I have suppressed. My God, I almost died! Kim is looking at me. Am I all right now?

I give her the high sign. Yes, I am all right. We finish the dive, though I have trouble concentrating. I am glad when it is over. When we get to the beach, I collapse. My whole body is shaking.

"That was weird," she says. She tells me that somehow the

air hose had gotten twisted around, so that it was hanging down behind my left shoulder. "I didn't know that could happen," she says. "It took a while to find it. Are you all right?"

"I think so," I say.

"You're shivering."

"I think I'm just cold."

I take a hot shower. Alone in my room, I have a terrible urge for sex, a compulsive desire. I think: this is a cliche — escape death and seek procreation. But it's true. I am feeling it. And here I am with my sister, for Pete's sake.

Michael Crichton (rhymes with "frighten") was born in Chicago in 1942. He was educated at Harvard College and Harvard Medical School. He is the author of many novels including The Andromeda Strain, Congo, Sphere, Jurassic Park, *and* Rising Sun. *He is also the author of four works of nonfiction:* Five Patients, Jasper Johns, Electronic Life, *and* Travels. *Among the films he has directed are* Westworld, Coma, *and the movie version of his own* The Great Train Robbery.

✳

The novelist Mary Gordon once said her most rewarding moment of motherhood came when she and her daughter read *Little Women* and sobbed together over Beth's death. I can understand, because recently I shared an experience with my eight-year-old daughter that, while less literary, was equally gratifying. Kate and I are holding hands and floating in a bright blue, tropical sea. Through our face masks, we discover a world of wonders: the white sand of the ocean floor blooms up in a coral garden that teems with fantastic plants and creatures—life forms so flamboyantly improbable that they might have been invented by Dr. Seuss.

From behind the mouthpiece of her snorkel, Kate squeaks excitedly; she points toward a crayon-bright assemblage of scales and fins. My daughter has spied her first stoplight parrotfish. As any snorkeler knows, these creatures are a dime a dozen around tropical reefs, the undersea equivalent of pigeons. But they are new to Kate, and she is stunned by the gaudy miracle of their existence....

I had awaited such a moment for a long time.

—Ann Banks, "Amazing Nature Adventures," *Family Fun*

KATE MEARNS,
AS TOLD TO ABBY ELLIN

⋆ ✶ ⋆

Six Months in Paradise

An overworked, overwhelmed Ohio family
finds the nerve to check out for a while —
and change their lives forever.

ONE DAY, MY HUSBAND DREW AND I WERE STROLLING ALONG
the banks of Lake Erie with our longtime friends Anne and
Steve, who live in New Zealand. We were telling them how
our lives in Cleveland were out of control: I was in nursing
school full-time, and Drew was all but living at his law office.
Plus, we had three young children, all under seven. We were
exhausted.

"Why don't you pack up the kids and come to New Zealand
for a few months?" Steve asked. Drew and I had dreamed of
running away, but it had always seemed impossible. At that
moment, though, something just felt right. We were young (I
was 34; Drew was 40) and healthy, and we had some money
in the bank. I turned to Drew and said, "Let's do it!"

And that was that. I completed my second year of nursing
school; Drew, who had been thinking about changing his line
of work anyway, resigned from his law firm. Then, our family
was on the way to Waiheke Island, the small, remote spot (about
a 30-minute ferry ride from Auckland) where our friends lived.

Waiheke is a haven for artists and people on a spiritual journey, which in a way we were. Our goal was to simplify our lives, to center ourselves. It was perfect. The two-bedroom house we rented was within walking distance of the beach and cost only $250 U.S. a month. (The entire six-month sabbatical ran us about $15,000.)

The kids had a ball from the start, and with our blessing they went barefoot like the local children. The only toys we'd brought were Legos and a stuffed bunny, so they relied on their imagination to create fun. Oversize palm leaves became sleds (perfect for gliding down sand dunes); they found crystals and rocks replaced marbles.

The easier pace meant we all had time to make plenty of friends. On weekends, when the kids were off from school, our family hopped into a minivan and traveled the country, seeing the sights. To save money we slept at campgrounds. At night we'd lie on our back and search the sky for shooting stars and the Southern Cross. Spending so much time together made the family stronger.

Toward the end of our stay in New Zealand, Drew and I panicked a little about getting work in the States. But by making some long-distance phone calls, we were both able to land jobs in the resort industry. We moved to Williamsburg, Virginia, where the weather is nicer than in Cleveland. I'm a spa manager and Drew is a financial consultant.

Once we were back in the United States, we found we missed our laid-back life. But for the most part, we managed to bring with us the tranquility we'd found on our trip. I never know when a word or a sight will trigger a wonderful memory of our six-month escape. As my grandmother used to tell me, "Travel is something no one can ever take away from you."

Would I do it again? Absolutely. The trip gave us a chance to reconnect and start fresh, to slow down and really examine what's important in life. Obviously we're still busy—especially because now we have two more children—but we don't run around as much as we did before.... Most nights we're content just to sit on our porch and gaze up at the northern stars.

Kate Mearns is a spa director in Williamsburg, Virginia, and the mother of five. Abby Ellin is a freelance writer in New York City.

*

Thirty-four years later, we still talk about it in mystical terms: The Trip To England. I was sixteen and my sister Becky was fourteen when our Midwestern family boarded the S.S. *United States* and sailed for Southampton. We saw 500-year-old cathedrals, funny little cars that drove on the wrong side of the road, people with strange accents who were entirely ignorant of the Chicago Cubs.

For a clean-cut Hoosier kid, it was a life-changing experience. Horizons irrevocably broadened, I applied to Stanford instead of settling for the small Indiana college I'd been thinking about. (To my astonishment, I was accepted.) I developed a passion for travel that has taken me to every continent, shaped my career, and enriched my life beyond measure. It all started, I'm convinced, with that family trip to England. Every kid should be so lucky.

So put off the new minivan for a few years and drop the personal trainer. Instead, spend that money on something really important, something your kids will still be talking about in the year 2033.

—David Noland, "It's a Big, Big, Big World,"
Outside Family Vacations

HUGO WILLIAMS

_{* * *}

Moving Heaven and Earth

An Englishman travels to France at
Christmas to maintain a family ritual.

IF YOU LOOK OUT OF THE WINDOW OF THE EUROSTAR AS IT
flashes across the countryside beyond Paris, you can catch a
glimpse of a high-towered village church near where my
wife lives for much of the year and where I am due to spend
Christmas.

Her house—our house—stands at the entrance to a little
farming village lost on a vast plain of sugar beet (in summer,
sunflowers). At night, drained of color, the landscape looks
like a frozen sea, with the Beghin Say sugar refinery standing
up like a monstrous lighthouse on the horizon. Added to the
hypnotic effect of the surrounding fields is a feeling of time-
lessness that hangs in the branches of the garden's chestnuts
and umbrella pines, the chiming of the church clock, the ringing of the school bell, like something out of *Le Grand
Meaulnes*. *"Vous êtes bien tranquilles ici,"* says my taxi driver, only
half admiringly, as he drops me at the front gates. I see the yard
is still ankle-deep in leaves, so I won't be deprived of my favorite
recreation. They look too wet to burn, though.

Christmas Eve. My wife has set out her grandparents' ancient Nativity scene, found in the attic. Our presents are shoved into our shoes in front of the fire in the French way. There is homemade carrot soup, Lagavulin whisky and Christmas cake from Marks and Spencer. We are ready for midnight mass, which is being held in a neighboring village this year. We set off on foot across the dark, oceanic countryside, through which cars crawl in straight lines. The big black sky is brightly lit at the edges, like a battlefield. People and cars converge on a little packed church where there is no room for us to sit together. *Venite Adoremus* and *Gloria in Excelsis Deo* have familiar tunes.

Christmas Day. The striking bells of the church come through on Radio Four as beeps, so they must be worked electronically, which is a bit disappointing. There used to be a café in the village when we were married here in 1965, but now there is only a butcher-caterer's, Madame Noël, from whom we have ordered a ready-made Christmas dinner, to be collected before lunch. We sit down opposite each other to feast on roast guinea fowl and chestnut stuffing. We even light the Christmas pudding.

There is something wonderfully soothing about raking leaves. It is like combing the old year out of your brain. I can understand why Zen Buddhists practice raking as an aid to meditation. After you have been doing it for a while, you notice that the raked leaves are a kind of mulch and that what is really being moved is earth from one place to another, a metaphor for all human endeavor. Every year my rake catches in the same root, for which I have developed an affection. Every year I wonder slightly at the same mysterious hole. Every year I think of Hardy's "Only thin smoke without flame/From the heaps of couch-grass;/Yet this will go onward the same/Though Dynasties pass," as I fail to light the bonfire.

Wet leaves are heavy to transport if they won't burn, but dry leaves are more of a nuisance to dispose of, because they tend to have a life of their own. They lie perfectly still until you touch them with a rake, then they suddenly wake up, and the slightest breeze sends them cartwheeling back over the area you have just cleared. The wind is getting up now and much of my work is being undone, putting my Zen wisdom to the test.

What I like about gardening is that you never have to hurry. The essence of it is that you plod about the place, pushing a wheelbarrow. You are doing such important work, the understanding is, that no one could possibly blame you for taking it easy. This means that you spend most of the time just walking along doing virtually nothing, with the result that you never get tired and have the impression that you have never been fitter in your life.

Just after five o'clock, the new sodium street lanterns flicker on pale pink, then gradually glow orange; time to go inside. Recreations in this telly-free house include chess and French billiards. *"Le billard, c'est un jeu très difficile,"* says our neighbor. We wouldn't know. Like chess, billiards is a game of chance for us, but that doesn't spoil our fun.

December 27. Now that I have raked the leaves together, they have to be loaded into an ancient trolley and taken outside the walls of the garden to be spread on a patch of wasteland. This is my least favorite part of the operation because it brings me into contact with a gang of pre-adolescent skinheads who have found out that I am English and thus capable of providing a major diversion in these parts. Last year, my wife let them into the house to play, hoping to diffuse their aggression, but they broke her guitar and stole various things, so she had to ban them. Now, when they see me coming with my homemade barrow, they start yelling things in English. Like a fool, I decided to ignore them and this has made matters worse. Now they have got a new game—throwing mud at me. First, they look through the grille to see where I am working, then they lob mud balls over the wall and run off. Another game is running across the garden, and dragging aside one of the old carpets we use to keep weeds off the paths. Nothing too vicious perhaps, but it is enough to make me step outside my leafy dream and catch a glimpse of myself as they must see me, a grim-faced foreigner going about some joyless grown-up task in his spacious garden where all the tallest trees grow. I think of Stephen Spender's poem about the "children who were rough" who first "threw words like stones," "copied my lisp behind me on the road," then "threw mud/while I looked the other way, pretending to smile."

Back home in London now, I think of them swarming over our shuttered *château*, dancing victory on the billiard table. It isn't surprising they are attracted to the place, but they don't find the welcome there that their parents found, or at least not yet. The last people before us to live in the house were my wife's grandparents, who ruled the village for years, the only bourgeois for miles. Such marauding children were unheard of then, perhaps because the old lady would have them into the house to sing carols and rehearse a Nativity play.

A former retainer, now a friend of ours, remembered the lovers' tiffs the old people used to have. When they were both well into their nineties (he died at age 102), he would complain about the darns in her cardigans and general lack of coquettishness. *"Je te la laisse, ta baraque (hovel),"* he would explode. *"Le retourne à Paris."* (He stopped driving when he was 97). Later, his wife would demand access to the massive safe housed in a room of its own off his study. This was where her pearls were kept against such an emergency. It wouldn't be long before she was having trouble putting them on and seeking her husband's assistance. As she picked up the few remain-

ing hairs at the back of her neck for him to fasten the catch
for her, their maid would be amazed to see him planting a
forgiving kiss.

*Hugo Williams is a freelance poet, television, theater and film critic,
and author of several books, including* Freelancing: Adventures of a
Poet *and* Dock Leaves. *He writes a regular column for the* Times
(of London) Literary Supplement.

✳

The first time I ever descended into the dark recesses of the prehistoric caves of France, a little girl—the seven-year-old daughter of a
friend—led the way. Noticing that I was edging myself extremely
slowly down the narrow stairway, whose view of the cavern below was
giving me a sudden case of claustrophobia, she blurted out, "If I can
do this, so can you!"

I will always be grateful to her for shaming me into entering,
flashlight in hand, a pale ivory sanctuary where, in half-trance, I saw
white stalactites hanging from the ceilings, golden stalagmites rising
from the ground. As I listened to an eerie underworld silence punctuated by the sound of dripping pings of water, I had the uncanny sensation that the animals pictured on the cave walls—floating deer,
prancing horses, retreating bison, charging bulls—were actually
moving in the flickering shadowy light.

I remember holding my breath at the sight of the ancient footprints, heel marks of barefoot children (probably not much older than
my friend's daughter) deeply imprinted in the mud and preserved in
the hard surfaces of frozen time. Noticing the wrinkled patterns of
those small feet, I thought, "This is my childhood." And then: "This
is our childhood"—the childhood of the race.

—Jonathan Cott, "Where Art Began,"
Travel Holiday

My Child, Our Vacation

*A mother takes her handicapped son on all
family trips. Sometimes her biggest
hurdles are well-meaning friends.*

A FRIEND CALLS. WE'VE BEEN ON VACATION WITH HER FAMILY
before. She wants us to go camping with them. It sounds like
fun. I consider the place she suggests and wonder aloud, "Are
there any pathways that will be paved or smooth enough for
our son's wheelchair to safely cruise along? Will the campground have an area flat enough for him to maneuver without
assistance? Can he get to the marina so he can fish?"

For our family, these are the types of questions that we think
about before we go anywhere. Such concerns seem normal to
me. I'm not distressed or particularly frustrated by them, so
I'm surprised when my friend perceives my questions differently. She heaves a deep sigh as if to say, "What a burden for
you!" Then she proceeds with a suggestion that stuns me:
"Have you ever thought about not taking Mahlon? Maybe
leaving him somewhere…"

I want to laugh: Leave him? Where? On the roadside?
Home alone?

At the same time, I want to cry because it's so hard to get

people to understand that Mahlon is family. I want to shout at her—as if that would make her understand more easily. "A family vacation without part of the family? Are you kidding? He's our child! He likes to be with us and do the things we do. He likes to camp and fish and ride in the boat. He likes to gather with everyone around the campfire to sing and listen to jokes."

Misjudging my silence as consensus, my friend plunges forward to explain that it would be good for us to do some things without our son to hold us back. It would relieve our burden, free us from the obligation to tend to his needs.

Whoa—now I'm insulted! As if my sixteen years as the parent of a child with cerebral palsy hasn't taught me that I have to take care of myself....

Would she also suggest excluding a child who has obnoxious habits? I have been on group outings where I had to endure other people's children who were far more troublesome than the relatively simple logistical problems posed by my son's wheelchair.

I try to put my hurt feelings aside. I tell myself that my friend's suggestion arose from her lack of experience rather than any malicious intent. I realize that she is

The Americans with Disabilities Act of 1990 has not only improved matters for travelers needing wheelchair access, it's also marked the beginning of a new kind of tolerance in the United States for travelers of all kinds. You may have challenges to solve on your travels that other parents can't even conceive, but you owe it to yourself and your child to do what you can to overcome them.

◆

—Claire Tristram with Lucille Tristram, Have Kid, Will Travel: 101 Survival Strategies for Vacationing with Babies and Young Children

looking at my life from the outside and imagining herself in my place. The tasks, the special preparations, and the efforts that I have come to take for granted seem overwhelming to her. Or maybe she can't imagine herself in my position because it's unsettling and uncomfortable for her to look at my life.

I want to tell her that I was uncomfortable at first, too. I didn't think I would be any good at this kind of parenting, but I've learned along the way. When I chose to become a mother, I decided that I was willing to take any child I got. Since then, I have asked myself what I would have done if I had known before he was born that Mahlon would have special needs. I don't have an answer....

Our family can't enter every building through the front door, but we've sometimes found it far more interesting to enter through the back. When we toured the White House, my son was able to enter through the kitchen and ride in the President's elevator to join the tour group on the second floor. He watched the kitchen staff prepare the President's lunch and discovered that the President himself had used the same elevator just ten minutes before—quite a thrill for a boy who loves American history!

On that same trip, we got to enter the National Archives building through a service entrance. We walked past cases of documents that were no longer on public display and some that were waiting to be catalogued. It was fascinating for all of us. Sometimes just finding an accessible door or an elevator is an adventure in itself. Other times it's annoying. We have done it for so long that we don't think about it much anymore....

I don't think we'll go camping with my friend again.... We'll try something more dramatic—like journeying by train through Europe. Maybe, by seeing that, my friend will realize that we are willing to make things work. We are a family who enjoys traveling and sharing experiences. Where we go, when we go, and how we go will always be affected by the fact that one family member is in a wheelchair. But one thing is certain: as long as our children want to travel with us, we'll go on family vacations with the entire family.

Kate Divine McAnaney lives with her husband Patrick in Carmel Valley, California. Her son Mahlon is now a history major at UC Berkeley and her other son Michael is a film major at the Academy of Art in San Francisco. Kate is the author of I Wish: Dreams and Realities of Parenting a Child with Special Needs. *When she is not substitute teaching, she is traveling—with and without her children.*

★

I was in a car accident and suffered spinal cord injury. I never would have thought that taking a vacation would be part of the healing process in dealing with my disability. But when my sister, Sue, came to me with the idea of traveling to Oahu, my first reaction was "it will never happen." I did not want to admit that traveling away from my comfort zone was terrifying, along with thinking that I could never have as much fun on vacation in a wheelchair.

At least 100 questions popped into my head to keep me from going. What if the long flight to Hawaii is too uncomfortable? What if I get sick? What if I sit around while everyone else has fun? The what-ifs continued. Luckily, Sue was so excited about getting us there that she wouldn't listen to any of my arguments. Besides, some able-bodied people have the same apprehensions about traveling.

At last we were in Hawaii. I was overwhelmed by all the things to do. There were dinner cruises, whale watching, luaus, a tour of Pearl Harbor, shopping, and much more.

Our main reason for going to Hanauma Bay was for the snorkeling. All the trolleys that take you to the beach area had ramps. And they had special wheelchairs that could roll right into the water. I cannot describe how exciting it was to be able to be pushed into the water. Even though I didn't snorkel, I could still see all the different wildlife in the bay.

The vacation was even more satisfying because I realized the many things I took for granted on trips in the past.

And I learned that my limitations were only as big as I made them. Because of Waikiki and Sue, I put my fears behind me and experienced more living.

—Raymond Cheever, "Stacy Goes Waikiki,"
Accent on Living

SUSAN LYN MCCOMBS

✦ ✦ ✦

Connections

*Teaching English in Thailand, a daughter
reaches across thousands of miles to
touch the parents she left behind.*

EVERYTHING ABOUT THAILAND IRRITATES ME THIS MORNING: the heat-laden air that kept me up through the night only to wake me again after an hour of sleep; the elephant that chased me from the watermelon stand and my morning meal, because she could not wait for her keeper to finish bargaining with the seller; and, now, my high school students, who are smiling and calling out to me in practiced English, as I hurry past their classrooms on my way to the post office. "Teacher, where are you going? Hello. Where are you going?"

If I knew the appropriate response to "Where are you going?"—a greeting as common in Thailand as "How are you?" is in the United States—I might feel less annoyed. But, after five months of living here, this everyday exchange remains an enigma to me. Sometimes the question is answered, other times it is merely repeated back:

"Where are you going?"

"Where are you going?"

Without slowing my pace, I check my watch. A drop of

sweat falls from my chin onto my chest, then slips under the collar of my blue cotton dress. It is ten-thirty in the morning. Already the glare of the Thai sun is melting the sun block off my face. Ten-thirty a.m. in Thailand, which makes it eight-thirty p.m. in California. Dad is probably watching television, but it is past my mother's bed time. I say a prayer to God, Buddha, and motherly instincts that she has found a good book to keep her awake until I call.

Outside the school gate, I hurry past the hut where the foreigner-hating dog lives. The mongrel has either heard the clicking of my sandals on the pavement, or he caught my scent. A snarling mass races out from the shadows of the raised hut. I let out a growl of my own, and pretend to pick up a rock. The trick works. The dog runs away, barking to warn the community that the foreigner is coming.

Ignoring the growing sweat stain on the front of my dress, I increase my pace to a half jog. The steep roof of the post office becomes visible through a grove of palm trees. Maybe there will be mail for me today. My mother tries to write to me at least once a week. And my father, who used to sign *and Dad* at the bottom of Mom's notes, now writes two and three page letters of his own.

My letters home are filled with exotic, everyday events, events that do not produce more than a smile of acknowledgment from my Thai co-workers. "Dear Mom and Dad, Because the school is on temple grounds, I have been given a nun's meditation hut to live in. With its red-tinged walls, my wooden house has all the look and feel of a sauna. My bed, the bottom half of a sawed off bunk bed, takes up most of the room…."

"Dear Mom and Dad, While the school waits another year for a permanent structure to be built, my classes are taught beneath rows of red and blue striped canopies. Praying mantis

and rhinoceros beetles the size of golf balls fly and land between the cross work of tent supports, providing visual aids for
impromptu language lessons...."

I stop to catch my breath
at the main road that winds
through the rural district
where I live. The local bus,
a pickup truck with two
long benches, passes in front
of me. Passengers twist in
their seats and stare. I un-
stick my dress from my
chest and thighs before
walking across the street to
a dirt road.

> *I*n Thailand, if you have
> the urge to pat a child's
> head, don't—it is considered
> the abode of the soul.
>
> ◆
>
> —James O'Reilly and
> Larry Habegger,
> *Travelers' Tales Thailand*

The weather-beaten ground curves around the palm grove,
and I arrive at the bottom of polished tile steps that lead up to
the post office. Its gold and red roof shimmers under the
morning sun. Inside, I tell the postal clerk that I want to make
a phone call to the United States. He motions for me to walk
around the counter and offers me a chair near the rotating fan
on his desk. I fall back against the plastic seat and exhale. The
clerk picks up the telephone to place my call.

Closing my eyes, I allow the fan's breeze to cool my body,
and the image of the coming conversation to cool my mind. I
imagine my father picking up the phone in the kitchen. When
he hears my voice, his face will flush from smiling. And, I will
not be able to stop smiling just from the relief of talking with
someone who is so familiar that I can see him from halfway
around the world.

On the other side of the whirring fan, I hear the young
clerk repeating my father's name, which means he has managed to reach the international operator. If all goes well, the

phone will soon be ringing in my parents' home. I laugh when I think of Dad shouting into the telephone: "Susie! How are you? Mary, pick up the phone. It's Susie! Susie, it's great to hear from you. How are you?" And, then, when I tell him I'm fine, he will yell once more, "Mary, the phone!" In his excitement, he will miss hearing the click of the extension being picked up.

"I'm here John, stop shouting." I can see Mom slipping a bookmark between the pages of her latest read. "Hi honey, how are things?" she asks, and the connection is complete.

The postal clerk clears his throat, bringing me back to the post office and the plastic chair. We exchange smiles when he hands me the phone. Then he leaves his desk, and I am alone with my family. Filling up on their words of love and pride, until I regain my sense of belonging, and am, once more, ready to return to my life in Thailand.

Susan Lyn McCombs is a freelance writer and winner of the 1997 Book Passage Travel Writers' Conference Competition. Her articles have appeared in many magazines and newspapers including Alaska Airlines Magazine *and* Reno Air Approach. *In addition to writing and roaming the planet, she teaches elementary school students how to make their own connections around the world. She is currently writing adventure travel stories for children.*

✳

Pregnant women may not go to a cremation, and may not go to visit persons seriously ill. This is probably protection against thinking too much, which might cause fear and loss of confidence. They are also forbidden to go and see other women give birth, because it will make delivery impossible, the children in the womb being embarrassed by one another and so refusing to be born.

There is another belief connected with pregnancy. If she would like to rear her child easily, a pregnant woman must seek an opportunity to walk under the belly of an elephant, but is necessary to choose an elephant with a kind disposition. If she has passed under the belly of an elephant, the child that is born will be easy to rear.

—Phya Anuman Rajadhon, *Some Traditions of the Thai*

EDDY L. HARRIS

★ ★ ★

South of
Haunted Dreams

Light is shed on a dark family legacy.

THIS IS WHAT I KNOW ABOUT MY GREAT–GREAT–GREAT–
grandfather.

He was a slave. His name was Joseph. He made and mended
harnesses. Born in 1795, he was owned—inasmuch as one
man can own any other—by a man named John—John
Harris of Goochland, Virginia.

In 1832 Joseph was legally manumitted. The reasons are not
clear. Family rumor has it that Joe might have been—even
must have been—John's son. What other reason could there
have been for the emancipation, for Joe's light complexion, and
for the fact that Joe, a slave, had been taught to read and knew
how to write? His master John Harris could do neither.

I had seen the last will and testament that Joseph recorded
in Shelby County, Tennessee—written in Joe's own hand and
signed by him. It is a document that has floated around the
family for years.

A copy of the emancipation deed I found in Richmond,
Virginia, in the State Library and Archives. It was not signed

by John Harris. He could only make his mark—a small but steady X.

> Know all men by these presents that I John Harris serv. of the County of Goochland and State of Virginia, have manumitted, emancipation and set free, and by these presents do manumit, emancipate and set free, a negro man slave named Joseph and sometimes called Joseph Harris, who was born my property, and I do hereby declare the said Joseph Harris to be entirely liberated from slavery, and entitled to all the rights and privileges of a free person with which it is in my power to vest him. He the said Joseph Harris hereby emancipated is a man of yellow complexion about five feet seven inches high and was thirty seven years of age on the 12th day of July last.
>
> In testimony whereof, I have hereunto set my hand and affixed my seal this 5th day of September Eighteen hundred and thirty two.
>
>   his
> Signed, sealed and delivered   John X Harris
>   mark
> in the presence of
> <u>NW Miller</u>
>
> In Goochland County Clerks Office 5th September 1832
>
> This Deed of Emancipation was this day presented to me in the said Office and acknowledged by John Harris serv to be his act and deed, and admitted to records
>
>   Teste, <u>NW Miller</u>

The language of the deed suggests that Joseph had already been granted his freedom. He might have bought it. He might have been given it. But he seems already to have had it. For some reason now he was being given it explicitly, perhaps because he had earned it, and like a son with his inheritance, wanted to leave with it.

Of course everything was subject to the discretion of the slave-holder. John's son or not, Joseph remained legally a slave. And even if Joseph had earned his freedom, or saved up money to buy his freedom, still he would have been hostage to the kindness of the man whose property he was. After all, the property of a man's property, his time and the fruits of his labor, is that man's possession as well.

But often slaves were allowed to earn and keep extra pay for doing extra jobs or for growing and selling crops on their own time. Many slaves were hired out—to work on other farms, in other homes, in factories. Many were given Saturday afternoons and Sundays off. What money they might have earned working these

The head must bow and the back will have to bend, wherever the darkey may go.

◆

—"My Old Kentucky Home"

extra hours, many would have been allowed to keep. That money, earned and squirreled away behind a loose board or beneath a few rocks, could have bought freedom.

As a skilled laborer Joseph might very well have been hired out—and often. John might have kept part of the wages, the rest he should have given to Joe.

Perhaps John was an honorable man, setting a price and then living up to his word, letting Joseph buy his freedom with the money saved. Perhaps he then let Joseph stay on, working for the lower wages that a black harness marker would charge. Working for John and for others in the county,

Joseph could save still more money before setting off down the road to find whatever adventures awaited.

And now with enough money saved, Joseph wanted to leave. He wanted to find his place and his fortune in the wide world. He wanted his freedom. And John, true to his word, let Joseph have it.

But in the deed there is no mention of the price of Joe's freedom. If this had been a cash transaction, the price should have been recorded.

But it doesn't matter. Whatever the case, whether he bought his freedom or was given it as some sort of birthright, before leaving the land that had been his home Joseph needed an official document to prove he was no longer a slave.

Patrollers roamed the countryside and lurked in the cities looking for runaway slaves. They made sure you were who you said you were, where you were allowed to be, doing what you were supposed to be doing. They stopped blacks routinely. Any slave caught without a pass was likely to be arrested and whipped.

Free blacks if challenged had to prove their freedom, either that they had been emancipated or—since freedom could only be inherited maternally—that either mother or grandmother had been born free. They lived, after all, in a society that equated black skin with slavery.

Free blacks were not entirely free, were slaves without masters, limited by what they could and could not do, where they could and could not go. In many southern cities they had to register their names and occupations. Often they had to wear badges. Free blacks arrested in faraway places without proof of freedom were apt to be forced back into slavery. Sometimes, proof was not enough.

But the allure of the city was worth the risk, worth the insult and subordination. The allure of the city was obvious.

There was opportunity there. There were jobs and money there. And there was freedom.

Not every runaway slave went north. Many escaped simply to anonymity in the closest southern city.

Cities like Richmond in Virginia and Charleston in South Carolina swarmed with black faces. The air was alive with black sounds—music, laughter, voices.

Away from the city, free blacks continuing to work on the farm were not much better than slaves. Some whites assumed that any black they saw was a slave, and dealt with him accordingly.

But in the city every black was not a slave and was not treated as one; nor was every black unskilled or unambitious. In the city there were blacks of every stripe.

In the city a black man could get lost in the crowd. In the city, free blacks and black slaves hustled along the sidewalks, bought and sold, shoved and shouted along with whites. The city was a more cheerful place. It was, perhaps, enough to know that slavery did not have to be a permanent condition. There was hope.

And there was life.

Fifty percent of Charleston's population was black, 40 percent of Richmond's, and the unskilled labor force in those two cities was 70 percent black—although in Charleston three out of four black men worked at skilled trades. The unskilled labor pool was 50 percent black in Mobile, 40 percent black in Nashville.

Blacks worked in tobacco factories, ironworks, construction crews, railroad companies. They were in the shops and on the streets. Blacks were plentiful. And they were conspicuous.

In the mornings the cities belonged to the blacks. Workers ran to the docks and hurried to the factories. Domestic workers went to the market. Drivers raced their wagons and carts noisily through the streets. Laborers repaired the roads, dug the ditches, manned the textile mills. The black presence was powerful and essential.

Free blacks were carpenters, millwrights, barbers, and tailors. Free blacks owned property, houses and farms and grocery shops. Free blacks owned slaves.

Free blacks made shoes, free blacks made perfume, free blacks made harnesses.

Goochland is only thirty miles from Richmond. Able to read and write, intelligent, Joseph surely would have accompanied John into town from time to time. He would have seen the possibilities afforded blacks in the urban environment. He would have wanted to test himself in those waters. If he had been living as a free man, he would need formal proof. An official deed of manumission was required.

And so one late-summer afternoon, John rode over to the Goochland County Courthouse and freed his son—if indeed he *was* John's son.

If he was John's son…the phrase causes me to stumble. Both pride and shame are bound up in it.

For days I pored over genealogy records in the State Library and Archives. I checked marriages, deaths, deeds, wills. I checked the census and the tax rolls, everything that was recorded by Goochland County for the State of Virginia. I followed a trail of property deeds and title transfers until finally I found John Harris's family and traced it as far back as the early 18th century, back to when this country was still England's and the land prices were still in pounds and shillings and pence. Probably John's family, possibly my family, had been here long before I found them.

His family, possibly my family, were speculators. They bought land and then sold it.

His family, possibly my family, were English or they were Scottish.

His family, possibly my family, were merchants. And they were successful. And I ought to be proud of them.

But my pride cannot outweigh my guilt.

John Harris's family, possibly my family, were also slave owners.

If Joseph Harris was indeed the son of John, then not just the blood of slaves but the blood of slavers ran in Joseph as now it runs in me.

If I am to be proud of what others have done before me, proud of these things I did not do, then I must feel guilt and shame as well for the horrors I did not do.

And which shame, that of slave or of slaveholder, should be the greater?

I was thinking for some reason of Joseph's mother. I know nothing about her. I wonder who she was and how she was, wonder as well how she endured being torn between joy and sorrow. She had conceived and for nine months would carry the joy that would be born a slave. The world her child would enter would not be the world she wanted for it. What a hopeful and strong woman she must have been.

No wonder John was attracted by her and drawn to her. No wonder he wanted her.

She likely had been a slave on the Harris farm. Although the southern edict has always been against black men loving white women, white men could do as they pleased. And one warm October night, John, wanting company, wanting a woman's warmth, walked in the darkness to where this nameless woman of my past sat, and he entered without knocking.

John Harris owned only 325 acres. His was no great plantation. He only held four or five slaves. He was probably a very humane man. His slaves might very well have liked him. He might have carried on regularly with the women on his farm before he married, and again after the death of his first wife and before his remarriage. So far there had been no accidents.

But on this October night, the moon and the stars were aligned; the woman was fertile. John's lust was strong. And that night when he entered without knocking and took hold of his property, in a moment as fleeting, as stirring and mysterious as a heartbeat, the blood of slaves and the blood of slavers mingled. The act was both momentous and casual, so casual in fact that it was being repeated at the very same time on countless farms all over the South.

I wonder if John would have stayed the night. Or did he take his pleasure quickly? I try to imagine his face, his manner, his way of walking. But I can see nothing. It must have been a very dark night.

The following July, Joseph Harris was born.

This man's face I can see clearly. I see him in the eyes of my father. His smile lives in my father's smile, his laughter in my father's joyful noise. When I look at my father, in the same way that I see myself, I also see my great-grandfather Joseph. When I look for Joseph against the night sky, it is my own face I see. I hear his voice in the whispering of the wind, and it is my voice as well. I feel his hand press against my heart.

---

*W*ithin the scholarly world, the acceptance of a Thomas Jefferson-Sally Hemings liaison had been gaining ground over recent years. Now that it has been proven beyond any reasonable doubt, the net effect is to reinforce the critical picture of Jefferson as an inherently elusive and deeply duplicitous character. We already know he lived the great paradox of American history. Which is to say he could walk past the slave quarters at Monticello thinking grand thoughts about human equality and never notice the disjunction.

◆

—Joseph J. Ellis, "When a Saint Becomes a Sinner," *U.S. News & World Report*

Joseph. I call him and he answers me.

So. It was not the voice of addiction that had urged me on. It was the soft voice of a man I had never met until now.

Until now I never knew him. Until now I never understood.

From the distance of centuries and the distance of different worlds, Joseph Harris at first seemed a coward to me. And my voice was accusing when I cried out to him.

Great-Grandfather, why did you suffer the hardship and humiliation of slavery? You could have fought against it. The arrogant blood that runs in me, that I took from my father and will give to my children, surely it came from you. Where was your courage and your pride when time came to rise up against injustice and pain? Why did you not think of me and the effect your actions would have on my life? Why this cowardice? Where would we be now if you had stood bravely and said no?

When I think of my great-grandfather with his head lowered and his eyes to the ground, I think of my father who in his day was also forced to bow his head and avert his eyes. And I am shamed. Having inherited arrogance, my father inherited cowardice as well. Having gone south to tempt fate and to test his limits, he learned his limits and had to eat his pride. And oh! how that must have hurt him.

If it hurts me now, how it must have hurt them then, proud men reduced to groveling, backs bent, heads bowed and eyes averted, voices humble and trembling with fear. When I think of them I feel their pain. How easy it is to hate them for it.

I ask myself how they could have done it.

I ask myself if my great-grandfather was a coward and the answer has always been yes. Of course he was a coward. But then again, he had to be.

He had been a slave. As fortunate as he was, still he carried the burdens of slavery, the insecurities of slavery. You don't go overnight from slave to free man in your thinking.

As free as he was, as light-skinned as he was, he was still a black man. He thought like a black man, was still plagued with the worries and fears of a black man.

When he moved to Richmond, he would not have wanted to draw attention to himself. Like other black men he would have wanted a low profile, would have tried to be as anonymous as possible. He disappeared from the tax rolls; the census takers could not find him. When he sought housing it would have been where the other blacks did, in back alleys, in stables and warehouses, in shacks on the edges of town. Where white residents refused to dwell, blacks both free and slave came together and formed communities. Comforts and services were few, but these hubs were vibrant.

In the cities slaves had been hiring out on their own time since at least as early as 1712. That year the South Carolina legislature complained that the practice of slaves hiring themselves out would grant them too much independence, and a chance to indulge in drunken behavior, to entertain evil ideas and develop bad habits. Slaves negotiating for pay, for housing, and for food struck many white southerners as undermining the very foundation of slavery. But the practice continued, and the white working man had to compete with the hired slave the same as he had to compete with the slave working for no wages.

(Naturally, resentment and hostility grew between blacks and poor whites. And violence often broke out as factory owners used blacks as strikebreakers—but still nothing like the great race riots that erupted in Boston and Philadelphia and other northern cities.)

As the southern economy expanded and the purchase price of slaves increased, those who could not afford to own slaves had to hire them. Cities hired slaves to collect trash, build bridges, maintain roads. Slave owners could cut expenses by letting others provide food and housing and clothing for slaves, as well as payment for their work. The slave owners could take in fifty cents a day for a slave. And if the slave could bargain for more than that, or find a job that paid more, he could satisfy his owner and still have a little money for himself. With this little bit extra he could set up house on his own and live away from his master. He could even hope one day to buy his freedom.

Until then, living out—as it was called—was liberty enough for the slaves, even if their lodgings were nothing more than squalid huts and makeshift shacks, dingy and dreary.

But they were away from the masters' gaze.

Some slaves were fortunate enough to rent houses, and while many families had never before found themselves in such favorable circumstances, these lodgings were often not much better than the shacks and huts the poorest of them stayed in. They were rickety and cheap, but still they afforded a degree of privacy and independence. And if a husband and his wife were owned by different masters, living out in these shacks and rented houses enabled them and their families to stay together.

In many cities, blacks were not restricted to certain areas by their race. Blacks lived in all parts of most southern cities. Not until after the Civil War would the South learn the strict segregation it would become noted for. And it would look north to places like New York, Boston, Pittsburgh, and Chicago to learn it.

Until then, as strange as it sounds, blacks were an accepted and integral part of the community at large. Considering the social climate, free blacks, because of their skills and their enterprise, had earned a rather high degree of respect and approval in cities all across the South.

At the same time blacks had their own community as well.

Free blacks and slave blacks visited freely. They got together for church activities, interacted at social affairs. They assembled in public houses for drinking and for lively conversation. There were dances and weddings, they celebrated new life, they buried the dead. They were a community that had in common work and race and circumstance. They had the same oppressors and the same fears. They lived in the same two societies— the one black, the other one white.

And the white society was dependent on the black one. The white society lorded over the black one. And the white society was afraid of the black one.

Blacks free and slave could have divided, but they didn't. There was more that bound them than separated them. They associated freely. And the white society feared this as well.

In 1822, Denmark Vesey gave them reason to fear.

Vesey was a blacksmith who had purchased his freedom in 1820. He lived in Charleston. It was his plan for blacks both free and slave to rebel, to assemble on the night of June 16, attack the guardhouse, and take the arsenal. Then they would murder the whites, pillage and set fire to Charleston. Afterward they would make their way to islands in the Caribbean.

The plot was discovered. Thirty-five blacks were executed. But the hysteria didn't die. Concerns grew about the association of free blacks and slave blacks. It was feared that free blacks would inflame the slaves and preach rebellion, that free blacks would deliver freedom papers from ex-slaves living in the North to slaves still in the South, that free blacks would hide fugitive slaves. For the sake of white safety and for the sake of slavery itself, laws were passed attempting to limit contact between free black and slave, to keep blacks out of the transportation trade, and to restrict alcohol from slave blacks. The laws were not strictly enforced.

Not until the 1830s.

On a Sunday night in 1831, Nat Turner stole up to his master's house and took the master's baby and killed it. There were 40 men with him. They went to another house, killed a schoolteacher, went on and killed many more. During a month of rampage and rebellion and hiding out, Nat Turner and his followers killed 55 white people in southern Virginia, after which the South and black-white interaction changed forever.

William Lloyd Garrison's abolitionist newspaper, *The Liberator*, had appeared in Boston. Slaves found courage. The rest of the world pointed an angry finger at the institution of slavery. White southerners fell back and insulated themselves. Many had considered slavery an evil institution. They had hoped and assumed it would eventually disappear. Now suddenly they rallied to its defense and praised it as part of what made the South and its way of life different and good and pure.

Upon the shoulders of slavery now rested southern honor and trust and a way of life. Into slavery's palms men and women of the South placed their fortunes and their futures, their lives and eventually the lives of their sons.

Laws that had been on the books for a long time but never enforced were now seen in a different light. South Carolina began executing a law that prohibited the manumission of slaves. Any black person who could not prove he had been free before 1822 was forced back into slavery.

By the late 1830s state legislatures would allow manumission only by judicial decree. By the late 1850s most southern states wouldn't permit manumission at all.

In Richmond the ability of slaves to hire themselves out was eliminated. Blacks could not assemble without white authorities present. Free blacks and slaves both were restricted from entering certain parts of the city. Blacks could not smoke, stand on the sidewalk, or carry canes. Jails, hospitals, cemeteries were now segregated, public schools, restaurants, and hotels were declared off-limits to blacks. The railroads kept separate cars for black travelers. There was even a law in Virginia that all free black men had to leave the state within 60 days of their emancipation.

Segregation had arrived and being black suddenly became a bigger crime. And slavery suddenly became even more hopeless.

This was the backdrop against which Joseph Harris won his fragile freedom in September 1832. And still freedom was valuable enough to him that he left the Harris farm and made his way to the city.

Joseph Harris remained in the area for twelve more years. He showed up on census records from time to time, but the last record I saw of him in Virginia was in 1844, the year John Harris died.

Not including the 325 acres of land, John left an estate valued at $2,965.86. Among his property were beds and furniture, two cultivators and a black bull, thirty head of sheep and an ox cart, a deep red cow, nine hogs and nine slaves. It obviously had not been for humanitarian reasons that John had emancipated Joseph. John died a slave owner.

As best I can make out from the blurred handwriting:

> Mahala and 4 children Tom, Louisa,
> Rose, and Frances $1125.00
> Toryan a Negro Man...........400.00
> John Ditto 500.00
> Bob Ditto. 400.00
> Sulpha a Negro Woman.......150.00

Nothing about them apart from this is noted, no mention of who the people were or what became of them, or of the too many others like them.

As for Joseph, he was not mentioned in the will, and maybe he did or maybe he did not attend his daddy's funeral, but he was there on October 31, 1844, when John's property was sold at auction. County probate records show that for thirty-seven cents Joseph bought horse collars and a harness.

And then what became of him?

Did he go to Richmond and try to lose himself in the city, pass as a white man, take a job at the Tredegar Ironworks? The hours were long and the work was hard, but with bonuses and overtime Joseph could make much more as an ironworker than as a harness mender, maybe close to $100 a year. Maybe Joseph had a plan to make the most of his freedom. To travel the land and find a home. To take the name of his former owner, which was the only name he had, and get on with his life. Not to forget about the past—how could he ever do that?—but to leave it where it belonged, behind him.

When he had saved enough, when he had had enough of Virginia with its sour memories, perhaps he pushed further south toward Raleigh and the Carolina coast. Perhaps he tried his hand as a fisherman, or maybe he ran a ferryboat between the islands.

And each time the wind shifted, he carried on, down through Georgia and into Florida, across Alabama and Mississippi, and on until the great river blocked his path, and then north but not too far north, to Tennessee, where the rich soil was deep enough for a wandering man to plant his roots. There Joseph Harris found his home.

He took the money he had saved, applied his skills as a horseman, and started a stagecoach line. He bought land. He prospered. And in the same way that my father is happiest when his kids are home and around him, Joseph surrounded himself with his children and was happy.

Much of this is conjecture, of course, but by the time Joseph died in 1875, he had indeed started and operated a stagecoach line in western Tennessee. He had amassed a sizeable wealth and 317 acres of land.

The land is still there. They call it Harris Hill. When Joseph died it was divided among his children according to terms set forth in a will of such sophistication that I wonder at it now, sounding like every white man who has ever asked me how it is that a black man travels the world and has as his hobbies skiing and scuba diving and fly fishing:

How in the world did a black man, a former slave, acquire wealth enough to leave behind at the time of his death five pages of final will and testament and 317 acres of land: 50 acres each to his daughter Martha and son Cornelius, 50 acres each to his daughters Mary and Lettie, 30 acres to his wife, Milly. The remaining 87 acres to be sold at public out-cry for one-third cash, the balance due in one and two years with interest and approved security. Where did a black man, former slave, gain such financial shrewdness?

Joseph ordered that the cash be doled out in equal shares among his children—except to his son James, to whom he willed ten dollars and nothing more.

Perhaps James was a bit of a goof-off. Perhaps he was a man, not unlike his father, with wanderlust in his soul. His father wanted James to settle down, be a farmer or a businessman, be respectable. James had different ideas. They fought.

Certain that James would only squander his share and amount to little, Joseph left him little.

James was the man who fathered Samuel, the man who fathered Melvin, the man who fathered another Samuel—my father. His blood is in my veins, and perhaps I am like him.

(My father also worried about me and my place in the world. For a long time he expected little from me, a writer, a dreamer, the one with different ideas. And we too have argued. But that is another story.)

James's brother Peter must have danced with uncommon visions as well. He left the hill and set off to find his own way in the world. Along the way he settled in the area known as the Delta in western Mississippi. He was a founding father of an all-black town called Mound Bayou.

It was a long way from the Harris plantation in Virginia to Harris Hill in Tennessee, and beyond; a long way from being a slave to being a landowner to founding a town. A long way to now. But here I stand, many generations and many fortunes hence. The torch has been passed. I carry Joseph's flame.

The mist recedes further from the mirror. The darkness brightens. I can see a bit clearer.

In all the kingdoms of the biological world, the instinct to survive surpasses every other. There is in mankind an intense instinct to survive. Joseph with his head bowed and his back bent was surviving. My father, when it was his turn, his eyes averted and his voice trembling, he was surviving. At the same time, it was more than survival of self. It has to be.

When Joseph stepped a free man out of the Goochland County Courthouse that September afternoon the day was very warm. It was a partly overcast sky, the clouds billowing up from dark bottoms to threaten rain. But the tops of the clouds boiled into the heavens and the sun struck them there and they gleamed almost golden. The light that late afternoon had such an amber quality that Joseph's skin darkened and seemed almost tan.

John went home without him. Joseph wanted to be alone. It was one of those moments best savored in quiet solitude.

Joseph did not shout his joy. He took his pleasure quietly, almost portentously, as he looked backward and forward at the same time. He stood on the hill of the courthouse and remembered. And then he looked forward and thought about his children and his grandchildren and his great-grandchildren, the same as he had thought about them every day of his captive life. He had been thinking about me.

I was the reason Joseph endured, the reason he could not stand up and say, "No, I refuse, I will do your bidding no more and you will just have to kill me." He would have died, and the future would have died with him.

"The struggle of today is not altogether for today," as Abraham Lincoln said in 1862. *"It is for a vast future also."*

I like to think that if I had been a slave, if slavery had rested on my shoulders and the shoulders of others like me, then slavery would have ended early. There can be no slavery without the complicity of the slave. I would rather have died. But then, I am not very forward-looking. I cannot see much farther than next week. I cannot see six generations from now, as Joseph and the others could, do not seem to care about the future as much as Joseph and the others did, would not sacrifice even half as much.

I turn to face the whispering wind, turn to thank my great-grandfather for what he endured for my sake. I turn to ask his forgiveness for not knowing sooner. And for not holding the torch higher or carrying it farther, for not having more to show for the pains he endured for my sake.

I'm sorry, Joseph.

There is no sound in the trees, no noise in the air, but I feel his gentle caress upon my face.

Joseph. I call out and wonder if he can hear the love in my voice.

I climb on the bike and ride west out of Richmond. Joseph rides with me. Along Monument Avenue the statues of Lee and Stuart and Jefferson Davis do not seem so chilling as before, not so frightening in their symbolism, for now I have a symbol of my own. I have a champion.

Eddy L. Harris graduated from Stanford University and has been a screenwriter and journalist. His first book, the critically acclaimed Mississippi Solo, *was followed by* Native Stranger *and* South of Haunted Dreams: A Ride Through Slavery's Old Back Yard, *from which this story was excerpted. At work in New York City on a new book on Harlem, Eddy Harris now divides his time between the East Coast and his hometown, St. Louis, Missouri.*

✴

I had crossed the line, I was free; but there was no one to welcome me to the land of freedom. I was a stranger in a strange land; and my home, after all, was down in Maryland; because my father, my mother, my brothers, and sisters, and friends were there. But I was free, and they should be free. I would make a home in the North and bring them there, God helping me.

—Harriet Tubman (1869)

PART FOUR

IN THE SHADOWS

ANDRÉ ACIMAN

Alexandria's Ghosts

The author returns to the Egypt
of his childhood.

To those who asked, I said I went back to touch and
breathe again the past, to walk in shoes I hadn't worn in years.
This, after all, was what everyone said when they returned
from Alexandria—the walk down memory lane, the visit to
the old house, the knocking at doors history had sealed off but
might pry open again. The visit to the old temple, the visit to
uncle so-and-so's home, the old school, the old haunts, the
smell of the dirty wooden banister on days you rushed and
almost glided downstairs on your way to a movie. And then,
of course, the tears, the final reckoning, the big themes: the
return of the native, the romance of the past, the redemption
of time.

I decide to visit my great-grandmother's house. As soon as
I near her neighborhood, I find myself almost thrust into the
old marketplace. It too hasn't changed since my childhood.
The pushcarts and open shops are still in place, as is the unforgettable stench of fish and meat, the masses of people throng-
ing between stacks of food and crates of live chickens.

I could go upstairs, I think, once I reach the building on Rue Thebes, but people are watching me fiddle with my camera, and someone actually pops his head out of the window and stares. I decide to leave. Then, having walked to the next block, I change my mind and come back again, trying to let the building come into view gradually, so as to hold that magical moment when remembrance becomes recovery. I am resolved not to be intimidated this time and make my way straight into the main doorway.

A woman appears with a child in her arms; she is the caretaker's wife; the caretaker died a few years ago; she is the caretaker now. A man also shows up. He lives on the street floor, he says in English, and has lived there since the early '50s. I tell him I too lived here once, at number 15. He thinks for a moment, then says he doesn't remember who lives there now. I tell the caretaker that I want to knock at apartment 15. She smiles and looks at me with suspicion. She is thinking. *"Sit Vivi,"* she says. Mme. Vivi. I am almost on the verge of shaking. Vivi was my great-aunt. "They left," she says. Of course they left, I want to shout, we all left 30 years ago! "May I knock at the door?" I ask. "You may," she replies, with the same smile, "but no one is there." When will they be back? She looks at me with a blank stare. No one has occupied the apartment since.

I know that if I push the matter and tip her well, I might persuade her to show me the apartment. But the thought of a dark apartment where no one's been for three decades frightens me. Who knows what I'd find creeping about the floor, or crawling on the walls. It's all well and good for a German to go digging for the ghost of Troy or sifting through Helen's jewels. But no Trojan ever went back to Troy.

When I point to the elevator and ask her whether this still works, she laughs. This had died long ago. And she adds, with inimitable Egyptian humor, *"Allah Yerhamu."* May God have mercy on its soul.

I step into the main courtyard and look up to our old service entrance; I can almost hear our cook screaming at the maid, my mother screaming at the cook, and our poor maid's heartrending yelp each time the tumor on her liver pressed against her spine. I am trying to decide whether I should insist and ask to be taken upstairs, or perhaps she could show me another apartment in the same line. I see a cat playing in the foyer; next to it is a dead mouse. The caretaker does not notice it. Even the man from the first floor doesn't seem to notice, doesn't care.

I know I'll regret not insisting, and also that this is typical of my perfunctory, weak-willed attempts at adventure. But I am tired of these ruins, and the smell of the old wood panels in the foyer is overpowering. Besides, this is how I always travel: not to experience anything at the time of my tour, but to plot the itinerary of a possible return trip. This, it occurs to me, is also how I live.

> *R*umors easily become legend in Alexandria, as the ancient city, mostly unexplored beneath the modern one, constantly reminds Alexandrians of their heritage. A bizarre occurrence took place within living memory when a bride, in her wedding procession, fell down a hole in the road. Searches proved of no use and the bride was never seen again— one more treasure lost beneath the modern city.
>
> ◆
>
> —Anthony Sattin and Sylvie Franquet, *Fodor's Exploring Egypt*

Outside, I spot an old woman with a shopping basket; she looks European. I ask her whether she speaks French. She says she does. She is Greek. I am almost ready to tell her about my entire life, everything about my grandparents, my mother, our apartment that was never lived in since the day we left so many years ago, and all these ruins scattered everywhere, but I break in midsentence, hail a cab.

I am a terrible nostographer. Instead of experiencing returns, I rush through them like a tourist on a one-day bus tour. I must try to find the cemetery, where my grandfather is buried.

Turb'al Yahud, Alexandria's Jewish cemetery, is located at the opposite end of the Armenian cemetery and lies only a few steps away from the Greek Orthodox. Farther down the quiet, dusty, tree-lined road is the Catholic cemetery. Magdi, a native Alexandrian who is employed by the American school I attended as a child, swears that Turb'al Yahud must be somewhere close by but can't remember where. "I come here only once a year—for my mother," he explains, pointing to the Coptic cemetery not far along the same road.

Magdi double-parks and says he will ask directions from the warden of the Armenian cemetery. We have been driving around for more than two hours in search of my parents' old summer beachside home, but here too without luck. Either it's been razed or lies buried in a chaos of concrete highrises and avenues built on what used to be vast stretches of desert sand.

Soon Magdi comes out looking perplexed. There are, as it turns out, not one but two Jewish cemeteries in the area.

"Which one has a gate on the left?" I say, remembering my early childhood visits to my grandfather's grave four decades ago. "That's the problem," says Magdi, drawing on his cigarette. "Both have gates to the right."

I am dismayed. I can situate the grave only in relation to the left gate. We decide to try the nearest cemetery.

Magdi starts the car, waits awhile, then immediately speeds ahead, leaving a cloud of dust behind us. In a matter of minutes, we have parked on a sidewalk and ambled up to a metal gate that looks locked. Magdi does not know; he pounds. I hear a bark, and after a series of squeaks, a man in his early 50s appears at the door. I try to explain in broken Arabic the reason for my visit, but Magdi interrupts and takes over, saying I have come to see my grandfather's grave. The warden is at a loss. Do I know where the grave is, he asks? I say no. Do I know the name then?

I say a name, but it means nothing to him. I try to explain about the door to the left, but my words are getting all jumbled together. All I seem to remember is a pebbled alleyway that started at the left gate and crossed the breadth of the cemetery.

The warden has a three-year-old son wearing a very faded red sweatshirt bearing the initials CCCP—not unusual in a place where ancient relics come in handy. Their dog, fleeced from the neck down, has a large bleeding ulcer on his back.

"Oh, that door," the warden responds when I point to another, much smaller gate at the opposite end of the cemetery. "It's locked, it's never been used." Indeed, the gate at the end of the alleyway looks welded in place. I am almost too nervous to hope. But I pick my way to the end of the path and, having reached the left gate, climb over a wild bush whose dried leaves stick to my trousers, turning with a sense of certainty that I am trying to distrust, fearing the worst.

"Is this it?" asks Magdi.

I am reluctant to answer, still doubting that this could be the spot, or this the marble slab, which feels as warm and smooth to the touch as I knew it would each time I rehearsed this moment over the years. Even the name looks dubious.

"Yes," I say, pointing to the letters, which I realize he can't read.

The warden knows I am pleased. His son trails behind him. A fly is crawling around his nose. Both of them, as well as the warden's wife, are barefoot, Bedouin style.

I take out my camera. Everyone is staring at me, including

the warden's ten-year-old daughter, who has come to see for herself. It turns out that no Jew ever visits here. "No one?" I ask. *"Walla wahid,"* answers the daughter emphatically. Not one.

There are, it occurs to me, far more dead Jews in this city than there will ever again be living ones. This reminds me of what I saw in a box at the main temple earlier this morning: more skullcaps than Jews to wear them in all of Egypt.

The warden asks whether I would like to wash the tombstone. I know Magdi has to go back to work; he is a bus driver and school ends soon. I shake my head.

"Why?" asks the warden. *"Lazem."* You must.

I have lived my entire life outside rituals. Now I am being asked to observe one that seems so overplayed and so foreign to me that I almost want to laugh, especially since I feel I'm about to perform it for them, not for me. Even Magdi sides with the warden. *"Lazem,"* he echoes.

I am thinking of another ritual, dating back to those days when my father and I would come on quiet early morning visits to the cemetery. It was a simple ritual. We would stand before my grandfather's grave and talk; then my father would say he wished to be alone awhile, and, when he was finished, hoist me up and help me kiss the marble. One day, without reason, I refused to kiss the stone. He didn't insist, but I knew he was hurt.

I pay the warden's family no heed and continue to take pictures, not because I really want to, but because in looking through the viewfinder and pretending to take forever to focus, I can forget the commotion around me, stand still, stop time, stare into the distance, and think of my childhood, and of being here, and of my grandfather.

I am almost to the point of forgetting those present when in totters the warden lugging a huge tin drum filled with water. He hoists it on a shoulder and then splashes the dried slab, flooding the whole area, wetting my clothes, Magdi's, and the little boy's feet, allowing the stone to glisten for the first time in who knows how many decades. With eager palms, we all go about the motions of wiping the slab clean. I like the ritual. Magdi helps out silently, but I want it to be my job. I don't want it to end. I am even pleased that my clothes are wet and dirty.

I still can't believe I was able to find my grandfather's grave so quickly. Memories are supposed to distort, to lie. I am at once comforted and bewildered.

"Are you happy now?" I want to ask my grandfather, rubbing the stone some more, remembering a tradition practiced among Muslims of tapping one's finger ever so gently on a tombstone to tell the dead that their loved ones are present, that they miss them and think of them. I want to speak to him, to say something, if only in a whisper. But I am too embarrassed. Perhaps this is why people say prayers instead.

I pretend to want to take another picture and ask Magdi, the warden, and his family to pose in front of one of the palm trees, hoping they will stay there after the picture and leave me alone awhile. I can feel my throat tighten, and I want to hide the tears welling inside me, and I am, once again, glad to cover my eyes with the viewfinder. The warden's daughter comes closer. She wants a picture by herself. I smile and say something about her pretty eyes. I give her father a good tip.

Everyone thinks it's been a good visit.

On my last evening in Alexandria, as I'm looking out from my balcony, I think of the young man I used to be, and of myself now, and of the person I might have been had I stayed here 30 years ago. I think of the strange life I'd have led, of the wife I would have, and of my other children. Where would I be living? I suppose in my great-grandmother's apartment—it would have fallen to me. And I think of this imaginary self who never strayed or did the things I probably regret having done but would have done anyway and don't wish to disown; a self who never left Egypt or ever lost ground and who, on nights such as these, still dreams of the world abroad and of faraway America, the way I, over the years, have longed for life right here whenever I find I don't fit anywhere else.

I wonder if this other self would understand about him and me, and being here and now and on the other bank as well— the other life, the one that we never live and conjure up when the one we have is not the one we want.

This, at least, has never changed, I think, in my mind drifting to my father years ago, when we would stop the car and walk along the Corniche at night, thinking of the worst that surely lay ahead, each trying to give up this city and the life that came with it in the way he knew how. This is what I was doing now as well, thinking of the years ahead when I would look back to this very evening and remember how, standing on the cluttered balcony at the Cecil, I had hoped finally to let go of this city, knowing all the while that the longing would start again soon enough, that one never washes away anything, and that this marooned and spectral city would eventually find newer, ever more beguiling ways to remind me that here is where my mind always turns, that here, to quote this century's most famous Alexandrian poet, Constantine Cavafy, I'll always end up, even if I never come back:

> For you won't find a new country,
> won't find a new shore,
> The city will always pursue you,
> And no ship will ever take you away...
> from yourself.

And then I remembered. With all the confusion in the cemetery, I had forgotten to kiss my grandfather's grave.

André Aciman is the author of Out of Egypt: A Memoir. *He was born in Alexandria and has lived in Egypt, Italy, and France. Educated at Harvard, he has taught at Princeton and now teaches at Bard College. He is the recipient of a Whiting Writer's Award and a Guggenheim Fellowship. A contributor to* The New York Times, The New Yorker, The New Republic, The New York Review of Books, *and* Commentary, *he is currently working on a novel entitled* Over the Footbridge. *He is the editor of* Letters of Transit *and* Spirit of Place, *his collected essays on exile, travel, and memory, is due to appear in 2000.*

✳

My daughter Arwen and I take a shuttle bus down to the great temple of Karnak. It's huge—probably the size of the entire Roman Forum, except this is a single temple. There are huge forests of massive columns, fields of tumbled blocks. We fall in love with one statue of a pharaoh standing with either his wife or his daughter much smaller in front of him. (One guidebook says it is his wife; another his daughter.) On the chance that the daughter story is the right one, we mug for the camera in front of the great stone pair.

We go that night to the Luxor temple and sit for about an hour in the inner courtyard (where they staged *Aida* a few years ago), resting on the stump of a 3500-year old column, enjoying the balmy breezes while meditating on Ozymandias. When we first saw this temple in the middle of town, we were disappointed. The modern city crowds in around it—there's even a playground, complete with swings and slides, right next to the temple! But once you're inside, it's pure magic. The familiar world disappears. It turns out to be one of our favorite spots in Egypt.

We return again each night, just to sit. One night, I bring my laptop to write email, and Arwen brings her homework.

Our favorite statue here is not one that speaks of Pharaonic majesty, but one that reminds us of the essential humanity of the temple's ancient creators, and makes us wish that my wife Christina, Arwen's mother, were also traveling with us. Outside, huge statues speak of Pharaoh's power. As you enter the inner courtyards, though, a smaller alabaster statue shows pharaoh's hand tender on the shoulder of his wife.

—Tim O'Reilly, "Travels with Arwen"

JIM DODSON

* * *

Death of a Small Civilization

When the author's marriage broke up,
he hit the road with his young
daughter Maggie.

EMERSON SAID WE DO NOT LIVE AN EQUAL LIFE, BUT ONE OF
contrast and patchwork; now a little joy, then a sorrow. Someone
else said a divorce is like the death of a small civilization.

That's exactly how I felt watching our children's faces on
the morning we broke the news to them about the divorce.
Eight-year-old Jack sat rigidly on my lap and finally began to
shake with tears. Seven-year-old Maggie, sitting with her
mother in my favorite green faded reading chair, squeezed her
own arms and refused to make eye contact with either of her
parents, staring in stunned disbelief at a bookshelf. She had
combed her own hair and pinned it up beautifully; she looked
like a young princess being betrayed.

Her mother spoke eloquently and bravely—it was perhaps
her best moment ever, explaining how broken-hearted both of
their parents were that things had come to this moment, but
revealing our shared determination to create a better, perhaps
even happier life from this unhappy time. Mom and Dad...
love each other, she said, but they couldn't live together and

didn't wish the two people they loved most to be caught in the crossfire. It was time, she added, for everybody to start healing. Then I took a turn at explaining the unexplainable, trying to calmly reassure our children that everything their mother said was true, that… in time the pain would subside…. It was perfectly natural to be sad, I said, afraid and angry and worried.

I said these words with great conviction, and may have even believed them. But it still felt like a civilization was dying. After a little while and a lot of tears, they went out with their mother to see their new place on the salt marsh and Amos, my fourteen-year-old dog, and I got in Old Blue, my ten-year-old truck, and drove to L.L. Bean to purchase a canoe.

A week later, around noon on a Sunday, I finished packing up the truck. Maggie was going west with me, Jack was accompanying his mother to Nantucket. That was the plan. This was the Brave New World of loving co-parenting.

All travel, someone said, is a vanishing act. You decide to go and disappear down the rabbit hole.

Two hours later, we crossed the great steel span over the Pisquataqua River into New Hampshire….

"Dad," she said, looking over, "please put on your shoulder harness."

I'm always forgetting to put on my shoulder harness.

> *T*raveling is not just seeing the new; it is also leaving behind. Not just opening doors; also closing them behind you, never to return. But the place you have left forever is always there for you to see whenever you shut your eyes.
>
> ◆
>
> —Jan Myrdal, *The Silk Road*

I obeyed and asked her if she planned to nag me about that for the next six weeks or 5,000 miles, whichever came first.

"If I have to," she assured me with a big toothy grin.

It struck me, as I said the words "six weeks," that we really were leaving home and heading to God knows where. Modern families didn't go on vacations like my family had—just hop in the car and go where the spirit leads them, with no reservations of any kind, seeing what they could kick up. They made airplane and hotel reservations, booked a car, bought the theme park tickets months in advance, made sure the restaurants accepted their brand of plastic, and took out trip insurance in case the whole thing was a flop....

On one hand, the idea of what we were biting off was downright thrilling. On the other, utterly terrifying.

"Dad, you look worried."

"Do I? It's this awful traffic...."

The larger truth: ...I was worried about the world we were leaving behind, and worried about the world we would come home to inherit. Too sad to stay but anxious to go, I was suddenly sorely tempted to turn Old Blue around and just go straight home and water my roses, forget this nutty idea of driving all the way out to Yellowstone Park because the embarrassing truth was, I had no idea where we'd go after reaching Boston.... I'd been so preoccupied with throwing together this hasty expedition, I'd somehow neglected to choose an actual starting point for our great camping trip west. It had never felt real—or for that matter necessary—until this very moment.

"Cinchy. Why don't you take another road?"

My daughter pointed to an exit ramp just ahead of us on the highway. Cinchy was her hip first-grade word for any question that had a simple or obvious answer.

I smiled at her, took the exit, and soon found us on a highway I once knew very well, a winding blacktop road that led us... through small towns with green commons and stone soldiers facing south, where Independence Day flags still hung from porches and geraniums bloomed in cemeteries.

Old Blue cooled down and Amos hung his big head out the window to let the rushing wind flap his jowls. Maggie sang along with Trisha Yearwood, a lovely torch song about somebody aching to hit the road after a love affair gone wrong, anxious to get out from under a rain cloud and find a way to live again. Funny how some perfect stranger can sing your deepest thoughts. The sound of my fishergirl's sweet voice made my anxiety begin to lift like Portland, Maine fog.

A few minutes later, it suddenly came to me where we could go—someplace I'd almost forgotten about, a beautiful river where I'd once begun another life and somehow found my way here.

Cinchy.

And with that, we slipped down the rabbit hole.

Jim Dodson is an award-winning columnist for Golf. *His work has appeared in* GQ, Outside, *and* Reader's Digest. *He is the author of* Final Rounds, *a memoir that chronicles his love of golf and love of his father and how he came to terms with his father's death. This excerpt is from his book,* Faithful Travelers: A Father, A Daughter, A Fly-Fishing Journey of the Heart.

⁂

When our sons Jonathan and Clayton were much younger, they always initially hated it when my wife and I decided to get off the interstate, particularly as we were headed back to the realm of television, Nintendos, and computers.

"Not now, Dad!" they would cry. "Let's get home."

"But we're off on an adventure," we would reply. And on most of these trips, getting off the superhighways did cost us time. During those often confusing rambles down poorly-marked state roads, we usually got lost. But what made it all worthwhile was what we found: quaint towns whose charm and color hadn't been diluted by the homogenization around the interstate exchanges and wonderful festivals too small to catch the notice of the big-city papers. We came across roadside attractions that captured the attention of the Nintendomaniacs in back: towering statues of extinct reptiles at Dinosaur Land near White Post, Virginia; reenactments of Civil War battles in the South; mysterious and spooky caves that welcome visitors; and even flying circuses of biplanes and hot air balloons.

The boys are grown now, and prefer to drive their own cars. But we suspect that some day, when they have their own children, our sons will also ignore the grumbling from the backseat and take the next exit off the superhighway. And then they and their family will discover what we learned many times over: you may get lost, but you just might discover what you've been searching for all your life.

—Larry Fox, travel columnist,
The Washington Post

✦ ✦ ✦

Forgiveness

*It took crossing an ocean for
a daughter to leave
her pain behind.*

FOR AS LONG AS I CAN REMEMBER, EVEN AS A TINY CHILD, I always felt I was the mother to my mother. She'd call for an Anacin and a half-glass of water when one of her "sick headaches" would come on. She'd curl up into a ball on the couch. I'd deliver the medicine, then go back to the business of childhood. Or try. It wasn't easy or simple. The child in me ached for a real mommy who'd smile lovingly and tell me what a good girl I was. Who'd hold me close when I was hurting and help me feel everything would be all right. Who'd take care of me instead of forcing me to take care of her.

On the surface of our lives, everything looked fine. I was fed and clothed and sent to school. We appeared to the outside world as if we were the perfect family. Knowing that the socially visible didn't match the truth only intensified my confusion and loneliness. My little girl heart was broken. Why didn't Mommy love me? Why didn't she ever touch me—except to yank my hair in a rage? What was wrong with me?

By the time I was thirteen, I had emotionally divorced myself from her. I was civil, but detached. I pretended things were fine. But they weren't. When her stinging criticism and biting sarcasm were whirled at me, I felt numb. It was the only way to keep the peace.

As soon as I could, I left. Went to college and then moved to New York City—about as far from the upstate New York farm as I could get. I aggressively abdicated Mom-care.

Occasionally, I'd visit. Spend a few hours. But her cutting remarks were constant. Crying and ranting on the way back to the city, I felt a hard, mean anger growing inside. I was beginning to hate my mother. She made it so difficult to love her.

And this was painful, too. Because, in spite of all I had been through, I had a conflicting need to be a good daughter.

After my first year of independence in New York, my army-officer brother was stationed in Germany. My mom hinted that she'd like to visit him. Then hinted again. Like many women of her generation, she hadn't traveled much. I knew I was being manipulated into taking her.

I landed us two seats on a military transport plane. In the window seat, I was cramped and miserable. "God," I wondered over and over again, "What have I gotten myself into? Will I ever be free of her demands?"

My mother, in the middle seat—boxed in by a young mother and her baby—was oblivious to my discomfort. That didn't surprise me. What did startle me was how she kept her good cheer. I couldn't believe my eyes or ears. Flying across the Atlantic was a different woman than the one I grew up with: she was softer, lighter. "I have to pinch myself to believe we're really going," she said several times.

Our first day trip was to go, by train, to Stuttgart, the bright city set in a golden-green valley 40 miles or so east of Schwäbisch Gmund. We arrived, late morning, at the train station, the Haupbahnhof. Glancing up at its soaring ceiling, my mother looked in my eyes and smiled broadly. It was an unguarded moment. And I felt as though we were a far, far distance from the farm—and all its sad memories.

We strolled the Konigstrasse, exploring the historical buildings. My mother commented pleasantly on the wide streets and verdant parks, so clean and obviously cherished. Even the sky looked pristine—blue with little white puffs of cottonball clouds scudding across. I told myself to loosen up.

My brother's wife gave us a long list of must-do's. But before we could find a single spot, we stumbled on Altes Schloss (Old Castle). Inside this museum, we moved effortlessly among four floors of galleries—filled with rare tapestries, ceramic craftwork, silver tableware, old costumes—all things we both coincidentally adored. Each time we entered a gallery that looked out over the Renaissance Courtyard, we stopped to admire together its beauty, and to share our great good fortune in stumbling on this place. We were genuinely agreeing.

Last stop was the exquisite clocks gallery. We had several treasured antique timepieces at home, but we'd never seen anything like these. We were the only people in the room. Listening to the thrum, tick, and chunk of the different clocks, we grew quiet. These instruments were created hundreds of years ago to monitor lives. I felt the ancient owners' spirits, and sensed that I, too, was merely a fleeting visitor on Earth. I could measure my time, but like those nameless clockmakers, could do no more to control it than I could control the weather.

My mother then made a solo circuit of the room. I stood in the corner of the gallery, near the window now bathed in the early afternoon light, and watched her move. Most certainly, I felt it wasn't the 20th century anymore. It could have been the 19th or 18th.

Moments like these, the ones that take us out of our own worries and concerns, are crossroads. Choices get made, seeds planted. Out of time, out of familiar surroundings, freed from the bonds of our former life, I saw my mother in a new way. As she exclaimed over the delicate miniature clocks, I got a glimpse of her own fragility, her—I gulped—humanity. My mother's childhood hadn't been wonderful either. She had faced disappointment and tragedy—a mother who beat her with a belt, a beloved sister who died young of cancer.

The hard place in my heart began to soften. As the sun warmed my shoulders, this trip's medicine, already making such a difference in my mother, began to work on me as well. Like the gong of a grandfather clock that moved a large brass hand from one hour to the next, I dared to look at her, and my life, with a deep breath.

It was possible to heal from a childhood that was unhappy, I heard myself say quietly. I could open my heart to forgiveness. Of course, forgiveness of this magnitude isn't an event— it's a process that can take years. But that day, in that lovely museum that took us out of our present time, our space, and even our own history, I made the most important choice of my life—to begin again.

Karen Cummings is a pseudonym for a New York City writer. She's the mother of three children, with whom she shares great happiness.

★

If you take revenge, you will regret it; if you forgive, you will rejoice.
—*Talmud*, Derekh Erets Zuta I:29

LESLIE EHM

✶ ✶ ✶

My Doctor, My Sister

Tragedy turns to blessing.

Two days before my husband Bob and I left for our Tunisian holiday, I discovered I was pregnant. My doctor reassured me that travel would not pose a problem. She was almost right.

We had a wonderful week in the sun. The day before we were to return to London, my cramps began and I bled slightly. By the next morning, both my pain and panic had increased and the hotel doctor directed Bob and me to a clinic.

After much gesturing of hands and broken French, I was admitted—then pretty much left to suffer in a small room. Eventually, the doctor-on-call paid us a visit.

She was young, no older than I. Happily, she spoke some English along with her French and we were able to communicate without too much effort. She explained that she would like to treat me in her private downtown office—it would be easier. She called her husband and, with him and her young daughter in the car, we were driven to the city. On route, she introduced herself properly as Dr. Safia Zemni.

At her office, I wept in her arms. She examined me and then confirmed my fears. Yes, I was, in fact, miscarrying. She recommended that I not fly back to England as planned. It was too dangerous!

I burst into tears again and whimpered, "I just want to go home."

"Don't worry," she kept saying, "don't worry. I am here. I am your sister. I will take care of you."

She prepared some mild painkillers, gave me her cellular phone number, drove me back to the hotel, and promised to check with me that evening.

Within a couple of hours the bleeding increased and my pain became unbearable. I called Safia. She explained that she was over two hours away, but she was turning her car around and heading back to the clinic. Bob and I were to meet her there.

From that point, it became pretty much a blur. After what seemed like a very long time, I opened my eyes to find Safia standing there, the same warm compassionate look on her face. She held my hand while I suffered through an internal scan and then she poured over the results. Evidently, she felt that the worst was not over and she had me admitted into the hospital. As I drifted in and out of sleep, Safia sat by my bed, telling Bob and me stories about Tunisia, her past, and her attitudes towards medicine.

I woke the next morning to discover I had miscarried fully, and thankfully the pain was gone. Safia discharged me and drove me back to the hotel. Before returning to work, she asked whether Bob and I would be interested in joining her and her husband for dinner that evening. Obviously, she was intent on keeping our minds off our loss.

With the help of the hotel, we arranged for a huge bouquet of flowers. Using my limited French to explain our senti-ments, I composed a card for my modern-day angel.

When Safia and her husband arrived at the hotel bar that evening, my husband and I were already waiting, the flowers hidden behind a chair. And, just when I thought that this wonderful woman could not possibly do anything more to amaze or impress us, I saw that she was holding a gift-wrapped package in her hands.

"For you," she said simply.

I reached behind and pulled out the bouquet. "And for you," I said.

Our eyes met—the bond of sisterhood so real, so potent. We laughed and wiped our eyes. I opened her gift—a traditional Tunisian coffee pot and an ornate little mirror in the shape of a hand.

"So you always see who you are," she explained.

During that last evening together, the four of us talked of life, love, tradition, family. Our hosts took us on a tour of the oldest and most beautiful parts of the city, culminating in a walk through an old port.

They drove us back to our hotel and we said our good-byes, exchanging addresses and phone numbers and promising to stay in touch. Safia and I embraced, holding each other tightly, my gratitude to her beyond words. She stroked my back and nodded...no words necessary. With a wave, she was gone.

Leslie Ehm, a United Kingdom TV host, globetrotter, and scriptdoctor, has recently returned to her native Canada, where she's finally given herself over to just writing. "It's novels or death," she says.

✳

After the verb "to love," "to help" is the most beautiful verb in the world!

—Bertha von Suttner, *Ground Arms* (1892)

LUIS ALBERTO URREA

✦ ✦ ✦

Tough Love

*A writer chronicles the desperate
journey of an unusual
Mexican family.*

NOBODY KNEW WHAT HAPPENED TO THE BOYS' PARENTS. NOT
even the boys—Chacho, Eduardo, Jorge, and Carlos—could
explain what had happened to them. As is so often the case
on the border, one day the boys woke up and their parents
were gone. Papá had apparently gone across the wire, into the
United States. Mamá blew away like a puff of smoke. The four
brothers were alone in the Tijuana garbage dump.

For a few nights the younger boys wept as Chacho, the
fierce elder brother, pulled together a small homestead amid
the garbage. They went hungry for a while, not having any
dump survival skills. The trash-pickers gave them what food
they could spare, but that wasn't much. And missionaries came
to the dump with goodies, but Chacho didn't trust gringos,
so he kept the boys away. Besides, the gringos gave baths, and
nobody was going to get Chacho naked.

One day an old man appeared in the dump. He wore grimy
old suits and had no past and no home. His left arm had come
out of the socket years before, and he had wandered, a half

cripple, from dump to dump, looking for people to care for him. Although there is no lack of ferocity in the *dompes*, there is also a high degree of compassion and fraternity. Still, if you have no food or room to spare, what can you do? Slip him a gringo doughnut (*una dona*) and see him off with a blessing. The evil ones, circling through the waters of night, kicked him around for fun, stole the *dona,* and left him in the dirt.

Chacho came across him after one such beating. He made the old man a deal: if he would look out for the younger boys, Chacho and Eduardo would share their trash-pickings with him. And Chacho would beat up anyone who threatened the old man. They engineered a new family unit that day.

The old man, keeping his part of the bargain, scrounged a cast-off Maytag appliance box. He cut a door in its side and upended it, open top to the ground. Then he carpeted the dirt floor with newspaper, plastic bags, and cardboard. They used scavenged clothes and rags for a mattress and blankets. The little ones played in the dirt outside while the old man lay in the dark box crying, hallucinating, and seeing visions—dead women he had loved, angels, demons, strange creatures, his mother coming to feed him, gringos with bags of beans, which turned out to be us, though I was never sure if he knew he wasn't dreaming.

He had a passion for avocados, and he collected them in rotting mounds inside the box.

For his part, Chacho built a real shack out of scrap wood, and he placed it on a low rise near the Maytag house, where he could watch over his brothers. For whatever reason, it never occurred to him to build them a house—that was the old man's job. Somehow Chacho acquired a pistol. Then he stole a pony from a neighboring ranch and built it a corral made of bedsprings and stolen wood. Chacho was a small warlord, surveying his kingdom.

His brothers watched the clean kids coming out of the gringo baths. They didn't envy the washed faces or clean clothes. They envied the doughnuts and chocolate milk and bananas. They marched into the bathing room and took off their blackened clothes.

Eduardo brought home animals—unwanted puppies, piglets swiped or bartered, a pathetic skeletal cat.

Chacho used his pony to steal cows. Nobody knows what happened to the old man. He was such a phantom that he passed through this story without a name. Perhaps he grew tired of being a dad, of living on a floor of smashed avocados and mud. Or he simply forgot them as the rising tide of mania and tequila ate his brain. Or he was taken by a car in the gloom of the highway canyons. Maybe he tried to go across the border. Any guess, any guess at all, is valid. The boys were out working the trash, and when they came home, he was gone. He had taken their ball of twine, so they knew he had tied his arm to his side. This suggested to them that he was planning a substantial journey.

Like abandoned children everywhere, they felt fear and talked themselves into feeling hope. *He'll be back. Maybe he'll bring us some food.* They huddled around the door of the box all night. When morning came, they knew they were alone again.

They marched up to Chacho's bandit's roost to seek help, to move in with him at least. But Chacho was a busy man. He was a *pistolero* and a cattle rustler, and he was suspected of being an undercover snitch for the police. He had *socios* (what we would call homeboys) running errands and fencing goods for him. He had a television. And he had his pistol.

Look, boys, he told them, the point is that life's shit. Who coddled me? Nobody. Who felt sorry for me? You see this house? These horses? This *pistola*? I did this. You've got to go out there and make your lives. Be tough or die.

This, in Chacho's eyes, was love.

Eduardo, Jorge, and Carlos failed to be moved by Chacho's warm sentiments. But they had to obey. He was, after all, their big brother. The closest thing to an elder they had. He was also macho, and they were afraid that if they whined too much, he'd pull his six-shooter and do them in. He wore it jammed in his belt, and even wore it to intimidate the missionaries. I once heard him say, near Pastor Von's van, "I'd better like these doughnuts. I'd hate to shoot anybody." This statement, as all macho bon mots, was delivered with a scowl that hid a tremendous laughter. Pancho Villa is the patron saint of machismo, and Pancho Villa is the in-dwelling spirit of every macho. Anyone who has survived in a tough area knows: machos are philosophers, and they are also weary judges of all they survey. If their variable code of ethics is betrayed, they are often called upon by their inner demons to be executioners. *A man's gotta*

I've gone to Tijuana for the past two summers. The first year I was part of a team that built a house for a family that was living in a shack made of cardboard, metal, and scraps of wood and plastic. Their gratitude for the house we built made me so glad I had given up my other summer plans. The second year, we stopped at the house we'd built the summer before. To our amazement, the family had moved back into their shack and turned the small house into a church! Their friends and neighbors had all worked together to build pews and a pulpit to furnish the church. This taught me an unforgettable lesson: these people, who had so little, gave to others out of their own need. Just think of all I could do with what I have.

◆

—Tim Williams, 15,
quoted in *Gutsy Mamas*
by Marybeth Bond

do what a man's gotta do. A macho can explode in unreasoning fury or act with benign munificence, at a moment's notice. Machos are sentimentalists, like all true fascists. Robin Hood or Vlad the Impaler—whichever it is, you have to have what it takes to back up the pose.

Chacho didn't like it, but he sent them away. That is not to say that Chacho lost any sleep over his brothers. Not yet.

Boys living on the edges of the dump have a vast playground of sorts. Collecting trash is hard work, even if the trash-picking is off to the side, where the small ones can go. The brothers played and romped in the mounds, found the occasional toy, found clothes and tins of food, found waterlogged magazines with pictures of nude women, which they took to Chacho. Once they even found a load of fetuses dumped on the edge of the trash. "Dead babies," everyone was saying. "A sacrifice." People were afraid, able to envision only something desperately evil, something monumental that would kill so many babies, then toss them into the dump. The boys poked at the cold fetuses with sticks. To them, living in such squalor, something even more squalid was a revelation.

Although Eduardo loved animals, for example, the sight of a diseased dog being pounced upon and eaten by other dogs was exciting.

The boys had rats to kill, fires to set, food to steal, huts to spy on. No wall in that neighborhood was particularly solid, and they could peek in through the cracks and see just about anything. And there were always the fights to watch: drunks and gang members and warring young turks from alien barrios and young women throwing punches like the meanest macho. Small Huck Finns on a sea of trash, they floated through life, avoiding schooling and being educated by the harsh classroom all around them.

They even had their own swimming hole.

On the hill above Chacho's horse pens, the city had built a huge *pila* to hold water for the downhill communities. The part of the reservoir above ground was the size of a *maquiladora* or a warehouse, and it didn't take long for the boys to break through an upper corner of the cinderblock structure. They climbed in through the hole with their pals and sat on the walkways in the shadows within. They loved to swim in that cool green water. They loved to urinate in the water, imagining their pee going down the hill to the fine stucco homes.

The one game they loved the most was the most dangerous. Everyone, even Chacho, warned them about it. Everyone told them to stop. But they loved it to the point of madness. The boys loved to jump on the backs of moving garbage trucks.

Eduardo thought he had a firm grip on the back of the big truck.

Retired from San Diego, the truck was rusty and dented. It was heavy with trash, and greasy fluids drained out of its sides like sweat. Its hunched back was dark with dirt, and its smokestack belched solid black clouds.

The boys had spent the morning running up behind the trucks as they entered the dump, hopping on the back ends, hanging on to any handhold they could grab. Sometimes, if they missed, they caught the sides and hung there like little spiders, swinging over the wheelwells as the trucks banged over the mounds.

Eduardo had run behind the truck, had flung himself at it and caught the upper edge of the open maw in back. He swung back and forth, doing an impromptu trapeze act, and the other boys called insults: "Faggot!" and "Coward!" He turned once to laugh at them, hanging by one hand and starting to flash them a hand sign. The truck slammed on its brakes. Eduardo flew inside, hit the steel wall, and was flung back out, hitting the ground on his back, hard enough to knock the breath out of him.

The boys were laughing wildly, and Eduardo tried to rise, pasting a game smile on his face though the blow must have hurt. He probably couldn't catch his breath. He lay back, just for an instant, to breathe.

The truck ground its gears and lurched into reverse. The boys yelled for Eduardo to get out of the way, but it must have sounded like more taunting. He raised one hand. The truck backed over him and the hand was twisted down to the ground, and the double wheels in the back made Eduardo disappear.

Carlos and Jorge stood staring, imagining somehow that Eduardo would get up after the truck had passed over him. But he was deep in the soil, in a puddle of his own mud. The truck driver shut off the engine and stepped out to unload the garbage, but he couldn't understand why the boys were screaming.

The dump people don't always knit together. Sheer survival makes it difficult to look out for their fellows. But death sometimes unites them, if the death is sad enough. Or the threat of death, if the threat is vivid enough.

Everyone knew Eduardo's story. They had all said at one time or another that someone should do something about those boys, but nobody had done much. They had all seen the Maytag box, the old man, the truck-surfing. Guilty and ashamed, the neighbors resolved to do something about Eduardo's death.

They collected money. *Centavos* came from hidden beer money, from the jar under the bed, from the schoolbook fund, from Christmas savings. The *Americanos* gave funds. People worked extra hard that day to get a few more *pesos*.

They bought Eduardo a small suit. His first and last fancy clothes. Some of the Mixtec men collected raw particleboard and hammered together a coffin. They set it inside the room where the missionaries gave baths. This was done very quickly. No undertaker ever saw Eduardo, no papers were ever signed. No official ever knew he had existed, and none would be told he had died.

Since he wasn't embalmed, they had to hurry. The suit was bought and pulled onto his twisted corpse by nightfall. The coffin was built by eight in the evening, and he was laid out under candles by nine. The women had washed his face. Eduardo was finally clean.

They would bury him in the morning.

Chacho took a bath. He stuck his pistol into his belt, got drunk, and walked over to weep over Eduardo. All the tough guys in the dump lost it over Eduardo. None of them knew how to deal with this tragedy. It was somehow worse than all the other tragedies. The men wept openly, inconsolably. Perhaps Eduardo had come to symbolize their own abandonment. Perhaps this small boy, thrown into the trash, left to die there, and facing a burial there, was too much like all of them. There was no way they were going to bury him in the trash too. In being killed, Eduardo had become everybody's son, everybody's brother. One family boasted that they had fed him often, another bragged that he wore their old shoes. Girls wrote his name on little torn bits of paper—hearts and flowers in blue Bic ink. Every boy there claimed Eduardo as his best friend. You would think somebody had actually loved him.

Chacho got one of his *socios* to drive a pickup. They hammered the lid on the box, then wrestled it up on their shoulders. The people who had not gone to work—mostly wives and daughters—stood silently. A woman or two worked her rosary beads. Some cried—nothing overwhelming, but there were tears. The boys lifted the box over the side and placed it carefully in the bed. Chacho and his remaining brothers climbed in with Eduardo.

We hired a boat and guide to take us to the floating reed islands [on Lake Titicaca] of the Uro Indians. Four oranges were all we had on hand, so that's what we took. When I saw how ravenous the children were, I wanted to rush back to the mainland for more fruit.

None of the little ones had clothes from the waist down, while we were glad to be wearing sweaters. A child walked to the edge of the island and peed into the water.

"Don't they have bathrooms?" asked Gino.

"No," Gene said. "It's like backpacking."

"If I was on this camping trip, I'd want to go home," Gino said. "It's too cold and windy here."

"But they are home," I said.

"I feel sorry for them," Gino said.

♦

—Mary Gaffney, "The Magic Side of Time," *A Mother's World*, edited by Marybeth Bond and Pamela Michael

Directly behind the pickup was a flatbed. It was filled to capacity with mourners. They passed a bottle of rum. Chacho would be drinking plenty that night and the next. People would steer clear of his robber's cabin, because Chacho would be in the mood to shoot.

Bringing up the rear of this funeral procession was one gringo van with a few missionaries. That one detail has lived on in the neighborhood, that the *Americanos* came to bury Eduardo. Nobody asked them. They just appeared. Mourning. It was the most anyone had ever done for the people on the hill.

Ironically, a busload of fresh-faced American Jesus Teens from some suburban church had pulled up and unloaded thirty happy campers into the middle of the funeral. They bounded about Praising the Lord and Ministering to the Poor. They were no doubt shocked to find the poor rather surly and unappreciative of their Witness. Their youth pastor, being no slouch, took the opportunity to send them into the shed before Eduardo was sealed into his box. He wanted the kids to learn what real life was like. For his part, Eduardo gave them a devastating sermon, lying there in his already dusty suit, flat and angry-looking. A mute testimony.

All the bounce gone out of their strides, the teens mounted their bus again and motored away, easy answers scrubbed right out of their skulls.

During all this, Carlos, the youngest of the brothers, stayed outside, playing marbles. He didn't show the least interest in Eduardo's corpse. As Chacho was standing beside the coffin, crying out his pain. Carlos used him as a sort of shield, peering around him at Eduardo. He reached out and prodded Eduardo's face with his fingers, apparently to make sure his brother was really dead. He then went outside and joined the marble game.

They could have been going to work, hauling some junk to the dump.

The small procession headed off across the hills, winding through small valleys and into regions never visited by gringos. They left the road entirely and drove across dead fields. Up a hill. Some of the dump people had created their own graveyard there. Little crosses made of sticks dotted the hill. The dead here were squatters. One day the landowner would find out. But really, how can you fight with the dead?

One American said, "It's Boot Hill."

The men traded turns with the shovel, cracking, then scraping out the rocky soil. It took quite a while to make the hole, but between them, they managed it. Nobody complained.

They manhandled the box into the hole and stood around looking at it. Chacho almost fell in, he cried so hard. The men quietly went back to work, pushing dirt and rocks back in. Others who couldn't get close to the shoveling went from grave to grave, pulling dry weeds and picking up paper. Some of the crosses needed straightening. A couple of guys made borders of rocks around unmarked graves.

Jorge never went near Eduardo's grave.

But if you paid close attention, you could see Carlos moving in behind Chacho. He peeked out from between Chacho's legs. Then, at the last possible moment, he grabbed a little handful of dust and pitched it into the hole.

Luis Alberto Urrea was born in Tijuana to an American mother and a Mexican father. He graduated from the University of California, did relief work on the Mexican border, and taught expository writing at Harvard. His first book, Across the Wire: Life and Hard Times on the Mexican Border, *was the winner of the 1994 Christopher Award and a* New York Times *Notable Book of the Year. Urrea is also the author of* In Search of Snow, *a novel, and* By the Lake of Sleeping Children: The Secret Life of the Mexican Border, *from which this story was excerpted. He divides his time between the American West and Central Mexico.*

★

In 1985, my wife Marti and I quit our jobs, sold our house, and took our four-year-old son, Chris to the Pine Ridge Indian Reservation in South Dakota to spend a year working with the Oglala Sioux.

Marti worked for the public health hospital doing outreach in occupational therapy for elderly Lakota and I worked as an attorney in economic development for the Oglala Sioux Tribal Council. Together we also worked as house parents for teenage Lakota boys, who came from abusive homes.

Chris was the only *wasicu* (white person) in his Montessori program at Red Cloud Indian School. He was introduced to Indian art and Pow Wow dancing and the tradition of storytelling by Lakota elders who would come into his class.

During our year on the reservation we attended many Pow Wows featuring native dancers and drummers and participated in healing ceremonies and sweats. We also saw dire poverty and it seemed like we lived in a Third World country just 100 miles from Rapid City. Pine Ridge is the second largest reservation in the United States and has high rates of unemployment, alcohol and drug abuse, infant mortality, and an annual income of approximately $2,500 for the average Lakota family.

Despite living in the poorest county in the United States, we experienced the richness of life among the Lakota and came to truly value their oral traditions, religious and healing ceremonies, view of nature and living in harmony with the "two-winged" and "four-legged" creatures around them. The Lakota have a rich saying: "*Mitakye Oyasin*," which means, "all my relation." The Lakota taught us to view life as interconnected between all forms of life and Mother Earth, and helped us discover new insights into the spiritual and material limitations of our own white culture.

—David Spicer, "Our Life on the Reservation"

✦ ✦ ✦

A View from
the Hospital

Illness leads to a hidden city.

AT FIRST WE THOUGHT IT WAS JUST A CASE OF BAD JET LAG. Our daughter Molly, ten years old at the time, hadn't slept on the flight to Rome and for the next couple of days she had drooped about. I'll admit that neither Molly nor her younger brother, Gus, had ever been known to hasten toward a museum. Still, Molly's persistent sluggishness began to worry me. Moreover, there was that annoying cough that brought every Roman grandmother within earshot to a standstill.

"La poverina," they cooed. *"Che tosse orribile!"*

But we were on vacation, a short jaunt through Italy before meeting up with 24 students from the college where my husband teaches art history. There simply wasn't time to get sick.

One tired morning in Florence, as we plodded toward the Museum of Science, the repository of Galileo's right index finger, Molly finally slowed to a halt.

"Mom," she said, "I really want to see that finger but I just have to sit down for a while." We sat on a cold stone doorstep while Molly leaned her head against my arm. I bundled her in my coat—it was late December—and noticed a blister erupt-ing on her lower lip. At lunch Molly ate one spoonful of her *pappa al pomodoro* and nodded off, her head just missing the steamy soup bowl. We took a cab back to the hotel and as I put Molly to bed, I noticed that her legs were covered with red spots. Moreover, her little body was warm as a hot water bottle.

As tourists, for the most part, we skim through cities; we speak politely to concierges; we order our meals; we hail taxi cabs. Our interactions with the local people are friendly and polite. The parameters of our needs are clear, predictable, temporal. But in a crisis, ground rules collapse. Credit cards and traveler's checks become superfluous because we cannot necessarily buy the sorts of things we need.

Our concierge called his family doctor, who arrived ten minutes later with black bag and blue loden coat. Dr. Valle was small and stooped, easily 80 years old. He felt Molly's hands, ran his fingers over the bumps on her legs, listened to her heartbeat, and tapped his spotted and wrinkled fingers on her back.

"La polmonite," he declared. "Most definitely. I have prac-ticed medicine for 45 years. I am absolutely certain."

Neither David nor I had heard this word before. Still we knew what it meant and to this day when I look back on that New Year's in Florence it was *la polmonite* and not pneumonia. Pneumonia is an American ailment: a good dose of antibiotics and you're up and about. But *la polmonite* is altogether different.

"You must go to the hospital," the doctor ordered. "I will call a cab." We thanked him and David pulled out his wallet to pay. But the doctor brushed aside our money, shook hands with us, and left.

I packed an overnight bag and the four of us filed into the lobby. We were no longer hotel guests, no longer tourists from abroad. Word of *la polmonite* had circulated throughout the staff. We were greeted with looks of profound concern. Could they wrap our daughter in a blanket for the ride? Would we like some tea while we waited for the cab?

Molly was given a bed in pediatrics with five other children. The mention of *la polmonite* brought a halt to the chatter of mothers and visiting relatives.

"La poverina," they said to each other as Molly lay listless in her bed. "You will have to spend some time in the mountains once she gets better," one of the mothers told me, "so your daughter can regain her strength."

Italian hospitals are a little like youth hostels. The management provides sheets, but you provide everything else: towels, soap, dish towels, toilet paper, pajamas, cups and dishes for the patient's meals, and sustenance for yourself.

Francesca's mother offered me a salami sandwich; Eduardo's brought me an espresso from the coffee machine two floors down. At 9 p.m. I followed my roommates to a storeroom filled with beach chairs, the kind that rent for $10 a day on the beaches of Positano. We set them up next to our children's beds.

At 10 the lights went out, and I settled into my beach chair for a fitful night. At 5 a.m. a team of nurses burst into the ward, handed each mother a thermometer, and the day began. We mothers felt anything but superfluous.

Molly seemed brighter. When the doctors came around I explained that we absolutely had to get back to Rome in three days to meet a group of students. The doctors balked—we were dealing with a serious illness—but they finally conceded that a nurse in Rome could administer the antibiotics.

David and Gus arrived at noon with a package for Molly: pajamas from the only shop in Florence that seemed to be open. With David temporarily in charge, I returned with Gus to our hotel. *"Signora,"* the grandmother behind the desk said. "How is the poor little girl?"

I explained that she was improving. "I have some things for you," she continued, and produced a shopping bag full of linens, dishes, tea towels, soap, toilet paper.

Gus showed me to a nearby restaurant where he and his dad had eaten the night before. Something of a gourmand, he didn't mind in the least that Florence was turning into a parade of meals with alternating parents.

The woman in charge was pleased to see that he'd returned. "And how is the poor little girl?" she asked me. I assured her Molly was out of the woods. For dessert the woman offered us the restaurant's special ricotta torte.

"We get dessert for free," Gus explained, "because of Molly."

We returned to the hospital for a festive afternoon. It was New Year's Eve. Platters of prosciutto and *crostini* were passed from bed to bed. Molly had finally perked up and was playing peekaboo with little Eduardo. The night head nurse arrived sporting a white silk bow tie and offered to postpone curfew until after midnight. Some of the fathers stayed and, once the children had fallen asleep, we congregated by a window to watch distant fireworks explode above the River Arno. Bottles of Asti Spumante appeared as if by magic.

As I turned in late that night, I noted that Molly's breathing was clearer. I slept soundly.

Meanwhile David and Gus had stumbled upon a restaurant that was welcoming in the new year with streamers, party hats and quantities of food. Mention of Gus's sister with *la polmonite* produced extra party favors, balloons, grappa, and a collective concern throughout the restaurant for Molly's well-being.

"Wake up, mothers, and take your children's temperatures," was our 5 a.m. bugle call. Molly's was normal. Eduardo was keeping his meals down better and Daniela was given her walking papers.

That morning David had found a nurse to help us in Rome, if we could figure out how to get there. Francesco's father had a cousin with a taxi who could take us to Rome off the meter for five hundred dollars. "Too expensive," my chorus of roommates intoned. In the midst of our transport trauma, Eduardo's mother pulled me aside and asked if her husband could drive us to Rome for free. He was heading south the next day to Gubbio.

It was an absurdly generous offer: true, Gubbio is south of Florence, but it is also two and a half hours north of Rome. This little side trip would easily add four hours to his drive.

"It was my husband's idea," she assured me. "He would like to help you." I returned to the hotel one more time. There was a phone message from Dr. Valle, who was still away for the holidays but wanted to make sure all was well with Molly. I settled our hotel bill, which came to half the amount I thought it should have been.

Eduardo's father flew down the *autostrada* as only an Italian behind the wheel of a Mercedes can fly. He dropped us off in front of our building, offered us a stash of his company's date books, and drove away. We were stunned by his generosity.

I gingerly guided Molly through a labyrinth of cars parked in front of our building, and just as we were about to walk inside, a frosty-haired grandmother wagged a sharp finger in front of my face and asked why my children weren't wearing hats.

"They'll catch *la polmonite*," she warned with a piercing look. "And then you'll be sorry!"

Libby Lubin lived in Italy for a year and continues to travel there frequently.

✳

Spending over two months in Europe for our honeymoon was a great experience. We have fond memories of Belgian chocolate, Irish salmon, French wine, and Norwegian goat cheese. But then something happened. The food didn't taste so good anymore. Our travels were then curtailed by my sudden inability to get on a bus. Those vistas we would scramble up a mountainside to get, well, now they just made me plain old nauseous. Yep, I was pregnant. The worst of it was in Rome. Through a friend, we were put up in a room on an empty floor of a hospital run by Little Sisters of the Poor. We had lots of privacy, including our own hospital beds. My husband had even more privacy, as he toured the sights alone! It was appropriate that we were in a hospital, as I needed to lay in bed most of the day. And it was so convenient to have a pregnancy test done "in house." We celebrated when a little white envelope was slipped under our door, with the result, "*positivo.*"

—Angelique Syversen, quoted in *Gutsy Mamas*
by Marybeth Bond

PART FIVE

THE LAST WORD

MAIRA KALMAN

Small Wonders

A mother's worldly wish.

WHEN I WAS LITTLE, WE TRAVELED OFTEN AND IN MANY DIF-
ferent ways. When I was twelve we went to Rome and stayed
at the Excelsior Hotel on the Via Veneto. Our room was the
size of Ohio, and the bathroom was all marble and had a white
and gold phone. My mother, my sister, and I had supper in
the opulent dining room. A man approached wearing a long,
black tunic and a gold medallion; he was carrying a black
leather book. We went into a quiet panic, having decided he
was a priest and that we would have to interact in ways we
could not comprehend. But he turned out to be the wine
steward, and my mother uncharacteristically ordered a bottle
of wine to celebrate our European travels.

We visited relatives in Tel Aviv some summers. For two
months, I would cavort on the beach, eat corn on the cob on
the promenade, visit shimmering mosques in Jerusalem, and
fight with my bratty, pie-faced cousin Orna, who grew up to
be a kind and dazzling beauty.

Now I have children, and we travel in varied ways. This is

what I want them to remember.

I want them to remember the crescent moon in Turkey and the man in a dapper white suit walking a black pig in the evening in Miami Beach. I want them to remember the hummingbirds in Belize and the mud-ball fight they had with a boy named Zen. I want them to remember that dog next to that bucket on that table next to that field with those blind rabbits. I would like them to remember the lobster on Cape Cod and the Dairy Queen Blizzard ice cream in Hatboro, Pennsylvania.

I would like them to remember that every time you leave the house to buy some milk it is an excursion. I would like them to be as good-humored as the Good Humor man. To make up their own stories. To realize that they are not the center of the universe. I want them to love traveling. To travel light. To take a journal, a sketchbook, and a camera. To not be too afraid of getting lost. To believe that there is magic in everything. And I would like them to feel that it is great to travel and great to come home.

Maira Kalman is an award-winning children's book author and illustrator.

⋆

You have brains in your head.
You have feet in your shoes.
You can steer yourself.
Any direction you choose.
                    —Dr. Seuss, *Oh, The Places You'll Go!*

Recommended Reading

We hope *Family Travel: The Farther You Go, The Closer You Get* has whet your appetite to journey with family members, and to learn how to do it with more ease and joy. Here are books—some inspirational, some practical—to start you on your way.

Ahlsmith, Scott. *The Complete Idiot's Guide to the Perfect Vacation.* Indianapolis: Alpha Books, 1995.

Bair, Diane, and Pamela Wright. *Places to Go With Children in New England.* San Francisco: Chronicle Books, 1990.

Barile, Mary, and Joanne Michaels. *Let's Take the Kids! Great Places to Go in New York's Hudson Valley.* New York: Griffin Press/St. Martin's, 1997.

Barker, Gayle, and Joanna Pinick. *Great Resorts for Parents and Kids.* Seattle: Editor's Ink, 1990.

Bond, Marybeth. *Gutsy Mamas: Travel Tips and Wisdom for Mothers on the Road.* San Francisco: Travelers' Tales, 1997.

Bond, Marybeth, and Pamela Michael, eds. *A Mother's World: Journeys of the Heart.* San Francisco: Travelers' Tales, 1998.

Boyle, Doe. *Connecticut Family Adventure: Great Things to See and Do for the Entire Family.* Old Saybrook, Conn.: Globe Pequot Press, 1995.

Butler, Arlene Kay. *Traveling with Children and Enjoying It.* Old Saybrook, Connecticut: Globe Pequot Press, 1991.

Cahill, Susan, ed. *Desiring Italy.* New York: Fawcette Columbine, 1997.

Clay, Rebecca. *Kidding Around Paris: A Young Person's Guide to the City.* Santa Fe, NM: John Muir Publications, 1991.

Cornell, Gwenda. *Cruising with Children.* Dobbs Ferry, NY: Sheridan House, 1992.

Crichton, Michael. *Travels.* New York: Ballentine Books, 1998.

Cullen, Paul. *Cook's Tour: A Haphazard Journey from Guangzhou to Dublin and Back Again.* Sydney: Allen & Unwin, 1995.

Davidson Dana, Kiki Davis, and Terry Lawhead. *Hawaii for Kids: A Family Guide to the Islands.* Honolulu: Bess Press, 1990.

Deutsch, Valerie Wolf, and Laura Sutherland. *Innocents Abroad: Traveling with Kids in Europe.* New York: Plume, 1991.

Dodson, James. *Faithful Travelers: A Father, His Daughter, A Flyfishing Journey of the Heart.* New York: Bantam, 1998.

Ford, Judy. *Wonderful Ways to Love a Teen…Even When it Seems Impossible.* Berkeley: Conari Press, 1996.

Franz, Carl. *The People's Guide to Mexico* (9th ed.). Santa Fe, NM: John Muir Publications, 1992.

Gallmann, Kuki. *I Dreamed of Africa.* New York: Penguin, 1991.

Gougaud, Henri, and Collette Gouvion. *Egypt Observed.* London: Gallery Books, 1980.

Graham, Robin Lee, and Derek L.T. Gill. *Dove.* New York: HarperCollins, 1972.

Hardyment, Christina. *Heidi's Alp: One Family's Search for Storybook Europe.* New York: Grove/Atlantic, 1987.

Harriman, Cynthia W. *How to Travel Safely (and Sanely) in Europe with Your Children.* Old Saybrook, Conn.: Globe Pequot Press, 1997.

Harris, Eddy L. *South of Haunted Dreams: A Ride Through Slavery's Old Back Yard.* New York: Simon & Schuster, 1993.

Hays, Daniel, and David Hays. *My Old Man and the Sea: A Father and Son Sail Around Cape Horn.* New York: Algonquin Books of Chapel Hill, 1995.

Helmericks, Constance. *Down the Wild River North.* Seattle: Seal Press, 1993.

Hitchcock, Susan Tyler. *Coming About: A Family Passage at Sea.* New York: Ballantine, 1998.

Holler, Anne. *New York Family Adventure Guide: Great Things to See and Do for the Entire Family.* Old Saybrook, Conn.: Globe Pequot Press, 1997.

Hughs, Holly. *Frommer's New York City with Kids.* New York: Macmillan, 1997.

Jeffrey, Nan, and Kevin Jeffrey. *Adventuring with Children.* San Francisco: Foghorn Press/Avalon House Publishing, 1992.

Jordon, Dorothy. *Great Adventure Vacations with Your Kids.* Hampstead, NH: World Leisure Corporation, 1997.

Juarez, Cheryl Lani, and Deborah Ann Johnson. *Places to Go with Children in Miami and South Florida.* San Francisco: Chronicle Books, 1990.

Kistner, Alzada Carlisle. *An Affair with Africa: Expeditions and*

Adventures Across a Continent. Washington, D.C.: A Shearwater Book, 1998.

Kottler, Jeffrey A., Ph.D. *Travel That Can Change Your Life*. San Francisco: Jossey-Bass, 1997.

Lansky, Bruce, ed. *If We'd Wanted Quiet, We Would Have Raised Goldfish*. Minnetonka, Minn.: Meadowbrook Press, 1994.

Lansky, Vicki. *Trouble-free Travel with Children: Helpful Hints for Parents on the Go*. Deephaven, Minn.: Book Peddlers, 1991.

Lee, Elaine, ed. *Go Girl!: The Black Woman's Book of Travel and Adventure*. Portland: The Eighth Mountain Press, 1997.

Lovett, Sarah. *Kidding Around the National Parks of the Southwest: A Young Person's Guide*. Santa Fe, NM: John Muir Publications, 1990.

Lovett, Sarah. *Kidding Around New York City: A Young Person's Guide*. Santa Fe, NM: John Muir Publications, 1989.

McConnell, Mary Mapes. *Outdoor Adventures with Kids*. Dallas: Taylor Publishing Company, 1996.

Matthiessen, Peter. *The Tree Where Man Was Born*. New York: Viking Press, 1972.

McCoy, Elin. *Where Should We Take the Kids? The Northeast*. New York: Fodor's Travel Publications, 1995.

Metcalf, Nancy Pappas. *Family Resorts of the Northeast: Carefree Vacations for All—Including Mom and Dad*. Woodstock, VT: The Countryman Press, 1991.

Meyers, Carole Terwilliger. *Miles of Smiles: 101 Great Car Games and Activities*. Albany, Calif.: Carousel Press, 1992.

Morris, Mary. *Nothing to Declare: Memoirs of a Woman Traveling Alone*. New York: Penguin, 1988.

Norton, Clark. *Where Should We Take the Kids? California*. New York: Fodor's Travel Publications, 1995.

O'Brien, Tim. *The Amusement Park Guide: Coast to Coast Thrills*. Old Saybrook, Conn.: Globe Pequot Press, 1997.

Parks, Tim. *An Italian Education: The Further Adventures of an Expatriate in Verona*. New York: Grove Press, 1995.

Portnoy, Sanford, and Joan Portnoy. *How to Take Great Trips with Your Kids*. Boston: The Harvard Common Press, 1995.

Robinson, Jane. *Unsuitable for Ladies: An Anthology of Women Travellers*. New York: Oxford University Press, 1994.

Ryan, Kathleen Jo. *Writing Down the River: Into the Heart of the Grand Canyon*. Flagstaff: Northland, 1998.

Reeves, Richard. *Family Travels: Around the World in Thirty (or so) Days*. Kansas City: Andrews & McMeel, 1997.

Reiser, Paul. *Babyhood*. New York: Rob Weisbach Books, 1997.

Sattin, Anthony, and Sylvie Franquet. *Fodor's Exploring Egypt*. New York: Fodor's Travel Publications, 1996.

Seuss, Dr. *Oh, the Places You'll Go!*. New York: Random House, 1993.

Shirk, Martha, and Nancy Klepper. *Super Family Vacations: Resort and Adventure Guide*. New York: HarperCollins, 1992.

Silverman, Goldie. *Backpacking with Babies and Small Children*. California: Wilderness Press, 1992.

Spencer, Gwynne. *Places to Go with Children in the Southwest*. San Francisco: Chronicle Books, 1990.

Spencer, Kelly. *Masachusetts Family Adventure Guide: Great Things to See and Do for the Entire Family*. Old Saybrook, Conn.: Globe Pequot Press, 1997.

Stapen, Candyce H. *Great Family Vacations Midwest and Rocky Mountain Region*. Old Saybrook, Conn.: Globe Pequot Press, 1997.

Stapen, Candyce H. *Great Family Vacations Northeast*. Old Saybrook, Conn.: Globe Pequot Press, 1997.

Stapen, Candyce H. *Great Family Vacations South*. Old Saybrook, Conn.: Globe Pequot Press, 1997.

Stapen, Candyce H. *Great Family Vacations West*. Old Saybrook, Conn.: Globe Pequot Press, 1997.

Sutherland, Laura. *The Best Family Ski Vacations in North America*. New York: St. Martin's Press, 1997.

Sutherland, Laura, and Valerie Wolf Deutsch. *The Best Bargain Family Vacations in the USA*. New York: St. Martin's Press, 1997.

Tice, Janet, and Jane Wilford. *100 Best Family Resorts in North America*. Old Saybrook, Conn.: Globe Pequot Press, 1995.

Tristram, Claire, with Lucille Tristram. *Have Kid, Will Travel: 101 Survival Strategies for Vacationing with Babies and Young Children*. Kansas City: Andrew & McMeel Publishing, 1997.

Urrea, Luis Alberto. *By the Lake of Sleeping Children: The Secret Life of the Mexican Border*. New York: Anchor Books, 1996.

Winokur, John, ed. *Fathers*. New York: Dutton, 1993.

Wurman, Richard Saul. *Hawaii Access*. New York: Access Press, 1997.

Index of Contributors

Acknowledgements

Thanks very much to series editor James O'Reilly, whose words—"That's a great book idea. Do it!"—were music to my ears. His skillful guidance and good humor, along with the keen insights of series editor Larry Habegger, are appreciated. And to superwoman Susan Brady, whose ace production and people skills sheparded this manuscript to publication. Also thanks to Deborah Greco, Jennifer Leo, Kathryn Heflin, and Susan Bailey for their production and design expertise.

Special hugs to Kate White and Gay Norton Edelman, whose wise women counsel on this and other editing ventures I cherish.

Heartfelt gratitude goes to my mom and dad, Jean and George Manske, who taught me the important value of family. And to my uncle, James Jana, who not only inspired a little Hoosier girl to see the world, but whose fun companionship on several recent trips has been memorable.

And my deep esteem to The Traveling Team—Chet, Max, and Natasha Lerner—who put their personal needs on hold during the final weeks of this project, when Macintosh and I were as one. They have given me immense support and joy.

"Blessed" by Mary Morris reprinted from the May 21, 1987 issue of *The New York Times*. Copyright © 1987 by The New York Times Company. Reprinted by permission of The New York Times Company.

"Road Scholars" by James O'Reilly excerpted from *Travelers' Tales France* edited by James O'Reilly, Larry Habegger and Sean O'Reilly. Copyright © 1995 by James O'Reilly. Reprinted by permission of the author.

"For the Birds" by George Kalogerakis originally appeared as "Travels with my Ancestor" in *Condé Nast Traveler*. Copyright © 1996 by George Kalogerakis. Reprinted by permission of the author.

"Pieve San Giacomo" by Jason Wilson excerpted from *Grand Tour: The Journal of Travel Literature*. Copyright © 1996 by Jason Wilson. Reprinted by permission of the author.

"Breakfast in a Vineyard" by Kathryn Makris published with permission from the author. Copyright © 1999 by Kathryn Makris.

"Wee Airborne Advice" by Paul Reiser excerpted from *Babyhood* by Paul Reiser.

the August 1994 issue of *Travel & Leisure*. Copyright © 1994 by William Stephen Cross. Reprinted by permission of the author.

"Team Spirit" by Calvin Trillin originally appeared in *Travel & Leisure*. Copyright © 1992 by Calvin Trillin. This usage is granted by permission of the author.

"Mike's Cane" by Mary Gaffney published with permission from the author. Copyright © 1999 by Mary Gaffney.

"A Storybook Adventure" by Ann Banks reprinted from the March, 1997 issue of *Family Fun*. Copyright © 1997 by Ann Banks. Reprinted by permission of the author.

"The Thrill of the Ride" by Marc Jacobson reprinted from the Summer Fun 1992 issue of *Parenting*. Copyright © 1992 by Marc Jacobson. Reprinted by permission of The Parenting Group.

"Into the Woods" by Greg Breining reprinted from the March/April 1996 issue of *Family Life Magazine*. Reprinted with permission from *Family Life Magazine*. Copyright © 1996 by Hachette Filipacchi Magazines, Inc.

"An Eye for an Eye" by Kuki Gallmann excerpted from *I Dreamed of Africa* by Kuki Gallmann. Copyright © 1991 by Kuki Gallmann. Used by permission of Viking Penguin, a division of Penguin Books USA, Inc.

"A Room in Oaxaca" by Chelsea Cain reprinted from the Fall/Winter 1997–1998 issue of *Grand Tour: The Journal of Travel Literature*. Copyright © 1997–1998 by Chelea Cain. Reprinted by permission of the author.

"A Seaside Birth" by Robin Lee Graham with Derek L.T. Gill excerpted from *Dove* by Robin Lee Graham and Derek L.T. Gill. Copyright © 1972 by Robin Lee Graham and Derek L.T. Gill. Reprinted by permission of HarperCollins Publishers, Inc.

"The Cheese Sandwich that Changed My Life" by Trams Hollingsworth published with permission from the author. Copyright © 1995 by Trams Hollingsworth.

"Paddling Right" by Leila Philip excerpted from *Writing Down the River: Into the Heart of the Grand Canyon* produced by Kathleen Jo Ryan. Copyright © 1998 by Leila Philip. Reprinted by permission of Leila Philip.

"Time Flies" by Leigh Montville originally appeared as "Completing a Cycle" in the February 22, 1993 issue of *Sports Illustrated*. Reprinted courtesy of *Sports Illustrated*. Copyright © 1993 by Time Inc. All rights reserved.

"Coming Up for Air" by Michael Crichton excerpted from *Travels* by Michael Crichton. Copyright © 1998 by Michael Crichton. Reprinted by permission of Ballentine Books, a division of Random House, Inc. and the author.

"Six Months in Paradise" by Kate Mearns, as told to Abby Ellin, reprinted from the August, 1997 issue of *McCall's*. Copyright © 1997 by Abby Ellin. Reprinted by permission of the author.

"Moving Heaven and Earth" by Hugo Williams reprinted from the January 9, 1998 issue of *The Times Literary Supplement*. Copyright © 1998 by Hugo Williams. Reprinted by permission of the author.

"My Child, Our Vacation" by Kate Divine McAnaney reprinted from the April, 1994 issue of *The Exceptional Parent*. Copyright © 1994 by Kate Divine McAnaney. Reprinted by permission of *Exceptional Parent Magazine*.

Acknowledgements

Selection from *The Complete Idiot's Guide to the Perfect Vacation* by Scott Ahlsmith. Reprinted by permission of Macmillan General Reference USA, a division of Ahsuog, Inc. Copyright © 1995 by Alpha Books.

Selection from *Cook's Tour: A Haphazard Journey from Guangzhou to Dublin and Back Again* by Paul Cullen copyright © 1995 by Paul Cullen. Reprinted by permission of Allen & Unwin Pty Ltd.

Selection by Barbara Grizzuti Harrison excerpted from *Desiring Italy*, edited by Susan Cahill. Reprinted by permission of Barbara Grizzuti Harrison. Copyright © 1997 by Barbara Grizzuti Harrison.

Selection from *Down the Wild River North* by Constance Helmericks copyright © 1968 by Constance Helmericks. Reprinted by permission of her daughters Jean Aspen and Ann Helmericks.

Selection from *Egypt Observed* by Henri Gougaud and Collette Gouvion, translated by Stephen Hardman and published by Kaye and Ward. Reprinted by permission of Reed Consumer Books. Text copyright © 1980 by Hachette, translation copyright © 1980 by Kaye & Ward.

Selection from "Escape Artists" by Gina Hyams originally published in Salon, at www.salon.com. Copyright © 1999 by Gina Hyams. Published with permission from the author.

Selection from "Family Vacations: Europe" by Judith Schultze reprinted from the May 18, 1997 issue of the *Los Angeles Times*. Copyright © 1997 by the *Los Angeles Times*. Reprinted by permission.

Selection by Christopher Buckley. Reprinted by permission of International Creative Management.

Selection by David Mamet reprinted from *Fathers*, edited by John Winokur, copyright © 1993.

Selection by Joyce Carol Oates, copyright © 1993 by Ontario Review, Inc. Reprinted by permission of John Hawkins & Associates, Inc.

Selection from "Fear of Crying" by Sue Warner reprinted from the May 21, 1995 issue of the *Los Angeles Times*. Copyright © 1995 by the *Los Angeles Times*. Reprinted by permission of the *Los Angeles Times*.

Selection from *Fodor's Exploring Egypt* by Anthony Sattin and Sylvie Franquet copyright © 1996 by The Automobile Association. Reprinted by permission of Fodor's Travel Publications, Inc., a subsidiary of Random House, Inc.

Selection by Larry Fox published with permission from the author. Copyright © 1999 by Larry Fox.

Selection from "Grand Guignol on the Grand Tour" by Catherine Calvert reprinted from the June 9, 1996 issue of *The New York Times*. Copyright © 1996 by The New York Times Company. Reprinted by permission.

Selection from Angelique Syversen excerpted from *Gutsy Mamas: Travel Tips and Wisdom for Mothers on the Road* by Marybeth Bond. Copyright © 1997. Reprinted by permission of Angelique Syversen.

Selection by Tim Williams excerpted from *Gutsy Mamas: Travel Tips and Wisdom for Mothers on the Road* by Marybeth Bond. Copyright © 1997. Reprinted by permission of Tim Williams.

Selection from *Have Kid, Will Travel: 101 Survival Strategies for Vacationing with*

Selection from "Our Life on the Reservation" by David Spicer published with permission from the author. Copyright © 1999 by David Spicer.

Selection from "Paddling with Mia" by Allen Noren published with permission from the author. Copyright © 1999 by Allen Noren.

Selection from *The People's Guide to Mexico* by Carl Franz copyright © 1992 by Carl Franz. Reprinted by permission of John Muir Publications.

Selection from "Picture Perfect" by Laura Muha reprinted from the July 10, 1994 issue of *Newsday*. Copyright © 1994 by Times-Mirror Syndication. Reprinted by permission of Times-Mirror Syndication.

Selection from *Some Traditions of the Thai* by Phya Anuman Rajadhon copyright © 1987 by the Thai Inter-Religious Commission for Development and Sathirakoses Nagapradipa Foundation.

Selection from "Stacy Goes Waikiki" by Raymond Cheever reprinted from the Fall 1996 issue of *Accent on Living*. Reprinted with permission. Copyright © 1996 by *Accent on Living Magazine*.

Selection from "Temples and Tortillas on a Mexican Tour" by Perri Klass and Larry Wolff reprinted from the December 13, 1987 issue of *The New York Times*. Copyright © 1987 by Dr. Perri Klass and Larry Wolff. Reprinted by permission of the authors.

Selections from *Travel That Can Change Your Life: How to Create a Transformative Experience* edited by Jeffrey A. Kottler, Ph.D. copyright © 1997 by Jeffrey A. Kottler.

Selection from *Travelers' Tales Italy* edited by Anne Calcagno copyright © 1998 by Anne Calcagno. Reprinted by permission.

Selection from *Travelers' Tales Thailand* edited by James O'Reilly and Larry Habegger copyright © 1993 by James O'Reilly and Larry Habegger. Reprinted by permission.

Selection from "Travels with Arwen" by Tim O'Reilly published with permission from the author. Copyright © 1999 by Tim O'Reilly.

Selection from *The Tree Where Man Was Born* by Peter Matthiessen, photographs by Eliot Porter, copyright © 1972 by *The New Yorker*, text. Used by permission of Dutton, a division of Penguin Putnam Inc. and the author.

Selection by Susan Ungaro published with permission from the author. Copyright © 1999 by Susan Ungaro.

Selection from "When a Saint Becomes a Sinner" by Joseph J. Ellis reprinted from the November 9, 1998 issue of *U.S. News & World Report*. Copyright © 1998 by *U.S. News & World Report*. Reprinted by permission.

Selection from "Where Art Began" by Jonathan Cott reprinted from the May 1991 issue of *Travel Holiday*. Reprinted by permission of the author. Copyright © 1991 by Jonathan Cott.

Selection by Kate White published with permission from the author. Copyright © 1999 by Kate White.

Selection from *Wonderful Ways to Love a Teen...Even When it Seems Impossible* by Judy Ford copyright © 1996 by Judy Ford. Reprinted by permission of Conari Press.

About the Editor

Laura Manske grew up in Knox, Indiana, near cornfields, red barns, and a wildlife game preserve. As a child, she listened to train whistles blow and dreamed of far-off lands, making her way through every book about adventure that the town's one-room library could provide.

On a school break from Indiana University, she stepped onto an airplane for the first time. Destination: the Big Apple (it was love at first sight). Ironically, her two young children, Max and Natasha, have already accrued hundreds of thousands of air miles around the world. What a difference a generation makes.

To this day, one of her favorite sensations is the moment an airplane's wheels lift off the runway and tuck—with a gentle but distinctive thump—into its underbelly. Aloft!

For the last twenty years, Manske has been an editor at many top magazines, most recently at *McCall's,* where, as editor-at-large, she writes about great family getaways, among other topics. As an expert on parenting and travel, she has frequently been interviewed on television and radio programs.

Manske lives with her husband, Chet Lerner, and kids in Manhattan. When wanderlust strikes and circumstances prevent immediate escape, she opens one of more than 30 marked Ziploc bags that contain sand collected from beaches around the world, and lets the grains run through her fingers.

Now, at night, instead of tuning into rural train whistles, Manske savors her home's fabulous view of the sparkling East River, and watches twinkling jets—departing Kennedy and La Guardia airports—soar skyward.

TRAVELERS' TALES GUIDES

LOOK FOR THESE TITLES IN THE SERIES

FOOTSTEPS: THE SOUL OF TRAVEL
A NEW IMPRINT FROM TRAVELERS' TALES GUIDES

An imprint of Travelers' Tales Guides, the Footsteps series unveils new works by first-time authors, established writers, and reprints of works whose time has come…again. Each book will fire your imagination, disturb your sleep, and feed your soul.

KITE STRINGS OF THE SOUTHERN CROSS
A Woman's Travel Odyssey
By Laurie Gough
ISBN 1-885211-30-9, 400 pages, $24.00, hardcover
A TRAVELERS' TALES FOOTSTEPS BOOK

ℐPECIAL INTEREST

THE PENNY PINCHER'S PASSPORT TO LUXURY TRAVEL
The Art of Cultivating Preferred Customer Status
By Joel L. Widzer
ISBN 1-885211-31-7, 253 pages, $12.95

DANGER!
Ttue Stories of Trouble and Survival
Edited by James O'Reilly, Larry Habegger, & Sean O'Reilly
ISBN 1-885211-32-5, 336 pages, $17.95

Check with your local bookstore for these titles
or call O'Reilly to order:
800-998-9938 (credit cards only—weekdays 6AM–5PM PST)
707-829-0515, or email: order@oreilly.com

$\mathscr{S}$PECIAL INTEREST

FAMILY TRAVEL:
The Farther You Go, the Closer You Get
Edited by Laura Manske
ISBN 1-885211-33-3, 375 pages, $17.95

THE GIFT OF TRAVEL:
The Best of Travelers' Tales
Edited by Larry Habegger, James O'Reilly & Sean O'Reilly
ISBN 1-885211-25-2, 240 pages, $14.95

THERE'S NO TOILET PAPER ON THE ROAD LESS TRAVELED:
The Best of Travel Humor and Misadventure
Edited by Doug Lansky
ISBN 1-885211-27-9, 207 pages, $12.95

A DOG'S WORLD:
True Stories of Man's Best Friend on the Road
Edited by Christine Hunsicker
ISBN 1-885211-23-6, 257 pages, $12.95

$\mathscr{W}$OMEN'S TRAVEL

SAFETY AND SECURITY FOR WOMEN WHO TRAVEL
By Sheila Swan & Peter Laufer
ISBN 1-885211-29-5, 159 pages, $12.95

$\mathcal{W}$OMEN'S TRAVEL

WOMEN IN THE WILD:
True Stories of Adventure and Connection
Edited by Lucy McCauley
ISBN 1-885211-21-X, 307 pages, $17.95

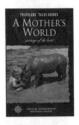

A MOTHER'S WORLD:
Journeys of the Heart
Edited by Marybeth Bond & Pamela Michael
ISBN 1-885211-26-0, 233 pages, $14.95

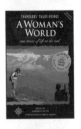

A WOMAN'S WORLD:
True Stories of Life on the Road

——— ★ ★ ★ ———
Winner of the Lowell
Thomas Award for Best
Travel Book – Society of
American Travel Writers

Edited by Marybeth Bond
Introduction by Dervla Murphy
ISBN 1-885211-06-6
475 pages, $17.95

GUTSY WOMEN:
Travel Tips and Wisdom for the Road
By Marybeth Bond
ISBN 1-885211-15-5,123 pages, $7.95

GUTSY MAMAS:
Travel Tips and Wisdom for
Mothers on the Road
By Marybeth Bond
ISBN 1-885211-20-1, 139 pages, $7.95

ℬODY & SOUL

THE ROAD WITHIN:
True Stories of Transformation and the Soul
Edited by Sean O'Reilly, James O'Reilly & Tim O'Reilly
ISBN 1-885211-19-8, 459 pages, $17.95

—★ ★ ★—
Small Press Book Award Winner and Benjamin Franklin Award Finalist

LOVE & ROMANCE:
True Stories of Passion on the Road
Edited by Judith Babcock Wylie
ISBN 1-885211-18-X, 319 pages, $17.95

FOOD:
A Taste of the Road
Edited by Richard Sterling
Introduction by Margo True
ISBN 1-885211-09-0
467 pages, $17.95

—★ ★ ★—
Silver Medal Winner of the Lowell Thomas Award for Best Travel Book—Society of American Travel Writers

THE FEARLESS DINER:
Travel Tips and Wisdom for Eating around the World
By Richard Sterling
ISBN 1-885211-22-8, 139 pages, $7.95

COUNTRY GUIDES

AMERICA

Edited by Fred Setterberg
ISBN 1-885211-28-7, 550 pages, $19.95

JAPAN

Edited by Donald W. George
& Amy Greimann Carlson
ISBN 1-885211-04-X, 437 pages, $17.95

ITALY

Edited by Anne Calcagno
Introduction by Jan Morris
ISBN 1-885211-16-3, 463 pages, $17.95

INDIA

Edited by James O'Reilly & Larry Habegger
ISBN 1-885211-01-5, 538 pages, $17.95

FRANCE

Edited by James O'Reilly, Larry Habegger
& Sean O'Reilly
ISBN 1-885211-02-3, 517 pages, $17.95

COUNTRY GUIDES

MEXICO

Edited by James O'Reilly & Larry Habegger
ISBN 1-885211-00-7, 463 pages, $17.95

THAILAND

Edited by James O'Reilly
& Larry Habegger
ISBN 1-885211-05-8
483 pages, $17.95

———★ ★ ★———

Winner of the Lowell
Thomas Award for Best
Travel Book—Society of
American Travel Writers

SPAIN

Edited by Lucy McCauley
ISBN 1-885211-07-4, 495 pages, $17.95

NEPAL

Edited by Rajendra S. Khadka
ISBN 1-885211-14-7, 423 pages, $17.95

BRAZIL

Edited by Annette Haddad & Scott Doggett
Introduction by Alex Shoumatoff
ISBN 1-885211-11-2
452 pages, $17.95

———★ ★ ★———

Benjamin Franklin
Award Winner

REGIONAL GUIDES

HAWAI'I
True Stories of the Island Spirit
Edited by Rick & Marcie Carroll
ISBN 1-885211-35-X, 375 pages, $17.95

GRAND CANYON
True Stories of Life Below the Rim
Edited by Sean O'Reilly & James O'Reilly
ISBN 1-885211-34-1, 375 pages, $17.95

CITY GUIDES

HONG KONG
Edited by James O'Reilly, Larry Habegger & Sean O'Reilly
ISBN 1-885211-03-1, 439 pages, $17.95

PARIS
Edited by James O'Reilly, Larry Habegger & Sean O'Reilly
ISBN 1-885211-10-4, 417 pages, $17.95

SAN FRANCISCO
Edited by James O'Reilly, Larry Habegger & Sean O'Reilly
ISBN 1-885211-08-2, 491 pages, $17.95

Submit Your Own Travel Tale

Do you have a tale of your own that you would like to submit to Travelers' Tales? We highly recommend that you first read one or more of our books to get a feel for the kind of story we're looking for. For submission guidelines and a list of titles in the works, send a SASE to:

Travelers' Tales Submission Guidelines
330 Townsend Street, Suite 208, San Francisco, CA 94107

or send email to *guidelines@travelerstales.com*
or visit our Web site at **www.travelerstales.com**

You can send your story to the address above or via email to *submit@travelerstales.com*. On the outside of the envelope, *please indicate what country/topic your story is about*. If your story is selected for one of our titles, we will contact you about rights and payment.

We hope to hear from you. In the meantime, enjoy the stories!

JOURNEY WITH THE WORLD'S BEST TRAVEL WRITERS

Fill in this card and we'll let you know about the best travel stories we've found.

Which book did this card come from? _____

Name _____

Company (optional) _____

Mailing Address _____

City/State _____

Zip/Country _____

Telephone _____

Email address _____

What was your favorite story in this book? _____
_____

We have other Travelers' Tales Guides in the works. What other countries, regions, or topics would you like to see us cover? _____
_____

Why did you buy this book?
☐ Prepare for a trip   ☐ Class/Seminar   ☐ Armchair Travel
☐ Interest in a specific region or topic   ☐ Gift

Where did you purchase your copy?
☐ Bookstore ☐ Direct from O'Reilly ☐ Received as gift ☐ Online ☐ Other

☐ Please send me the Travelers' Tales Catalog
☐ I do not want my name given to outside mailing lists

Please give us three names and addresses of people you think would like Travelers' Tales.

Name _____
Address _____
City/State/Zip _____

Name _____
Address _____
City/State/Zip _____

Name _____
Address _____
City/State/Zip _____

BUSINESS REPLY MAIL

FIRST CLASS MAIL   PERMIT NO. 80   SEBASTOPOL, CA

Postage will be paid by addressee

TRAVELERS' TALES

c/o O'Reilly & Associates, Inc.
101 Morris Street
Sebastopol, CA 95472-9902